MW00587904

ELEPHANTS IN THE COTTONFIELDS

ALSO BY WAYNE GREENHAW

The Golfer

The Making of a Hero

Watch Out for George Wallace

Wayne Greenhaw

MACMILLAN PUBLISHING CO., INC. New York

COLLIER MACMILLAN PUBLISHERS London

ELEPHANTS IN THE COTTONFIELDS

RONALD REAGAN AND THE NEW REPUBLICAN SOUTH

Copyright © 1982 by Wayne Greenhaw

All rights reserved. No part of this book may be reproduced or transmitted in any form or by any means, electronic or mechanical, including photocopying, recording or by any information storage and retrieval system, without permission in writing from the Publisher.

Macmillan Publishing Co., Inc.
866 Third Avenue, New York, N.Y. 10022
Collier Macmillan Canada, Inc.

Library of Congress Cataloging in Publication Data
Greenhaw, Wayne, (date)
Elephants in the cottonfields.
Bibliography: p.
Includes index.
1. Southern States—Politics and government—1951– . 2. Reagan, Ronald. 3. Republican Party (U.S.) I. Title.
F216.2.G73 1982 975′.043 82-9907
ISBN 0-02-545500-1 AACR2

10 9 8 7 6 5 4 3 2 1

Designed by Jack Meserole

Printed in the United States of America

The author gratefully acknowledges permission to quote from the following:

The Charlotte Observer, news articles and portions thereof; permission granted February 15, 1982.

Conservative Digest (July 1981), 7777 Leesburg Pike, Falls Church, Va. 22043. Copyright © 1981 by Viguerie Communications.

Howard Covington, city editor, *Greensboro* (N.C.) *Daily News*, for his articles and columns appearing in *The Charlotte Observer*.

From "Politics: The Professional Baker" by Richard Reeves (*Esquire*, January 1980). Copyright © 1979 by Esquire Publishing Inc.

From "Don't Overrule the Court" by Archibald Cox (*Newsweek*, September 28, 1981). Copyright © 1981 by Newsweek Inc. All rights reserved. Reprinted by permission.

Copyright 1887, 1901, 1952, 1960, 1964, 1969, 1970 by The New York Times Company. Reprinted by permission.

The South Old and New by Francis Butler Simpkins. Copyright © 1948, Alfred A. Knopf Inc. Reprinted by permission.

The Washington Post, article by Myra MacPherson, December 7, 1980. Copyright © The Washington Post.

Special permission granted by U.S. Representative Trent Lott for Op-Ed article from *The Washington Post*, April 14, 1981. Copyright © The Washington Post.

To Sally
with love

Contents

Acknowledgments, xi

1 The First Republican, 1

2 Groundwork for a Winner, 9

3 A Mixture of Madness, 15

4 Republican Takeover, 25

5 Compromised Reconstruction, 34

6 A New Division, 48

7 Enter: The Good Guy, 63

8 Dixie Republicans Rise Again, 71

9 The Southern Strategist, 77

10 A Conversion to Republicanism, 87

11 Mississippi by a Mile, 98

12 A Kinetic Chaos, 110

13 New Southern Strategist, 117

14 Marching toward Victory, 132

15 Jesse the Juggernaut, 146

16 The Way to the Top, 161

17 Southern Sex Czar, 170

18 The Damning of Dixie, 181

19 The New Religious Right, 189

20 The New Old Republican Order, 202

21 The Long-Distance Runner, 214

22 Some Other Southern Republicans, 235

23 A Youthful Tomorrow, 248

Afterword, 261

Notes, 263

Selected Bibliography, 275

Index, 279

Acknowledgments

The writing of *Elephants in the Cottonfields* actually started many years ago. Like all writers, I draw upon knowledge collected from members of my family and handed down from generation to generation. While not a memoir, this book could not have been written without such remembrances. The memory of my father, Harold Reed Greenhaw, my maternal grandfather, H. D. "Bub" Able, and an uncle, Dr. Hugh L. Taylor, is particularly noted on many of the pages concerning the history of the Republican party in the South. With the help of my mother, Mrs. Lee Able Greenhaw Brown, and two aunts, Mrs. Ida Greenhaw Taylor and Miss Lucy Mae Greenhaw, I remembered parts of my early lifetime.

Without the years of friendship from an Alabama hill country populist Republican, Ira DeMent, former U.S. Attorney for the middle district of Alabama, I would have started totally cold in my research. With his many stories and his guidance I became aware of the differences among Southern Republicans.

Years of friendship and tutelage from a man whom I consider a master journalist, Ray Jenkins, are greatly appreciated. One of the staunchest and strongest believing Democrats I know, this former member of President Jimmy Carter's White House staff is a loyal friend and has never turned away when I needed his advice.

I want to go back a decade to a time when I first considered writing about the South other than articles for a daily newspaper. I had the good fortune to be awarded a Nieman Fellowship at Harvard University, where curator James Thomson and his wife Diana were guiding intellectual forces. There were too many people at the school who were important to me to list here, but I want to thank particularly two professors, Thomas Pettigrew and Frank Freidel, who offered sharp insight into Southern problems and history. Also, I would like to thank the people at the Kennedy Institute of Politics, who gave me and fellow Fellow Ed Williams, a highly respected editor at *The Charlotte Observer*, the opportunity to teach their first seminar in Southern Politics.

While working on a grant several years ago from the Fund for Investigative Journalism, I picked up much information that ultimately went into this book. Howard Bray at the Fund helped during that time, and I appreciate it very much.

Much needed support has been given to me as a journalist during the years from the Southern Regional Council in Atlanta and its executive director, Steve Suitts, a knowledgeable student of the South.

My good friend Tom Cork, journalist and raconteur, read through the manuscript and offered needed and valued advice.

Another good friend, Joe Azbell, an astute political observer and long-time worker behind the scenes in many campaigns throughout the South, offered advice, observations, and brainstormed the title, *Elephants in the Cottonfields*, during one of our countless breakfast meetings.

Scores of newspeople contributed to the making of this book, including Claude Duncan of the Montgomery *Advertiser*, Virginia Gibson of the Pensacola *Journal*, Jack Nelson of the Los Angeles *Times*, Howell Raines of the *New York Times*, Peggy Roberson of the Montgomery *Advertiser*'s Washington Bureau, Phil Smith of the *Newhouse News Service* in Washington, Remer Tyson of the Detroit *Free Press*, Patrick Owens of *Newsday*, and so many others I unfortunately could not possibly list them all here.

Bob Wyrick of *Newsday* and his lovely wife Kathy stayed up so many nights and listened and gave advice.

Randall Williams of the Southern Poverty Law Center's *KlanWatch* offered insight into the political operations of the Ku Klux Klan in the South today.

Starr Smith, friend and philosopher, mapped the way toward numerous journeys into Republicanism.

The staffs of the senators, congressmen, governors, and other politicians I concentrated on in my efforts were all courteous and prompt, and I appreciate the efficiency with which they did their jobs.

My good friend, former Alabama Attorney General Bill Baxley, has given generously of his time and observations on historical as well as current political events. A true-believing Democrat, he has experienced the creeping power of the elephants in the cottonfields.

The personnel of the Library of Congress and the Montgomery Public Library were always willing to fill my requests. I particularly wish to thank Tommy Anderson of the reference section of the Montgomery Library, who helped time after time with dozens of newspaper and magazine articles.

My research assistant, Fredd Frost, helped beyond the call of duty with his many chores during my researching and writing.

My agent, Charles D. "Chuck" Taylor, is a super person without whose help I could not have started in the very beginning. And my editor, Jane Cullen, has been a delight without whose help I could not have finished.

Lastly, I want to thank my darling wife Sally who continued to be my best critic and my number-one fan.

ELEPHANTS IN THE COTTONFIELDS

The First Republican

When I was a little boy, I spent most summers with my Granddaddy and Nanny, my mother's parents, on their farm in Shelby County, Alabama. I was about seven when on a Saturday morning during one of these visits, Granddaddy awakened me before the first crack of sunshine. "Come on, son, we're going to town," he said, and I dressed hurriedly in the semidarkness of the lantern-lighted room.

After Nanny served Granddaddy and Uncle Baxter cups of steaming coffee and I had my milk, I climbed up between them in the cab of a pickup. In the vibrant early-morning chilliness Uncle Baxter rolled a Prince Albert from a can and Granddaddy broke off a chaw of Redman and stuck it into his cheek. I sat back and peered over the dusty dash into the fog, cut by the beams of the headlights, and I smelled the varying odors of the tobacco and the dank mustiness of the imitation-leather seatcovers, and I listened to their talk.

Uncle Baxter talked about how President Harry S Truman was not as good as Franklin Delano Roosevelt, and Granddaddy said it was no wonder because nobody could ever be as good as Roosevelt. "Roosevelt got us jobs when we had to have jobs, or all of us poor people would have starved to death," Granddaddy allowed. He went on about how the Republicans never cared one hoot in hell about the poor people like us.

"Old Herbert Hoover just sat his big fat ass up there in the White House and didn't do one thing for anybody as far as I could tell," Uncle Baxter said.

And Granddaddy put in, "Except take care of the rich birds with the big oil companies and the automobile manufacturers and such."

I looked from one to the other; one was chewing and the other drawing, and they both were talking while the sun peeped up over the far eastern edge of Red Mountain. Its pinkish red glow lighted the high iron statue of Vulcan, whose torch was green, which meant there had been nobody killed on the highways that night. "Old Harry Truman does tell them where to get off when they get too nosy, carrying on about that daughter of his or saying how he can't play a piano," Granddaddy said, and I wondered what that had to do with politics.

They kept on about the state of the nation, and I got to thinking, and I realized before I knew it, before the old truck rumbled down the hillside on Twentieth Street into the city of Birmingham, that I had never before in all my life even seen a Republican except in *Life* magazine or *Time* or some other periodical that printed a picture of Mr. Thomas E. Dewey, who had run against Mr. Roosevelt and who everybody said was about to run against Mr. Truman, making an appearance at some big dinner or something. And then I remembered that one time when Mama had brought me in to the movie in Homewood that I had seen the mustachioed, black-haired Dewey on the newsreel, and he grinned sort of like Professor Kermit Eversley at the Trussville Elementary School where I went to the third grade.

We got downtown, and Uncle Baxter pulled into a parking place near the wholesale warehouses and the curb market where we knew the vegetable farmers who sold their wares under the big tin roof. A half-dozen of the men sitting on Coca-Cola crates in a semicircle around this side of the red-glowing potbelly stove looked up and nodded and said, "Howdy," and Granddaddy pulled a crate over next to one tall man with a giant Adam's apple so they could share a spitting can that sat on the wooden floor halfway between them and the stove.

"They say old Tom Dewey's going to whip President Truman in November," Granddaddy allowed, and I reckoned he knew exactly how to get a conversation started, because all of the others commenced to talking at once. They agreed and disagreed, but not one let on that he was personally going to vote for a Republican.

"I imagine it's going to be a uphill battle for old Harry," one said, and another said, "It ain't ever easy when you're playing politics," and Granddaddy said, "I guess not," and another said, "Ain't nothing but a bunch of crooks no way." They spat, and I edged around to the corner and sat up next to somebody's sack of mule feed. Uncle Baxter slipped off and came back an hour later with a sack of goods he put in the cab of the pickup. Coming back inside, he eased another smaller sack out of his overall pouch. "Have a little nip of this, Bub? Warm you up down deep inside," he said, offering the sack that looked like it ought to hold candy; and Granddaddy shook his head. They talked on and on about politics, and most of the men agreed with Granddaddy that Truman wasn't doing as good a job as Roosevelt, and when they mentioned Roosevelt's name, they'd bow their heads just a little and hood their eyes, and now and then their voices would break slightly when they called his name; they still had the feeling that he had just died yesterday.

Sometime later in the morning a man with a heavy foot stepped up to the group. He seemed different from the others. He wore a dark, freshly pressed suit and a bleached-out, starched shirt and a silk tie with a diamond stickpin on the chest, and his shoes were low-cut and shiny. Granddaddy had on a suit, and his gray shirt—not his Sunday-go-to-meeting best—was buttoned to the neck, but he didn't wear a tie; and he still had on his everyday brogans like me and Uncle Baxter and the others. This man was a dude, and he smelled pretty, like a woman, and his hair was slicked back with some kind of grease, like Mr. Thomas E. Dewey. He spoke to everybody in a deep voice like ones I had heard on the radio, and when he saw me, his eyes sparkled and he said, "How you, boy?" and I said, "Right fine." His name was J. Edgar Corrington, according to Granddaddy, and for a few long minutes they talked about the weather and how Birmingham was getting too big for its britches. They didn't say much of anything that was of any real importance, and I wished he'd move on so the men would have a go at politics some more, but he lingered.

Way later, when we went across the floor to Mrs. Mary Ann Rutherford's booth and got some fresh biscuits and sorghum syrup, after Uncle Baxter snored a time or two and nearly fell off his Coca-Cola case, Granddaddy commented offhandedly, "You know, old Corrington's a Republican." And I nearly broke my neck straining it around where I could get another look at his shiny backside going through the parking lot. "They tell me he right smartly brags about voting for old Wendell Willkie," Granddaddy said, and some of the others at Mrs. Rutherford's agreed and said, "Yeah, and he'll probably vote for Dewey this time around," and Granddaddy said he was sure of it.

On the way home, the bed of the truck filled with our finds of the day—a scarred churn that didn't look nearly as good as the one Nanny used for years, a brand-new, chrome-plated flashlight that would be good on the cold, early-morning trips to the barn, a canvas Uncle Baxter said he hadn't found a use for yet but knew it would be good for most anything, and other goods—I asked Granddaddy, "What is it so bad about the Republicans?"

He rared back, clicked his false teeth together, and focused his eyes on me. "Son, the Republicans brought on the Great Depression. They don't care one whit about the workingman. They let us rot without jobs before the Democrats came along and Mr. Roosevelt created job programs, the CCC, WPA, and made it worthwhile for a farmer to live out on his land. The last Republican president, Mr. Herbert Hoover, just turned his back on the little people like us," he said with the utmost of surety.

And that was that. I never questioned one word of what Granddaddy told me. After all, he was Granddaddy, and that meant everything. I leaned back against the stiff-backed seat and closed my eyes. I was whipped to a frazzle. As I closed my eyes, I remembered the story he had told me about the clock that sat on his and Nanny's mantel in the living room. "Son, that's the finest clock in the whole wide world," he had told me. On the face were the tin figures of a fife player and two drummers. The hand of one drummer ticktocked loudly with every second's beat. The face was a circle formed in the middle of the ship's helm next to which stood President Roosevelt, shoulders wide, head aloof, and eyes focused on the future. Across the base of the clock was the inscription: FDR: THE MAN OF THE HOUR.

Granddaddy was crippled in those days. He hobbled about on a walking cane, injured when he fell more than 200 feet down an embankment while working on the construction of Wheeler Dam for the Tennessee Valley Authority. He was retired from the carpenter trade, but he liked to remember. "I'll never forget that night when I bought that clock. Me and your nanny and your mama were living in a tent in Sheffield. It was hard times back then. It was the middle of the Depression. I had worked every job I could get, but nothing came steady. We moved in a tent all over Alabama, Mississippi, and part of Tennessee. Your nanny and mama never complained. Every time

I'd get a new job, they'd pick up and we'd move." He told me about joining the labor union after Mr. Roosevelt gave him the job with the T.V.A., and the Friday after he got his first regular paycheck he stopped off to have a drink with the other union men, and they toasted the President of the United States with a drink of straight whiskey. He was walking home when "I saw that clock in the window of a drugstore. Franklin Delano Roosevelt was standing there." His voice almost cracked. "I don't think I even looked to see how much the price was. I went inside and bought it. I carried it home and put it next to my chair. Emma looked at it and shook her head. Your mama touched it very softly. I told 'em we'd have to keep that clock forever. It was a sign that everything would be all right."

Again, that was that. Granddaddy had spoken.

I slept. The next day, while I wandered beyond the barn into the pasture where Bossy the cow munched on her morning grass, I thought about that man from Birmingham. I pictured Mr. J. Edgar Corrington in his dark suit and his stiff-collared shirt and his evil-looking ways, and I wondered if there were any sure-enough Republicans down here in Shelby County.

Four years later I watched my first national political convention on the television that had become a part of our world. The Republicans gathered and appeared to pick General Dwight D. Eisenhower without much difficulty, although if you looked close, you could see a touch of sourness on the face of Mr. Robert Taft, who seemed to think he ought to be the nominee.

I didn't think General Eisenhower looked like a Republican, and Mama said she thought he should be a Democrat with his background of being born in Texas and raised in Kansas; and I knew he didn't appear to favor Mr. J. Edgar Corrington one iota. He seemed just like a real nice man with a soft voice and pleasant ways. His running mate was Richard Nixon from California, and I thought he looked more like Mr. Corrington.

A few weeks later the Democrats came on with their show, and I was glued to the television, and Mama said she was pulling for Senator Estes Kefauver for the nomination. Although you couldn't tell too much about it from the television, which showed only the hip-hoorah and speechmaking, the nomination was won by a man even kindlier looking than Ike, Governor Adlai Stevenson of Illinois, and Mama said that was all right because she had read where he was a very smart man. And, anyway, it didn't take long for me to get into the spirit of things when on the next night it was announced that Senator John Sparkman of Alabama would be Stevenson's vice-presidential nominee.

Talking with Mama, I thought it would be a cinch for the Stevenson-Sparkman ticket. I listened to every word I could fathom from the television commentors. I just knew the Democrats had a shoo-in, and I talked it up at school. But in junior high school when I was twelve years old, my classmates started looking at me out of the corners of their eyes. I got my friends together and asked if they wanted to participate in block politics, and they stared at me like I was crazy. I said, "You take your home block, campaign from door to door, and ask the people to vote for Adlai Stevenson and John Sparkman. And you can show the people the picture of Mr. Stevenson in *Life* magazine with holes worn in his shoes; that always gets a smile." But they turned away. "What's wrong?" I insisted.

"Is your mama and your daddy going to vote for them?" one asked.

I stopped. I had to think. I nodded. "I know my mama is," I said. I realized my daddy had never said one way or other.

"Well, ours are going to vote for Eisenhower," the boy said. After they left, I was forlorn. I couldn't believe these really good people, friends of mine, folks I knew, who had taken me to picture shows on Saturdays with their boys and girls and one of whom was even my Boy Scout master and another who taught Sunday school at the Covenant Presbyterian Church, would actually sure enough vote Republican, but I didn't figure my friends would lie either.

I talked seriously with Mama that night. Daddy had gone out of town. He was a traveling salesman and usually left on Monday mornings and didn't come home until Friday afternoons. Mama said that she didn't care what my friends said, she thought Adlai Stevenson would be the next president; we hadn't had a Republican president since Herbert Hoover, and she didn't imagine more than half the people wanted another Republican this close to the Great Depression.

At school I kept up my talk. I even took four one-dollar bets with my friends, including the little blonde-haired girl who lived on the corner down the street from us.

On the Monday before the election our homeroom teacher asked who was for Eisenhower, and nearly everybody stood. She counted the people and then asked who was for Stevenson. A handful of us stood, and there was a tittering giggle through the room. It made me mad enough that I took two more one-dollar bets at recess.

The next night Mama let me stay up to hear the returns. I was glued to the television set, and it made me sink close to the floor with unhappiness when I heard the first Alabama votes being counted overwhelmingly for Eisenhower, but Mama reassured me that that was the early boxes from the cities. "The cities in the South are already going Republican," she sighed.

Later in the night the count began to change in Alabama. It would almost certainly be a victory for Stevenson-Sparkman. But the picture in the rest of the country was bleak. All the large states like New York, California, Pennsylvania, and Ohio were leaning toward the Republicans. The next morning I found out that Stevenson carried only seven Southern states, including Alabama. At least I had that satisfaction. In the meantime, however, I had to empty my piggy bank of my savings and borrow two extra dollars from Mama. Each time I paid off I felt my stomach knot up a little more.

That Friday night, when I asked Daddy how he voted, he said, "Shoot, son, I never vote Democrat," and there was a fine cackle at the end of his voice. My stomach gripped tighter than it had when I was paying my friends. I stared at him and determined that he wasn't kidding me. The realization that all my life I had been living in the same house, loving someone who was a Republican, tore at me. It made me think long and hard about what was what in this political world. Later, Daddy told me, "Everybody in Town Creek [the little town in north Alabama where he was raised] voted Democratic when I was a boy. That's all they ever talked about. I swore way back then that I'd never vote Democratic if I could help it." Several years after that he told me he had heard stories when he was a boy about families in north Alabama being broken up because of political differences, and he said he had never thought politics was *that* important. But I figured he was just telling me that to try to mend something he might have damaged between us. Traveling from barbershop to beauty parlor, selling his goods, Daddy knew hundreds of people. Most of the folks liked him. They knew his big body on sight, and they'd holler out when they saw him coming, and he would reply in kind. Most of them never knew whether he was Republican or Democrat, and most never cared; he talked a good line and listened well, and I noticed that if ever the conversation dragged, which it seldom did around him, he interjected, "What y'all think about politics down here?" or "How's Big Jim Folsom doing in this part of the country?" and the folks would be off and talking.

I raised hell through the peace and prosperity days of Eisenhower in the fifties, growing up in Tuscaloosa High School, getting involved once in James E. "Kissin' Jim" Folsom's campaign for a second term as governor of Alabama. But that was only as a kid putting bumper stickers on cars, though I did get to meet the giant man. It was nearly eight years later before I worked in another of his campaigns—and this time a feisty welterweight with a loud voice and an egotistical pompadour, George C. Wallace, won his first term as governor. I had first met Wallace years before when I was traveling with my father through south Alabama. He was campaign manager in that area for Jim Folsom, but he was talking up a storm about himself in the barbershop where we saw him. After we left, Daddy predicted that some day he would be governor.

All of my experience up to 1980 had been in Democratic politics. That had always been the name of the game around my part of the world, and I never for one instant thought the Solid South would ever turn Republican. But in this day and time, when anything can happen, I discovered that even elephants can trample through the cottonfields. And every now and then a boll weevil will latch itself onto his stumplike legs and hang on for the ride.

Groundwork for a Winner

Southerners had generally liked Ronald Reagan since way back in the fifties, when he looked out of the television screen at them on the "General Electric Theatre" or "Death Valley Days." They liked movie stars, found them intriguing, mysterious, and glamorous. They especially liked the smooth-voiced, silky-faced lover boys of the old school in which Ronald Reagan held a front-row seat. And they admired the rough-and-tough heroes of the Old West into which Ronald Reagan had grown. He was still smooth, but he had that gruff, crusty-layered exterior. He looked you in the eye, and he was sincere.

Through the sixties Reagan was the advance scout forging out into unknown territory. While governor of California and afterward, he made trips into the Southland and spoke to chambers of commerce, groups of businessmen gathered in Brownsville, Lake Charles, Kosciusko, Johnson City, Cullman, Macon, Perry, and Falls Church, and places in between. He was an old-time politician with a Westerner's delight at new discoveries; and he had found the mother lode in the eyes that scrutinized his every move and then asked for autographs before he left. He knew that at some time, when that time was right, he would come back and collect on his findings.

Reagan stood up there in front of thirty-three people in Pontotoc, Mississippi, and he leaned his head to one side, lazylike, and he grinned just the way he had on the big silver screen when the five women in the audience were teenagers and knew doggone well they were in love with him. He spoke slow and nice, not drawly and nasal like the hill country folk, but easy like a man who had been up in the mountains and had lived off the wilderness and had come to know himself and his land. As much as anything these people who tilled the soil, sold insurance downtown, filled cars with gasoline at the corner station, and cooked three breakfasts every morning for the old man, the middle kids, and herself and the youngest ones, liked his eyes. They looked straight out at them, clear and without hesitation. He was perfectly groomed, as a movie star or an out-of-state politician should be. His hair was obviously tinted, the cosmetologist noted; it didn't have the gray a man's hair usually had or should have at age fifty-nine or sixty; but only she noticed things like that. And Abner Greene thought his ears were too big, and Doc Morgan the dentist wondered at his perfect teeth. What Ronald Reagan said was, "We're here together in a great land. We are pioneers seeking a better land for our children. We all want what we used to have—a great country for which we can have everlasting pride," and they clapped and stood and shook his hand and had their pictures made with him.

It wasn't by accident that Ronald Reagan, star of a hundred movies and host of a thousand thirty-minute television shows, came to Mississippi in 1974 as he had almost a decade earlier. He was touching base with a people he felt close to. He was laying groundwork for a garden to be grown here and harvested in the future. The quicker the better, but he knew, as the people around him were sure, his time would come.

"I knew Ronald Reagan would be president someday all the way back in the early 1960s, before I got into politics, while I was watching it and commenting on it and knowing what *our* people wanted and who they would vote for and why they would vote for him," commented the long-time Reagan-pusher, U.S. Senator Jesse Helms, who had witnessed the man's performance in a small meeting hall in the tobacco backfields of North Carolina. "He not only had the charisma that was necessary to win, he had the necessary will and the way which is essential. You can tell when a politician is proud and honest, and that's what Ronald Reagan was. He exuded honesty to his fellow man. He was humble honestly, and he spoke out the truth that the people wanted to hear; they were tired of the old-line liberal rhetoric that poured out of Washington for years and years and years. They were ready for a new, honest voice."[1]

While other Republicans heard that new and honest voice in Senator Barry Goldwater of Arizona in 1964, Helms and others, while not denying the candidate their support, "felt sure that other, more viable choices would come our way for a total and absolute swinging of the pendulum from the left to the right." While Helms was an individualist in his own right, he was also a leader of the breed. Too often these were called the new breed, or the New Right, when actually they came from a long line of sufferers in the South that reached back to a time even before the Civil War but who became prevalent after the War. They were the leadership that was manifested in John C. Calhoun, William Lowndes Yancy, William Bankhead, Cotton Tom Heflin, Pitchfork Ben Tillman, James K. Vardaman, and George C. Wallace, all of whom called themselves Democrats or Populists or States' Righters. In the years after he decided politics was the stage upon which he would continue to act, Ronald Reagan wooed the people who had voted for the likes of these leaders. In Hattiesburg, Mississippi, where Theodore G. Bilbo had carried his racist message from the piney woods to Washington, Ronald Reagan told them how he thought this country "should be turned back again to the old tried-and-true ways that our forefathers found to be the backbone of a new nation."[2] And in Clemson, South Carolina, where Strom Thurmond had been carrying the conservative banner for Democrats, States' Righters, and then Republicans since back in the forties, Reagan said, "We need to step hand-in-hand across a threshold into a future that will bring back the value system which has meant so much to so many."[3] His rhetoric was not too different from one meeting to the next. It all held the same simplistic conservative meaning. As one of his early advisers stated in a meeting in Orlando, Florida, "How in the world can anyone argue with mama, apple pie, and Ronald Reagan conservatism? If they do, they're destroying themselves."[4]

Southerners saw something in him they had seen in their earlier political heroes and something they saw in the former Golden Gloves champion George C. Wallace. The South felt a kinship to the West. Like the West it was a frontier. Westerners didn't cotton to folks sitting down on the job, hanging around, doing nothing, waiting for handouts, or at least that's the way Southerners viewed them, and that's what Ronald Reagan told them. And Southerners liked the idea of their leaders being ready, willing, and able to fight for them. Politicians, after all, were hired gunslingers. When the bad men threatened, George Wallace took them on. He had stood in the school-house door, hadn't he? He had gone up north and had toured the Ivy League campuses back in 1964, and he had told them, "As a Southerner, as an American, I stand before you in defiance of illegal and immoral edicts by federal judges who have no idea what the people of our country have to go through every day of their lives."[5]

Perhaps Ronald Reagan never stated his position as strongly, but they knew exactly what he meant when he spilled out his own brand of rhetoric. They felt as though they could send him out onto the street to face the bad guys. They felt confident that he would stand up to whatever evil forces might be lurking out there in the alley. After all, he was the rough and tough Westerner. In Charleston they didn't ask him about his divorce from Jane Wyman. In Waycross they didn't question his one-time stand for the left-wing Democrats in Hollywood. And in Lafayette they didn't probe into his past as a labor union leader with the Screen Actors Guild. While Reagan charmed their pants off with his trained intonations and his firm handshake, they were too kindhearted and hospitable to question his background. They did believe his words, as simple as they were; they grasped his personality. He was the kind of man the men could talk with, the kind of guy they wanted their sons to grow up and be like, a hero of sorts; and he was the kind of man the women wanted to love, the nice kind of fellow they had dreamed about and wished their daughters would grow up and marry. He was soft but forthright, he spoke well and loud enough to be heard, and he told them positive ideas about ideals they had been wanting to hear.

As he moved around the South in those days, moving quietly but forcefully, he was really and truly a living-room candidate; he came into their meeting halls, their convention auditoriums, their hotel banquet rooms, and their panel-lined dens. He rode easily across the territory, clearing the way for another day when he would bring the campaign troops for a showdown.

Ronald Reagan, a dream in alliteration, was the candidate of brightness in the sixties, when for many Southerners the time of Lyndon Baines Johnson was a New Reconstruction, a punishment for racist crimes committed in the past and present. For these Southerners LBJ was the dark candidate: They respected him as a politician just as they somehow respected Huey Long, Sam Rayburn, and John F. Kennedy, but he was darkness, and Ronald Reagan brought them light. LBJ represented black in their eyes while RR was white; whether it was race, land, ideas, economics, or general appearance. There were only a few with whom Reagan shared bourbon and branch water; to most he was the coffee-and-cake candidate, the nice fellow who came to call, who will spend his polite few minutes in the parlor and will never overstay his welcome and will call only when he needs us. LBJ was ever-present, showing off his gall bladder scar, drinking and raising cain, and too willing to give away everything these middle-class Southerners had worked for all these years. Then came along Hubert Horatio Humphrey, ever jubilant about any given issue—especially the prospects of giving away welfare to the needy. The Southerners just couldn't buy him and were glad when George Corley Wallace ran as a third-party candidate, because that way they wouldn't have to choose between Humphrey and Nixon. And in 1972 the mainstream Southern voter could not abide the liberalism of George McGovern even when his Dixieland supporters talked about how he was a good and decent son of a Methodist minister; there was no way in the world they were going to pull the lever for a man who proposed to give everybody in the country $1,000; they had to go with the incumbent Richard Nixon. All the while the sunshine candidate lurked in the wings, waiting for his time to come.

When Reagan ducked in and out of the one-horse towns referred to in Southern idiom as wide-places-in-the-road, he found no Republican organizations to speak of. For the most part in these states the Republican party had not placed any probate judges or county commissioners. There was a scattering for a few years in the mid-sixties, but they had ridden Barry Goldwater's coattails into office when the Deep South's average middle-class white voter rallied behind the senator from Arizona, and the officeholders were not beholden to party machinery for their success. What he had was the people. It was living room chitchat and one-on-one politics.

Reagan brought old-time Reagan Republican party maneuvering home to roost in a conservative Southland. He showed the professionals how the game was played by working the parlors and living rooms and kitchens, not getting headlines in the big-city newspapers but leaving satisfied listeners who would tell neighbors, "He's the kind of person we need in the White House."

In place after place he reinforced this kind of thinking. They had heard him earlier on television when he blasted out with his kind words for Barry Goldwater, and Barry Goldwater was their man back in 1964. He had told it like it was, and now . . .

In Gatlinburg, Tennessee, he told the Volunteer State Republicans, "There are a lot of people out there in our community that you and

I should be talking to, and all of those people are the unsung heroes of our world. They are made up of every race and religion, they are in every economic bracket, and they have every ethnic background." With his words he stunned them to silence. This was their sincere hero telling them about the people they needed to tuck beneath the wing of their party in order to win. And then he hooded his eyes with his elegant brows, zeroing in on the problem. "What I'm talking about," he said, "are all those hundreds of thousands of Americans out there, that great unsung body of Americans who have been carrying the load and paying the bills. They go to work, they send their kids to school, they contribute to their church and to their charity, and they make the wheels go around with their contributions, civic and otherwise. I think that our banner, if we want them to follow us, must be that we say to them, 'We offer equal opportunity at the starting line of life, but no compulsory tie for anyone at the finishing line.' "[6] And they whooped and hollered as politely as they could to his quiet words, while he stood there with his acrylic smile and looked down on them as his eyes opened wide. He knew exactly what he was saying and exactly where he was going. He was leading the Republican party in the South out of the dark ages; that's what he said, and that's what his people said, and that's what the Southern voters believed.

Only a few Southerners knew the history of the Republican party in their region. They did not realize the long tradition that existed, a hate-love relationship from the very beginning, but now it was making itself known and felt.

A Mixture of Madness

A tall man with graying, fashionably shaggy sideburns, a lawyer of considerable talent, a thoughtful conversationalist, and an enthusiastic Wisconsin Whig who spoke out with fiery glee against Jacksonian Democrats of the nineteenth century, Alvin E. Bovay was adamantly in favor of developing a new political party in the United States. Early in 1854, while visiting New York, Bovay sat down with his friend Horace Greeley, the editor of the *Tribune*, who had made a name for himself as a Whig spokesman first with a campaign paper called the *Constitution* and later with his own literary sheet he called the *New-Yorker*. Like Greeley, Bovay was disenchanted with the prevailing Democratic government under which the institution of slavery persisted. Most recently the Democratic-controlled Congress had passed the Kansas-Nebraska Act, permitting the extension of slavery into the new territories. "With all our political strength, we cannot permit the spread of slavery!" Bovay insisted in his Yankee-bent determination. Greeley agreed. And they bantered about possible names for a group that would include all abolitionists, Whigs, and others who were dissatisfied. Of all the names, Bovay said, "Republican is the only one that will serve all purposes present and future—the only one that will live and last."[1]

Bovay called a meeting. And on a warm springtime afternoon in Ripon, Wisconsin, the people gathered in a schoolhouse. On March 20, 1854, "we went into the meeting Whigs, Free-Soilers, and Democrats, and we came out of it Republicans," Bovay announced before the first convention under the oaks in Jackson, Michigan, on July 6. More than 300—too many for the town's largest hall—gathered amid victorious shouts and resolved that "in view of the necessity of battling for the first principles of Republican government, and against the schemes of an aristocracy, the most revolting and oppressive with which the earth was ever cursed, or man debased, we will cooperate and be known as Republicans until the contest be terminated."[2]

It was indeed a Yankee political organization, viewed from a distance by Southerners with something akin to bolshevik disdain for aristocracy. It was seen as humorous by the South until its first major victory came on February 2, 1856. For nearly two months and 133 ballots the contest for Speaker of the U.S. House of Representatives was locked in a dead heat between South Carolina slaveholder William Aiken and Massachusetts Free-Soiler turned Republican Nathaniel Banks, who had vigorously opposed the Kansas-Nebraska Bill. On the 134th ballot Banks was elected. And within several weeks, at its first truly national convention, the members of the Republican party screamed with shouts of joy in Pittsburgh's Lafayette Hall.

Southerners acted like spoiled schoolboys after the new kid in town got the best of them. At first they sulked and did not play the game, watching askance while Free-Soil Democrat Charles Sumner, the bushy-haired, baby-faced senator from Massachusetts took the floor in May, speaking eloquently and loudly with bombastic Yankee pride on "The Crime against Kansas," lambasting many Southerners including Senator Andrew Butler. Several days later Butler's nephew, Preston S. Brooks of South Carolina, came upon Sumner seated at his desk in the Senate chamber. Brooks rushed toward him, lifted his cane, swung it through the air, slashed Sumner across the ear, and then beat him insensible to the wooden floor. Several days later, recuperating from the wounds, Sumner declared that from that moment on he would be a Republican.

In June Sumner carried the banner for a military hero to the Republican national convention in Philadelphia, where on the second ballot John Charles Fremont, the Pathfinder explorer and general, was nominated as candidate for the presidency. The only real drama that emerged was the fight over the nomination for vice president. The strong candidate was New Jersey Senator William L. Dayton, who was challenged by a political newcomer, Abraham Lincoln of Illinois, who managed to win only 110 votes. In losing, young Lincoln showed that he was a true believer in Republicanism by declaring, "Let us, in building our new party, plant ourselves on the rock of the Declaration of Independence and the gates of hell shall not prevail against us."[3]

For the first time women campaigned in a presidential election. Clubs were formed where poor poetic praises of Fremont were read and where accolades were pronounced for the new political party. The literary giants of the North—Henry Ward Beecher, Ralph Waldo Emerson, Horace Greeley, Washington Irving, Walt Whitman, and John Greenleaf Whittier—sang out for a new day ahead for leadership in America. Young men's clubs called the Wide Awakes were formed in every little town across the Midwest. And while all this was happening, down South whispers were broadcast widely by the Democrats that Fremont was a communist and an advocate of free love. It was also said that if he was elected, the South would simply secede. The prevailing belief was that the Republican party was anti-South by its very nature.

The party burst forth with youthful two-year-old enthusiasm, but it suffered from virtually no effective organization and absolutely no support in the South. James Buchanan carried every slave state with the exception of Maryland, and he added Illinois, Indiana, and Pennsylvania, tallying 174 electoral votes to Fremont's 114.

Two years after this defeat had slapped it squarely in the face, the young party picked up a plurality of seats in the House of Representatives, won the governor's chairs in Wisconsin and Maine, and became respectable in Illinois, where Lincoln, who had been defeated in his bid for reelection to Congress, challenged Democratic incumbent U.S. Senator Stephen A. Douglas. In the first speech of the campaign Lincoln's words rang out loudly and clearly for the new party as well as American history:

> We are now far into the fifth year, since a policy was initiated, with the avowed object, and confident promise, of putting an end to slavery agitation. Under the operation of that policy, that agitation has not only not ceased but has constantly augmented. In my opinion, it will not cease, until a crisis shall have been reached, and passed. A house divided against itself cannot stand. I believe this government cannot endure permanently half slave and half free. I do not expect the Union to be dissolved. I do not expect the house to fall. But I do expect it will cease to be divided. It will become all one thing or all the other. Either the opponents of slavery will arrest the further spread of it, and place it where the public mind shall rest in the belief

that it is the course of ultimate extinction; or its advocates will push it forward till it shall become alike lawful in all states, old as well as new—North as well as South.[4]

In his debates with Douglas Lincoln articulated masterfully the words that made Southerners breathe fire and swear they would never live under "a Black Republican." In a speech in October in Quincy, Illinois, Lincoln stated,

> The difference is between the men who think slavery is wrong and those who do not think it wrong. The Republican party thinks it wrong . . . a moral, a social and a political wrong. We think it is a wrong not confining itself merely to the persons or the states where it exists, but that it is a wrong in its tendency, to say the least, that extends itself to the existence of the whole nation. Because we think it wrong, we propose a course of policy that shall deal with it as a wrong. We deal with it as with any other wrong, in so far as we can prevent its growing any larger and so deal with it that in the run of time there may be some promise of an end to it.[5]

Two years later Lincoln was considered a dark horse favorite son of Illinois by the *New York Times*, which supported William H. Seward for the nomination of the new party.

Horace White, secretary of the Republican state committee of Illinois, said of Lincoln:

> He was one of the shrewdest politicians of the state. Nobody had more experience in that way; nobody knew better than he what was passing in the minds of the people. Nobody knew better how to turn things to advantage politically, and nobody was readier to take such advantage, provided it did not involve dishonorable means. He could not cheat people out of their votes any more than out of their money. The Abraham Lincoln that some people have pictured to themselves, sitting in his dingy law office, working over his cases 'til the voice of duty roused him, never existed. If this had been his type, he never would have been called at all.[6]

Describing Lincoln's nomination in Chicago, a reporter wrote, "The response was absolutely terrific, the uproar was beyond description. Imagine all the hogs ever slaughtered in Cincinnati giving their death squeals together, a score of big steam whistles going, and you conceive something of the nature." After the nomination on the third ballot, the reporter continued, "There was a moment's silence. The nerves of thousands, which through the hours of deep suspense had been subjected to terrible tension, relaxed, and as deep breaths of relief were taken, there was a noise in the Wigwam like the rush of a great wind in the van of a storm—and in another breath, the storm was there. There were thousands cheering with the energy of insanity."[7]

Chosen as his running mate was former Jacksonian Democrat Hannibal Hamlin, who had switched parties and had been elected governor of Maine in 1857 as a Republican.

Southerners heard about the carrying on in Chicago, talked about it with utter disdain, and waited for the Democratic convention held in Charleston. But there fights broke out on the floor. Jefferson Davis spoke out in favor of Black Codes for all territories. William Lowndes Yancey, an articulate Alabama spokesman for the Dixie point of view, asked the party to proclaim "that slavery is right."[8] Delegations from eight Deep South states walked out and later nominated John C. Breckinridge, the Kentuckian who was then vice president under Buchanan; Senator Joseph Lane of Oregon was picked as his running mate.

A further split among Southerners came when the National Constitutional Union, the "gentlemen's party," was formed, and John Bell of Tennessee was nominated with Edward Everett of Massachusetts as his vice-presidential nominee.

The South viewed Lincoln with the same contempt that they watched the dashing but hostile figure of Charles Sumner, who on June 4, 1860, delivered a four-hour oration, "The Barbarism of Slavery," on the floor of the Senate. Most of the Deep South stayed with Breckinridge, giving him 849,781 popular votes and seventy-two electoral votes. The Outer South voted with Bell, giving him 588,879 popular and thirty-nine electoral votes. Democrat Stephen Douglas outpolled both with 1,376,957 popular but only twelve electoral votes. Lincoln, sweeping the North, won by a landslide 1,866,452 popular and 188 electoral votes.

While the South revolted, seceding from the Union almost immediately, beginning with South Carolina five days before Christmas in 1860, some Southerners such as Jefferson Davis of Mississippi and Alexander H. Stephens of Georgia attempted to talk their people into giving Lincoln a chance. But by February 1, 1861, South Carolina, Alabama, Mississippi, Florida, Louisiana, Georgia, and Texas had withdrawn from the United States, and a week later delegates from the seven states met in Montgomery, Alabama, and elected Davis president and Stephens vice president of the Confederacy. Holdout counties, which were to become Republican strongholds of the future, dotted the South; these included the free states of Winston in Alabama and Jones in Mississippi. These were hill counties where Unionist sympathies ran high. "They were the Republican cancers on the backside of the South, looked upon as a terrible disease that had to be cured,"[9] wrote Southern historian J. Langford Baggett. One of the reasons why the hill-country folk did not wish to secede—and in several instances tried to secede from the state and declare themselves still a part of the United States—was because the people did not own slaves and had no economic reason for owning slaves. Nevertheless, the residents were called "Black Republicans" by the Confederates.

A plan to colonize blacks outside the United States was drawn up and presented to the national Republican party by Virginian Francis P. Blair and his sons, Frank and Montgomery, who were abolitionist slaveowners. "Our stronghold in the South will be among the poor white people who cannot afford slaves. We can organize the poor white people in the Republican party as long as we can show them that we will move the slaves from their midst. The idea of liberating the slaves and allowing them to remain in the country is one that will never be tolerated,"[10] Blair said. When nonslaveholders of the South were convinced that freedom of blacks and removal of blacks would go hand in hand, Blair said, then the Republican party would emerge as a power in the region. He proposed that the American government purchase land in Central America, where blacks would be given free homesteads, free transportation, and financial aid in establishing themselves in agriculture or business. In speeches in New York, New England, and the Midwest Blair argued his idea, stating that when the former slaves would succeed, other blacks would be attracted to the place of settlement, and soon all blacks would have left the United States. Among the Republican leaders in Congress to support Blair's plan were Preston King, Henry Wilson, Lyman Trumbull, Hannibal Hamlin, Ben Wade, and James Ashley, while Republican newspapers including the *New York Times*, *New York Evening Post*, *Cleveland Leader*, *Chicago Tribune*, and *Boston Daily Bee* supported it. In his first state of the nation address Lincoln urged that Congress consider colonization as a solution "to free colored people and to aid them in their desire to leave the country."[11] At Lincoln's request Congress appropriated $100,000 on April 16, 1862, to aid in resettling persons of African descent.

In the meantime Tennessee, Arkansas, Virginia, and North Carolina joined in secession and in fighting the Civil War. Blair's scheme never came to fruition, although in January 1863, Lincoln's Emancipation Proclamation stated that in the next session of Congress the president would propose a practical measure to "colonize persons of African descent with their consent, upon this continent or elsewhere with the previously obtained consent of the government existing."[12]

Politically the South was in limbo during the war. It had its Confederate government. Leaders claimed the region was fighting for its independence, while in Washington Republican Charles Sumner proclaimed that when a state seceded "it commits suicide and thereafter its territory falls under the exclusive jurisdiction of Congress."[13] He set the stage for Radical Reconstruction. Later Sumner concluded that "the rebels of the South should be punished by giving civil and political rights to the Negroes and educating them in the same schools with the whites."[14] Fellow Republican Thaddeus Stevens spoke of the Confederacy as "conquered provinces" and stated that punishment of the rebels should be "longer remembered than death."[15] As early as December 8, 1863, Lincoln offered to pardon rebels who would sign oaths to support the Constitution of the United States. In sanctioning a moderate approach to Reconstruction Lincoln promised that if ten percent of the voting population of 1860 would qualify by taking such an oath and would establish a state government without slavery, he would recognize the state legal. He qualified his position by adding that suffrage should be extended only to Negroes who were "the very intelligent, and especially those who have fought gallantly in our ranks."[16]

The first state to be defeated, with Confederate troops abandoning it to Union soldiers, was Tennessee, where the first attempt was made to restore civil government. Lincoln sent Andrew Johnson back to his home state to serve as military governor. Not far behind was a former Tennessean who had been intense in his verbal fight for Unionism and Republicanism before the war. William G. "Parson" Brownlow, a tall, rawboned mountaineer carpenter turned itinerant Methodist preacher, had written, edited, and published the Knoxville *Whig*, the last remaining newspaper in the South to oppose secession and embrace Republicanism. Into the fall of 1861 he had been known as a fighter against the Confederacy, publishing diatribes against Jefferson Davis and other Confederate leaders. He roused groups to burn railroad bridges and destroy other means of transportation for the Southern troops. Although he suspended the publication of his paper in October, publicly inviting the army to arrest him, Davis and the others wanted to avoid making him a martyr. More than a thousand graycoats marched into East Tennessee, brought him secretly through the battlelines north, and released him to Union troops. It was reported that when he saw the flag, he shouted, "Glory be to God in the highest, on earth peace and good will to all men, except a few hell-born and hell-bound rebels down in Knoxville!"[17] An orator of more than average talent, he began a tour of the major cities of the North, spoke to vast audiences about the hell on earth in the South, drew pictures of the horror of slavery, and made his listeners weep and applaud. As soon as the Union army took Tennessee, he followed General Burnside's hoofbeats, started his presses rolling, published the Knoxville *Whig and Rebel Ventilator*, and after a new constitution was adopted under Andrew Johnson, was elected governor of the state.

But political success did not ease his fury. At first reticently attentive to Lincoln and Johnson's mild Reconstruction policy, Brownlow then sided with the Radical Republicans in Congress when they and the administration parted company. Brownlow led his Tennessee delegation to the convention for Southern Loyalists in Philadelphia in September 1866. Speaking out against President Johnson, Brownlow called for the extension of suffrage to blacks. Upon returning to Tennessee, he called a special session of the legislature through which he pushed the Fourteenth Amendment, later fraudulently obtaining a quorum to ratify it. He also encouraged the legislature to disfranchise former Confederates. He traveled the state promoting Republicanism, especially in his home area of East Tennessee. After serving four years as governor, he was elected to the U.S. Senate in 1869. Crippled, he sold his newspaper and served out his six-year term in Washington in a wheelchair. Until his death he was outspoken in favor of Radical Republicanism. However, during his term as governor there were no black officeholders; the legislature that he controlled did extend suffrage to blacks who in turn voted for Brownlow-backed white Republicans. After he went to the Senate, Republicans lost other elections in Tennessee even as the party was beginning to gain strength in other Southern states where, under Reconstruction, blacks were gaining ballot privileges. Without Brownlow's leadership the Republican party in Tennessee split between the blacks and the whites.

On the national scene the South lost the war piecemeal. Lincoln appointed military governors to Louisiana, Arkansas, and Virginia, and the last was given special political dispensation. Government was established in Alexandria under Francis H. Pierpont, slavery was abolished, and the Constitution was recognized. Since that precedent, not requiring a special election in the state to ratify its positions, Virginia continued to be given special privileges politically even into the 1980s, when the state was allowed more leeway on its reapportionment than any other in the South.

Lincoln and Congress continued to bicker about plans for Reconstruction until the night in April 1865 when he was assassinated.

Taking over as president, Andrew Johnson expressed the viewpoint that the Southern states had never legally been out of the Union and their constitutional relations to the federal government were therefore unaffected. He began to carry out the main thrust of Lincoln's May Amnesty Plan, which would grant pardons to anyone who would swear allegiance to the U.S. Constitution, with the exception of certain specified rebels such as top civil and military officers of the Confederacy, men who had resigned from federal service to join the rebels, and persons possessing more than $20,000 which he thought would make them rich enough to oppose the federal government.

In North Carolina William H. Holden was appointed provisional governor; he called for a constitutional convention, which set the stage for others in the Reconstruction states. Following the president's orders, it abolished slavery legally, repudiated the Ordinances of Secession, and rejected all Confederate war debt. Only in South Carolina was the final provision never carried out. When white, mostly Democratic leaders failed to carry out Johnson's orders to allow black men who were educated and who owned property to vote, the president did not push for black suffrage. There was only one Parson Brownlow. Most of the Southern white leaders attempted to undercut Johnson's moderate approach—apparently not knowing or caring to know the consequences.

The Radical Republicans of the North reacted angrily. In December 1865 Congress refused to seat members sent from the South. In rapid succession Congress formed the Freedmen's Bureau to assume authority over the blacks in the South and to make sure they were not treated unfairly, dispatched an army of occupation to suspend operation of civil authority in the Southern states, and created a fifteen-member Joint Committee on Reconstruction. Headed by Thaddeus Stevens, who announced during the initial session that he personally backed a plan to confiscate all rebel property and redistribute it among the black citizens, the committee heard 144 witnesses of whom more than 100 expressed strong bias against white Southerners.

The new white Democratic governments in the Southern states paid no attention to what was happening in Washington. They persisted in their insolence against Republican leadership. With the exception of Tennessee, all legislatures rejected the Fourteenth Amendment, which provided civil rights for blacks and a means to penalize states that refused to allow blacks to vote. Arguing vehemently for states' rights, the Southern legislators moved another step by shaking a fist in the face of authority by passing a series of Jim Crow Black Codes based on old vagrancy laws from the British West Indies. While abolishing slavery, most Southern legislatures wrote laws stating that those with one-eighth or more Negro blood were to be considered as "persons of color."[18] The laws mapped out specific provisions for marriage, most allowing blacks to marry only blacks. In Mississippi blacks could own land only in towns, while in Alabama and South Carolina they could own land only outside of townships. In some states blacks could testify only in court cases involving their own race, and in some they could only sue persons of their own color. Except under special circumstances and after obtaining a special license could a black in South Carolina work in any business other than husbandry or as domestic help. In Mississippi vagrancy laws affected blacks who did not have jobs and blacks "found assembling themselves together."[19]

The Republicans announced that under General Oliver O. Howard the Freedmen's Bureau would fight against such Southern Democratic-passed laws. It would see that food and other necessities were distributed among the blacks, act as an employment agency throughout the region, supervise labor contracts, transport the dislocated to their former homes, provide hospitals and other medical services, open schools, and protect the former slaves from social and legal discrimination. So angered at the passing of the Black Codes was the *Chicago Tribune* that it editorialized, "Tell the white men of Mississippi that the men of the North will convert the state of Mississippi into a frog-pond before they will allow such laws to disgrace one foot of soil over which the flag of freedom waves."[20] And pointing toward the Jim Crow laws, Stevens and Charles Sumner told their fellow Republicans that if the free blacks of the South were not enfranchised immediately, Democrats and former Confederates would soon control the national government.

Republican Takeover

Frightened by the warning sounds of the party's leadership, Congressional Republicans fell into line with Sumner and Stevens. Two years after Appomattox Radical Reconstruction was put into effect. The lawmaking body of the federal government declared that in ten of the eleven former Confederate states there was no legal local government that could or would protect life and property. The only exception was Tennessee because it had already, under Parson Brownlow, undergone reconstruction.

The South was divided into five military districts: Virginia; the two Carolinas; Georgia, Florida, and Alabama; Mississippi and Arkansas; and Louisiana and Texas. Each had a military commander with powers to make arrests, conduct trials by military commissions, suspend functions of civil government whenever necessary, and call delegates into convention to frame constitutions, make rules of suffrage, and have legislatures elected under the constitutions approve the Fourteenth Amendment.

A Supplementary Reconstruction Act, passed in July 1866 placed the commanders of the military districts under the control of General Ulysses S. Grant rather than the president as Commander-in-Chief.

Following Johnson's veto of the acts, which the Congress immediately overrode, the Radical Republicans attempted to impeach the president. Johnson vigorously defended his stand, spoke out in favor of the Southern portion of the United States being allowed to take up their previous position in the government, and criticized Radical Reconstruction as bad law. The impeachment resolutions were narrowly defeated, Johnson remained president, but Radical Republicans continued their plan of punishment for the upstart Southern Democratic leadership. Six governors were replaced, civil courts were suppressed, more than a thousand local elected officials were drummed out of office and supplanted by blacks and carpetbaggers who had smelled the perfume of power. Much state legislation that had recently been ramrodded through the lawmaking houses by the Democrats, including provisions to give free education and artificial limbs to crippled Confederate veterans, was set aside. Representatives of the Radicals rode through the Southland, organizing small units of the Republican party and preaching the uplifting influences of universal suffrage. The men who brought their changes of longjohns in their carpetbags sat around campfires in the shantytowns, talked about freedom and equal rights, made reference to the Declaration of Independence to the accompanying rhythm of the clanging of chains and the burning of sweet-smelling incense. "They did the hoodoo and the voodoo, and they made the blacks rear up, and they told them everything would be good and beautiful, and they said the Southern whites were Democratic and bad, and they said the only way for Negro people was the Republican way," wrote free slave Jackson Lee Morganville of Savannah, Georgia, in the first days of Radical Reconstruction.[1]

At the 1868 Republican national convention in Chicago four black delegates, one each from North Carolina, Louisiana, Texas, and South Carolina, became the first blacks in American history to attend a convention of a major political party. Moderate Republicans rallied their forces to nominate on the first ballot U.S. Grant over the darling of the Radicals, Chief Justice Salmon P. Chase, a champion of black suffrage. Picked as Grant's running mate was Schuyler Colfax, former speaker of the Indiana House of Representatives, who subsequently did most of the campaigning for the ticket.

After the Republicans won the general election, blacks from twenty-two states met in Washington, D.C., on January 12, 1869, to promote support in Congress of a Constitutional amendment for black suffrage. The Fifteenth Amendment soon received the necessary two-thirds vote in both houses and was sent out to the states for ratification. Blacks throughout the nation sang the praises of the Republican party.

On March 30, less than a month after he was sworn into office, Grant proclaimed the Fifteenth Amendment ratified. The Reconstruction governments of the South had all voted for ratification in elections that were closely guarded by federal troops and counted by the new black and white Republicans of the South. Frederick Douglass, the spokesman for hundreds of thousands of blacks, told the American Anti-Slavery Society ten days later, "I am a Republican! I am a black Republican dyed in the wool! And I never intend to belong to any other party than the party of freedom and progress."[2]

White Southern Democrats were aghast. Black Southern Republicans were delighted. "Douglass' speech did more for the recruitment of freedmen into the Republican party than any other single cause," stated black Tennessee politician James Everett Johnson, who rode horseback from small community to township organizing former slaves into Republican enclaves.[3]

Blacks of the South believed that Grant would be their political savior even more so than Lincoln. One black historian wrote:

> While the essence of Black Republicanism stems from progressive Republican measures up to 1870, it was during the era of Black Reconstruction, in which more and more black public officials served as symbols and examples of Republican concern, interest, and dedication to the idea of freedom, that Black Republicanism took even deeper roots. Black politicians themselves became the final link connecting the black community to the Republican party. They not only served the black community but helped to stimulate, motivate and maintain black allegiance to the Republican party.[4]

While on one hand Grant did not urge Radical Reconstruction, he took a hands-off attitude toward the South which tended to make all sides irritated if not angry. The foundations of the Republican party were laid after the passage of the Fifteenth Amendment. A coalition was formed between the scalawags (white Southerners who became Republicans during Reconstruction), carpetbaggers (white Northerners who came south after the Civil War and became Republican activists), and black former slaves who joined the Republican party.

Scalawags and carpetbaggers alike fought tooth and nail for power in the Republican party. In Georgia scalawag Governor Joseph E. Brown used his office to become president of a steamship company, a railroad company, and a coal and iron company. Antagonizing both scalawags and carpetbaggers, who tried to have him thrown out of office, he was taken care of by supporters to whom he had given positions within the party. In Mississippi the first Republican to be elected governor, James Alcorn, a scalawag, attempted to sell control of the state to the Whigs, but other scalawags, carpetbaggers, and blacks voted him out and put a carpetbagger into office.

Describing one element of this new political coalition, the Montgomery *Daily Advertiser* in 1865 wrote:

> Our scalawag is the local leper of the community. Unlike the carpetbagger, he is native, which is so much the worse. Once he was respected in this circle; his head was level, and he could look his neighbor in the face. Now, possessed of the itch of office and the salt rheum of Radicalism, he is a mangy dog, slinking through the alleys, haunting the governor's office, defiling with tobacco juice on the steps of the capitol, stretching his lazy carcass in the sun on the square, or the benches of the mayor's court. The tribe of scalawags is not numerous but its members are very pestiferous, like the frogs of Egypt, that crawled into the ovens and kneading troughs of the people. We long to write the obituary of the last of the scalawag.[5]

While no black was ever elected governor, the son of a former slave and a white planter, Pinckney Benton Stewart Pinchback, was acting governor of Louisiana from December 9, 1872, until January 13, 1873. Born in Macon, Georgia, he went along with his mother when she was sold to a plantation owner in Louisiana, where he was raised. Shortly after he left office the state legislature elected him U.S. senator. The Radical Republican leadership in Washington supported Pinchback, who was vehemently opposed by moderate Republicans and Democrats. He was never seated in Congress. But he remained in Washington until his death in 1921.

Mississippi, Louisiana, and South Carolina elected black lieutenant governors, and Mississippi elected two black U.S. senators, who were seated. The coalition government in South Carolina was described by James Shepherd Pike in *The Prostrate State*, expressing his shock at the state of the state:

> The Speaker is black, the Clerk is black, the doorkeepers are black, and the chaplain is coal-black. At some of the desks sit colored men whose types it would be hard to find outside of the Congo; whose costumes, visages, attitudes and expression only befit the forecastle of a buccaneer. Seven years ago these men were raising corn and cotton under the whip of the overseer. Today they are raising points of order and questions of privilege. Today they find that they can raise one as well as the other. They prefer the latter. It is easier, and better paid. It means escape and defense from the old oppressors. It means liberty. It means the destruction of prison walls only too real to them. It is the sunshine of their lives. It is their day of jubilee. It is their long-promised vision of the Lord God Almighty.[6]

In 1872, with Grant's silent support, Congress passed the Amnesty Act, which removed the political restrictions that had been put on the prewar leadership and restored to them the right to hold elected office. This act breathed new life back into the white Democrats, who had found themselves on the outside looking in during the first years of Radical Reconstruction. It also angered the Radical Republicans, who backed Democratic nominee Horace Greeley against Grant in the 1872 election.

But, as John Tweedy reported from the Philadelphia Republican national convention:

> The spacious academy was crowded with thousands of spectators in every part, and on the stage, in the parquet, and in tier upon tier of galleries, arose deafening prolonged, tremendous cheers, swelling from pit to dome. A perfect wilderness of hats, caps, and handkerchiefs waved to and fro in a surging mass. The band appeared to catch the prevailing enthusiasm and waved their instruments as though they had been flags, and then they struck up "Hail to the Chief." As the majestic stream of music came floating down from the balcony, a life-size equestrian portrait of General Grant came down, as if by magic, filling the entire space of the back scene, and the enthusiasm knew no bounds.[7]

And the enthusiasm continued through the election as Grant amassed three times more popular votes than he had in 1868, receiving 272 electoral votes to Greeley's sixty-three.

During Grant's second term the war-ravaged South was further hurt by runaway inflation, which caused U.S. money to weaken drastically. Southern white Democrats blamed the Republicans for all the problems. Then business scandals panicked Wall Street, and economic problems worsened.

In the North cartoonist Thomas Nast was having a satirical field day with the poor showing of Republican administration and Republican Senate. On November 2, 1874, Nast's elephant symbol for the Grand Old Party appeared for the first time in *Harper's Weekly*. The great elephant labeled "The Republican Vote" stampeded past other smaller animals, stepping across a dark pit labeled "Southern Claims and Chaos," over which was laid planks stamped "Inflation," "Repudiation," "Reconstruction," and "Reform–Tammany." After cartoonist Nast had the elephant fall into the pit, he showed that the only escape possible would be Grant's repudiation of third-term aspirations.

In the Republicans' fourteenth year in power Senator George F. Hoar of Massachusetts reviewed the party's accomplishments:

> [It] enacted a protective tariff which made the United States the greatest manufacturing nation on earth; it enlisted, organized and sent back to civil life a vast army; it created a great navy, constructed on principles not invented when it came into power; it put down a gigantic rebellion; it made freemen and citizens of four million slaves; it contrived the national banking system; it created a currency which circulates throughout the world on an equality with gold; it made the credit of the country the best in the world; it restored specie payment; it devised and inaugurated the beneficient homestead system; it built the Pacific railroads; it compelled France to depart from Mexico; it exacted apology and reparation from Great Britain; it overthrew the doctrine of perpetual allegiance and required the great powers of Europe hereafter to let our adopted citizens alone; it made honorable provision for invalid soldiers and sailors.[8]

In rebuttal a Southern politician remarked, "Apart from the Mexican War, all of these things that the Republican party did built up an overpowering centralized government, wrecked the economy, gave away land and money to people for no good reason, and made mockery of our military system. I think it is nothing to be proud of."[9]

Throughout the South white Democrats battled for control of the local governments. In Mississippi the state election of 1875 was one in which terror was wielded to recapture the political machinery. Blacks were run off their land and into swamps, or were induced to show up at the polls with Democratic ballots clutched in their hands, while white Republicans were shunned, their children hounded at school, and their wives dressed down as immoral in some churches. At the same time in Alabama Henry County landlords required their black laborers to sign political contracts stating that if they voted wrong or Republican it meant a loss of job, medical benefits, credit, food, and farm supplies.

According to at least one source, Lerone Bennett, Jr.'s *Before the Mayflower*, the new governments in the South and the sudden absence of federal troops to look over the shoulders of those in control "reduced Negroes to political impotence . . . by the boldest and most ruthless political operation in American history: by stealth and murder; by economic intimidation and political assassination; by whippings and maimings, cuttings and shootings; by the knife; by the whip; by the political use of terror . . . by fear."

Mississippi elected the first black to the U.S. Senate. Born in North Carolina, Hiram Rhoades Revels had led several black regiments for the Union in the Civil War. He settled in Natchez after the war and successfully lobbied the Radical Republican Mississippi legislature to elect him to take the U.S. Senate seat previously held by Confederate President Jefferson Davis. After a year in Washington he resigned to become president of Alcorn College in Mississippi. Expressing disgust with the heavy-handed tactics of the radical-dominated legislature, Revels joined with Democrats to defeat the carpetbag government. In an open letter to President Grant Revels declared that the combined forces of all good men of Mississippi—Democrat or Republican, black or white—had brought an end to the graft-laden Republican state government.

Mississippi also elected the first black to serve a full term in the U.S. Senate. Blanche K. Bruce, born in Virginia and raised in Missouri, moved to Mississippi in 1868, bought a Delta Plantation, became a successful cotton planter, and was elected to the Senate in 1875. Serving one term, he spoke out loudly and emphatically against election frauds promulgated by Southern whites, but he also attempted to remove what he thought was the excessive punishment against the Southern whites imposed by the Radical Republicans. On more than one occasion Bruce made speeches on the Senate floor in which he defended the rights of all minorities, including blacks, Southern white, Chinese, and American Indians. He worked to improve navigation on the Mississippi River, met with foreign emissaries to promote international trade, and after his term in office remained in Washington, where he accepted several federal appointments from Republican administrations.

When shortly after the Civil War Arkansas held its constitutional convention, General Albert Pike raised his voice against black suffrage, saying that it would make Little Rock and other Southern capitals "hell on earth, a hideous, horrid pandemonium filled with all the devils of vice, crime, pauperism, corruption, violence, political debauchery, and social anarchy."[10] Nevertheless, the suffrage amendment was carried by a preponderance of black and white Republicans, and the new constitution was ratified by a vote of 33,380 to forty-one. And by 1873 Arkansas passed one of the South's most stringent civil rights laws; it made hotels and other places of public amusement admit all persons, and it contained a punishment of fines up to $1,000 and imprisonment to twelve months. When the Democrats recaptured the state in 1874 the black state militia was attacked on the streets of Little Rock and aboard the one state boat in the Arkansas River. Several persons of both races were killed, and more than a dozen were injured. Tension prevailed, but the Democrats held on to take complete control, and Washington never intervened. Such violence was not unusual during these days in Arkansas, since only two years earlier two factions of Republicans had battled between themselves during a state convention, and one group had taken possession of the state capitol by force. The Democrats persuaded the victorious group to join them, and together they became the final ruling party—as Democrats—by the mid-1870s.

Alabama's Reconstruction government was less violent but no less confusing in 1870, when Governor William H. Smith, running for reelection, was defeated by Democratic nominee Robert Burns Lindsay. When Lindsay arrived in Montgomery on November 19 to assume control of the government, the state Republican leadership advised the incumbent not to vacate the capitol. The Republicans won a court injunction to keep the president of the state senate from opening the election returns for the offices of governor and treasurer. Democrats had also won the other state offices of lieutenant governor, secretary of state, and attorney general. After a long weekend of bickering Speaker of the House John H. Hubbard called a joint meeting of the legislature to order, Edward H. Moren was escorted to the speaker's rostrum, where he was sworn in as lieutenant governor. He then ordered the president of the senate to count the votes for governor and treasurer. Following a short recess Moren announced that Robert Burns Lindsay had been elected governor and J. F. Grant treasurer. Lindsay stepped forward and was sworn into office by Speaker Hubbard amid the noise of cheering mixed with catcalls. After being sworn in, Lindsay and the other Democrats proceeded to the governor's office, where they discovered Smith and incumbent treasurer Chester Arthur Bingham barricaded inside. While the Democrats banged on the door, Smith called in U.S. troops, who took possession of the capitol. During the next two weeks Lindsay wrote to Smith and requested his surrender; Smith wrote back his refusal, stating that the votes could not be counted because of the injunction; Lindsay rebutted that there could be no contest of the election unless the votes were counted; finally Smith agreed to allow the votes to be counted if the election could indeed be certified. After Smith and Bingham had been locked in the governor's office for two weeks, sustained by food handed to them through the windows, a circuit judge was called in. He ordered the Republicans out of the office, and Lindsay finally became governor on December 10, 1870.

When the Republican party of South Carolina held its first state convention in Charleston in 1867, it endorsed the Reconstruction Acts, as did most other local party organizations. After the party was formally structured, at a later meeting, in July in Columbia, forty-five of the sixty-nine delegates were blacks. Their platform called for universal suffrage, equal rights, economic reform, and a system of free education. By the November election about 69,000 registered blacks actually voted. Black Republicans won many state offices, and two years later the first black was elected to the U.S. House of Representatives. Joseph Hayne Rainey, the son of a barber from Georgetown, South Carolina, took his seat in Congress in 1869, spoke out in favor of Radical Reconstruction, championed civil rights legislation, and stated on the floor of the House that all people should have access to all public places. On his way home from Washington he stopped at an inn that had previously served only white clientele. When Rainey refused to leave the dining room where he was seated, white law-enforcement officers picked him up and bodily threw him out onto the road. He used the incident later to illustrate the need for stronger public-access laws, but his legislation was not accomplished in his lifetime. He returned to his birthplace in Georgetown, where he died in 1887.

Throughout this period the Ku Klux Klan continued their violent activities. In Dallas County, Alabama, in August 1874, robed Klansmen assassinated two Republican leaders, one black and one white. At Spring Hill near Eufaula, in Barbour County, Democrats stormed a polling place at twilight, shot out the lantern, fired at the Republican official who had been counting the votes, fatally wounded his sixteen-year-old son, and stole the ballot box which contained more than 1,700 mostly Republican votes. In Russell County on the state line Georgia Democrats crossed over and voted freely in the Alabama election.

During these years of political chaos in the South the Republican party, while attempting to help the poor black former slaves, put itself deeper and deeper into the Southern pit of despair. The elephant Thomas Nast created in his cartoons slipped badly in the cottonfields. The cotton farmer hated the sound of the name Republican as the price of his product dropped lower and lower during this period. In 1870 cotton sold for fifteen cents per pound, but by 1880 it was down to less than ten cents per pound, and ten years later it brought less than eight cents per pound. After charges for transportation, commissions to brokers and merchants, and deductions for substandard quality, Southern farmers received even less than the going rate for the once-lucrative crop.

Compromised Reconstruction

In 1876 the twenty-year-old Republican party had held the presidency for four full terms, and Thomas Nast's cartoons became stronger and stronger in their acid comments. Running on the ticket to keep the Grand Old Party in office was a graduate of Harvard Law School, four-time wounded veteran of the Civil War, former member of the House of Representatives, and three-time governor of Ohio. At the national convention Rutherford Birchard Hayes had appeared in opposition to a third term for U.S. Grant. Running with William A. Wheeler of New York, the Hayes ticket was shown by Nast as an elephant stomping the daylights out of Democratic nominees Samuel Tilden and Thomas Hendricks. But after the election on November 8, when Tilden-Hendricks outpolled the Republicans in popular votes and electoral votes, doubts were raised as to the validity of voting practices in Louisiana, South Carolina, Florida, and Oregon. A special commission appointed by the Congress found that irregularities had taken place in the Southern states, and it was recommended that Hayes be awarded 185 electoral votes to Tilden's 184. When the Democratic House threatened filibuster in which there would be loud shouts of scandal, a group of Hayes supporters met with Southern leaders at the Wormley House Hotel in Washington. After thrashing out possibilities, a compromise was struck. It was agreed that the Southerners would allow Hayes to take office. Upon taking office, Hayes would remove federal troops from state governments of South Carolina and Louisiana where they had been stationed to make sure Reconstruction Acts were adhered to. Hayes would also ask for appropriations for funds to be given for the completion of the Texas and Pacific Railroad as well as more money to be given for overall improvements of all the Southern states. He would also appoint a Southerner to his cabinet. In return Republican James A. Garfield would be elected Speaker of the House despite a Democratic majority.

After it was announced that Hayes would be the next president, Thomas Nast drew his elephant stumbling, battered and bandaged, through a battle-torn field. The tagline read: "Another such victory and I am undone . . ."[1]

As his people had promised, Hayes withdrew federal troops from the statehouses and countrysides of South Carolina and Louisiana on April 10, 1877. To the position of postmaster general he named conservative David M. Key, who began handing out jobs to his friends throughout the South. And Hayes began his rebuilding program by naming prosperous whites to other federal positions in the region. Telling blacks in Atlanta that "your rights and interests will be safer if intelligent white men were let alone by the general government,"[2] he considered that his moves would bring about a Southern fusion among Republicans—and he set the stage for future Republican actions in the South regarding blacks.

In September 1877 swinging through the South accompanied by South Carolina Governor Wade Hampton, Hayes told a number of people that he was accomplishing his grand purpose. In October, however, when Congress met in special session, Southern Democrats in the majority reneged on their agreement to elect Garfield to the Speaker's chair. Hayes then leaned back in his rocker in the Oval Office and said he would have to reconsider the matter of federally funding the Texas and Pacific Railroad.

During his first year in office Hayes was criticized by Yankee abolitionist William Lloyd Garrison, who said the President "believes the best way to protect sheep from being devoured is to give them over to the wolves."[3] In the off-year congressional elections Republicans dropped from ten to three seats in the South. Both predominantly black and white counties across Dixie went Democratic. As Garrison and other radical northerners insisted that "the bloody shirt" of stronger federal controls on Reconstruction be waved again, Southern Democrats in Congress attempted to repeal the Federal Elections Act of 1871. Hayes vetoed the repeal bills eight times, stating that there had to be federal election control, but all the while his pollwatchers in the South had become mere figureheads.

Assessing the Hayes administration, historian Benjamin B. Kendrick wrote that it was recognized "principally for the pacification policy adopted with respect to the Southern states, bringing about the end of the 'carpetbag governments.' This action brought Hayes into sharp conflict with many of the political leaders of the party. It, however, made more rapid the slow recovery of the South from the effects of the war and was beneficial to the nation."[4]

South Carolina Democratic Governor Wade Hampton, who had won his office on the promise of equal rights but who also employed the use of KKK-like Red Shirts to intimidate black Republicans, traveled to Washington to meet with President-elect Hayes after both Democrats and Republicans claimed a victory in the state elections. On election day Georgians and North Carolinians had been brought across the South Carolina border to vote for Hampton and the Democrats. After the meeting Hayes removed the federal troops from South Carolina and supported Hampton for governor.

For all practical purposes Hayes' actions destroyed the Republican party in South Carolina. When intimidation increased in 1877, Hampton and the Democrats pointed to a minor corruption involving several Republican officeholders to justify their night-riding, economic pressures, and ballot-box patrolling. When it became evident that President Hayes would not interfere in the local problem, the intimidation became even more intense and open. Before the elections of 1878 the Democrats passed a new law. All ballot boxes would be labeled for each office, and any ballot in the wrong box would be declared void. The Democrats knew that such a requirement would further repress the Republicans because a great percentage of the voting blacks were illiterate. During the year the Republicans split between Black Republicans and Lily-White Republicans. Similar splits occurred elsewhere in the South, the blacks calling their party the Black and Tan Republican party and the whites being known as the Lily-Whites.

The 1880 Republican National Convention, attended by black and white delegates from nearly every Southern state, was a cause for celebration of twenty years of Republican leadership in the White House. After former President U.S. Grant and James G. Blaine locked horns on the first ballot, James A. Garfield of Ohio became the dark-horse compromise and captured the nomination on the thirty-sixth ballot. After a childhood of poverty on a rundown farm near Orange, Ohio, Garfield graduated from Williams College, became a schoolteacher, read the law, fought in the Union Army, and was elected to Congress for eight terms. Earlier in 1880 he had been chosen to represent Ohio in the U.S. Senate. After he was nominated, Garfield became the first candidate of a major political party in the United States to take a significant part in his own campaign for the presidency. He made more than seventy speeches, a number before Southern audiences. Until his effort it had been customary for candidates to let their supporters do most of the campaigning. Also in this campaign the U.S. witnessed the first documented political dirty trick, when a short-lived Democratic publication entitled *TRUTH: The Whole Truth and Nothing But the Truth* published on its front page a letter that was represented as having been handwritten by Garfield on House of Representatives stationery. The letter expressed the candidate's subservience to big business as his largest contributor and advocated increasing immigration of cheap Chinese laborers. The publication of the letter caused an immediate and immense sensation, but within days it was proven to be a forgery. The writer of the letter was indicted, tried, and sent to prison for eight years. With Chester Alan Arthur as his running mate, Garfield won all the electoral votes he needed without question or controversy, but the popular vote was very close—4,449,053 to Democrat General Winfield S. Hancock's 4,442,030—with Republican votes in the South falling off as much as fifty percent in some states. It was obvious that the Southern Democrats had gained back most of the control they had had before the Civil War, and President Hayes' compromise had not won over to the Republicans the white support he had hoped for. Garfield wrote in a letter to an associate that the closeness of the election was due to "the distrust of the solid South." He tempered his words in his inauguration speech, saying that "under our institutions there is no middle ground for the Negro race between slavery and equal citizenship. There can be no permanent disfranchised peasantry in the United States," and adding that the question of an uneducated electorate in the South "is of supreme importance."[5]

Garfield was assassinated on September 19, 1881, and Arthur was sworn in the following day. A young lawyer who first attracted attention with his winning of the Lemmon Slave Case, in which it was established that blacks were automatically free and could shake off the shackles of their past when they stepped onto free soil, Chester

Arthur was no favorite of the South. Like his predecessors, he gave Southern patronage to well-to-do whites and disregarded the blacks who had voted for Garfield.

In his third try for the Republican nomination James G. Blaine became the party's standard bearer in 1884. A former Speaker of the House of Representatives and the U.S. senator from Pennsylvania, Blaine had been defeated twice for the nomination by dark-horse candidates. On election eve, when a Blaine supporter spoke to a group of New York clergymen, he stated emphatically, "We are Republicans and don't propose to leave our party and identify ourselves with a party whose antecedents have been rum, Romanism, and rebellion." Pro-Democratic newspapers in New York headlined the anti-Catholic slur and gave the impression that Blaine was personally responsible for the statement. On the next day Blaine lost the state's large Catholic vote, allowing Democrat Grover Cleveland to win the state by 1,500 votes. Cleveland also carried the solid South, Missouri, Illinois, Kentucky, West Virginia, Delaware, and Maryland. Blaine won fewer Southern votes than Hayes or Garfield. For the first time in twenty-four years a Democrat occupied the White House.

Losing the Southern states by such large percentages was not taken lightly. By the end of Cleveland's second year in office, when the Republicans were beginning to rebuild for a strong surge in 1888, an unnamed editorialist commented in the *New York Times*:

> Those Republican politicians who still think there is capital for their party in keeping up sectional agitation and firing the Northern heart with Southern outrages are trying desperately to make an issue of the alleged suppression of the Republican vote in Southern states. The difficulty which confronts them lies in the fact that the Northern people want no more sectional agitation and are entirely willing to leave the elections in Southern states to the control of the people in those states. This does not imply a lack of belief in some of the alleged wrongs, but it indicates a lack of faith in the efficacy of federal interference to right them, and a willingness to leave the South to work out its own political problems. Universal suffrage does not work to perfection in any state. It is beset with evils and abuses against which honest men are constantly contending, but it is generally admitted that the states must be left to cure these evils as best they can.
>
> Most candid men both North and South are forced to counteract the effect of the Negro vote where it is large enough materially to affect results. The original reason for this is to be found in the deplorable consequences that followed upon the enfranchisement of the colored race. Unprepared to exercise intelligently or conscientiously their newly acquired rights, the Negroes fell under the leadership of unscrupulous men and were arrayed against the

people who had the largest interest in the good order and good government of the reconstructed states. The result was incapacity, extravagance and fraud in public affairs, and a burlesque on popular government. The native Southern people, who felt that they had the right to control affairs in their own states, saw no salvation for their public or private interests except in overcoming the power which was thrust upon them. It could not be done by persuasion, and they were prepared to countenance almost any means by which it could be done. Even the federal power intrenched in the reconstruction acts could not prevent the violence and the outrages by which the control of three states was recovered by the men who paid the taxes and who had the intelligence and character to maintain decent government.

The North soon admitted that federal interference to sustain state governments which rested on the ignorant Negro vote and were managed mainly by greedy and unscrupulous adventurers could not be maintained. Public opinion withdrew all support, and nearly a dozen years ago the whole fabric went to pieces. By one means or another the Negro vote was to a large extent suppressed, and there is no question that in several states it has since been kept down so far as was necessary to enable the native Southerners, who owned property, who paid taxes, and who controlled intelligent public sentiment in their states, to direct the management of their public interests. This is a fact which most Southern men will privately admit and defend. On the other hand, most candid Northern men will admit that, given the same situation in any Northern state, the result would have been the same. This is the truth of the history of the last twenty years.

There is no need to go into the circumstances which inevitably arrayed the great mass of intelligent and property-owning citizens in the Southern states against the Republican Party so long as it controlled the National Administration. They were determined to control the political and public affairs of their states, and they were mostly Democrats. Outrage, violence, and election frauds diminished in proportion as the necessity for them ceased. For the last two years little has been heard of them, but election returns show that many votes are withheld from the ballot box for one reason or another. Colored voters may have become indifferent, after finding that the ills which they were taught to expect from Democratic ascendency did not befall them, and easily induced not to vote. More or less, also, they have begun to divide their votes between parties. In not voting or in voting for Democratic candidates they are probably influenced by no worse inducements than are used in Northern states to sway the action of voters whose intelligence and honesty are not sufficient to guide their political action.

There is but one helpful way of dissolving the Democratic solidity of the South. Slowly the political intelligence of the colored citizen increases. Gradually the colored vote is ceasing to be a solid Republican vote. As it divides, the motives which sustain the Democratic solidity will give way, and the questions which divide citizens in the North on national politics will divide them in the South, without regard to race. Every attempt to maintain sectional distinctions, every suggestion of new experiments of Federal intervention, will retard this process, and every such attempt or suggestion will find less and less support in the North. The Republican Party abandons its chance of making gains in the South and loses still more of its support in the North every time it insists anew upon its sectional attitude. The country is weary of the long contest and wishes to see both parties national in spirit and in purpose. There are electoral wrongs in the Southern states. They have been diminishing steadily for years, and the process will go on if no new antagonism is excited. Negro suffrage presents problems and difficulties of those states which cannot be settled at once, but they can only be settled at all by the people of the states in which they exist.[6]

During the next year, when the Republicans met in Chicago, enough of the delegates had read the *Times* editorial or had the same prevailing thoughts that they again turned away from James G. Blaine and nominated dark-horse candidate Benjamin Harrison, a U.S. senator from Indianapolis, Indiana, who was supported by Republican leaders who had spent time cultivating New South businessmen interested in a protective tariff. While incumbent President Cleveland amassed more popular votes, totalling 5,540,329 to Harrison's 5,439,853, Harrison counted more electoral votes. Again Cleveland carried the Solid South, but this time he did not win New York. While Harrison received even fewer votes in the South than did Blaine, he waved away those who wished to fly the bloody shirt of Radical Reconstruction all over again. Deciding that he lost the South because the Republican ticket could not register its full strength, Harrison concentrated his efforts behind a drive throughout the South to protect the voting rights of the Negro and register more of the minority. A bill was introduced in the House of Representatives by Henry Cabot Lodge of Massachusetts to give federal elections officials power to control registration and pass on the qualifications of challenged voters. Democrats labeled it the Force Bill, and it went on to pass the House, where the Republicans were in the majority, but got sidetracked in the Democratic Senate.

In 1892, when the disgruntled farmers of the South joined with Western ranchers to form the Populist party, Harrison attempted to fuse them with the Republicans. But in Georgia's October elections the Democrats whipped their Populist opponents so badly that Harrison was quoted in the *Atlanta Constitution* as saying, "I have washed my hands of the South. It is a land of rebels and traitors who care nothing for the sanctity of the ballot, and I will never be in favor of making an active campaign down there until we can place bayonets at the polls. I am now more than ever in favor of ramming a force bill down their throats."[7] Less than a month later Grover Cleveland, carrying the Democratic banner with his vice presidential nominee, General Adlai E. Stevenson of Illinois, won the South and defeated Harrison on the second try.

During this period, when the farmers formed their political coalition, Leonidas L. Polk, a leading agricultural writer, described it succinctly in the *Raleigh Progressive Farmer*, "The wheels have dropped out of balance. The railroads have never been as prosperous, and yet agriculture languishes. The banks have never done better or more profitable business, and yet agriculture languishes. Cities and towns flourish and 'boom' and grow and 'boom,' and yet agriculture languishes. Salaries and fees were never as temptingly high and desirable, and yet agriculture languishes."[8] Cotton that sold for 15.1 cents per pound in 1870 dropped to 9.1 cents in 1882, to 7.8 cents in 1890, and to 5.8 cents in 1894. The farmer, who paid as a consumer and received as a producer, had his prices regulated by the middleman brokers.

The first organization of farmers was founded by Oliver H. Kelley, clerk of the U.S. Bureau of Agriculture, who was distressed by the conditions of the Southern farms and founded the Patrons of Husbandry, or Grange. By 1873 the Grange had a membership of 210,000 in the Deep South. Another group formed the Farmers' Alliance in Lampasas, Texas, in 1875, becoming the Grand State Alliance and spreading throughout the South by 1889. One of the strongest mouthpieces to speak for the Alliance was South Carolina's Benjamin R. "Pitchfork Ben" Tillman, a one-eyed countryman who raged up and down the state preaching against the "hateful domination of the railroad machine" and screaming that the courthouse and statehouse "need to be cleaned out with a real good scrubbing." Running for governor, he proposed to bring the liquor business under the auspices of the state government, so that no whiskey could be consumed on the premises where it was sold and the amount sold to each customer was limited. "Old Pitchfork Ben will stop this evil sin of excess drinking,"[9] he promised the crowds who listened to his fiery speeches. And he stated that the profits from this liquor monopoly would result in other tax reductions, but after he was elected and the program was initiated, it produced only a series of scandals involving greedy officials who ran the state dispensary. However, Tillman did establish agricultural and mechanical colleges for women and men, instituted tax reforms, and regulated the railroad.

While he reduced blacks to abject political poverty, he increased the political strength of the poor white man by arousing him to new heights of political awareness through the Farmers' Alliance.

At the same time that Tillman was growing in power and being elected to the U.S. Senate while handpicking his successor in the state capitol, in Georgia Thomas E. Watson, speaking with waving hands and booming voice, became the powermonger. And in Alabama, Florida, Mississippi, and Tennessee the Alliance won control of the legislatures. Most of these lawmaking bodies passed poll taxes to further disfranchise the blacks who could not afford to pay to vote. However, The Alliance refused to listen to the advice of Ben Tillman, who told the group to stay in the Democratic party, and it lost in most states in 1892, when it bolted from Grover Cleveland's conservatism and formed the Populist party. Tillman, who championed the free coinage of silver to help the farmer secure higher prices for his commodities, lost his bid for the presidential nomination to William Jennings Bryan. In the meantime Republican William McKinley, an Ohio native of Scotch-Irish ancestry, visited the Georgia home of his campaign strategist Mark Hanna at Thomasville, where Southern Republicans consulted with him and agreed to back him at the national convention. While Bryan won the South in November, McKinley won the presidency and was indebted to the region. He outdid his predecessors in appointing token blacks to office, but he made little effort to develop a Southern strategy in the national elections. During his tours through the South in 1898 and 1901 his appeals to white Southerners were either sentimental pleas for reunion or prophecies of a rich future. He told the Georgia Legislature in the aftermath of the Spanish-American War, "Sectional lines no longer mar the map of the United States. The old flag again waves over us in peace, with new glories which your sons and ours have added this year to its sacred folds."[10] However, even in 1900, when his running mate was war hero Theodore Roosevelt, whose mother was a Bulloch from Georgia, the South continued to cast its presidential vote for the Democratic candidate.

When McKinley was assassinated in September 1901 Roosevelt at forty-two became the youngest man to occupy the White House. Within a few short months, after he invited Tuskegee Institute President Booker T. Washington to dinner at the executive mansion, white Southerners spoke of him venomously. Of the criticism in the press as well as the letters that flooded his office, Roosevelt wrote Henry Cabot Lodge, "In the Southern Atlantic and Gulf states there has really been no Republican party, simply a set of black and white scalawags concerned purely in getting the federal offices and sending to the national conventions delegates whose venality makes them a menace to the whole party."[11] Nevertheless he had to woo the South to win enough delegate strength to gain the nomination in 1904. He appointed a black as collector of customs in Charleston. And in Indianola, Mississippi, where he had appointed a black postmistress, a mob waved torches and threatened to burn down the building and the post office had to be closed.

Telling his fellow Democrats that total disfranchisement of the blacks would result in great gains for the Republican party in the South, U.S. Representative William Bankhead of Alabama stated in 1901:

> I am a Democrat, and in voting the Democratic ticket vote my sentiments, but I know that there are many men of wealth and social and business prominence in the South who affiliate with the Democratic party under protest. There has been a wonderful industrial development in Alabama, and many of the wealthy and prominent men engaged in business enterprises are at heart Republicans, and if conditions were such as to admit it, would vote with the Republican party. As long as the Negro is in politics, however, they cannot do so. They have to ignore every other consideration in politics when confronted with the danger of Negro domination.
>
> I feel no hesitation in saying that if the Negro question is eliminated, some of the most prominent men in Alabama will associate themselves with the Republican party, and as a Democrat I say that it would be better for the South and for the whole country if conditions were such as to admit of every man voting his sentiments on great questions of public policy without being held in bondage by a disturbing local condition.
>
> With the Negro out of politics, I believe the time would come when Alabama would be divided between two great parties of nearly equal strength, and that elections would be determined there by the candidates and the issues of the hour. This cannot be as long as the Negro question remains unsettled. That question renders it impossible for many who are prominent in business affairs, progressive and respected in the community—some of the best men we have—who are in sympathy with Republican politics, from acting with that party.
>
> If this obstacle were removed it would conduce to the welfare of the whole country, as well as of the South, giving the South a freedom of thought and action, magnifying its influence in public affairs while giving to the Republicans the advantage of the cooperation of all those who believe in its policy. If the elimination of the Negro question results in the Republicans dominating anywhere in the South, through the expression of the sentiments

of intelligent voters, we will have no reason to complain, but as long as the Negro is in politics the men who are now voting the Democratic ticket under protest will continue to vote it. [12]

During the same year Alabama, like other Southern states, addressed itself to a constitutional convention, where John B. Knox of Calhoun County was elected presiding officer. Stating the importance of the Negro voter as the key issue, Knox said, "So long as the Negro remains in insignificant minority, and votes the Republican ticket, our friends in the North tolerate him with complacency, but there is not a Northern state, and I might go further and say, there is not an intelligent white man in the North, not gangrened by sectional prejudice and hatred of the South who would consent for a single day to submit to Negro rule." [13] As similar conventions had announced in South Carolina, North Carolina, Mississippi, and Louisiana, the main problem was to rid themselves of black domination. They had been called upon, they said, to put out the fires set by Radical Republicanism. To illustrate his point that Northerners did not care for black people as much as did Southerners, Knox told the group meeting in Montgomery "a well-authenticated story from Kentucky":

An old darkey . . . after the war, influenced by the delusion that the only friends the Negro had were in the North, wandered up into Illinois, hoping to find an easy fortune. But here he soon found that while the people had much to say to him about the evils of slavery, and the destiny of his race, every one with whom he did business held him in a strict accountability. Trained, as he was, to the slow movement of the mule in the Southern cornfield and the cotton patch, he could not handle the complicated machinery, or keep pace with the quicker methods of farming in the West, and so he was soon cast adrift. When he asked for help he was told to go to work, and so he wandered, foot-sore and weary, back through Indiana and Ohio until he reached again the old Southern plantation in Kentucky. Finding the planter comfortably seated on his veranda, the old darkey approached, hat in hand, and asked for something to eat. "Why, you damned black rascal, what are you stopping here for? Go into the kitchen and tell the cook to give you something to eat," he was told. "Before God, master," the old darkey said, grinning from ear to ear, "them's the sweetest words I'se heard since I left old Dixie." The old man was home at last. He was among the people who understood him, and whom he understood. [14]

When Knox paused, the statehouse rafters rang with applause. The men stood and cheered and whooped and hollered. "Yes, sir! Yes, sir!" the cries sounded. And in the next sentence Knox told the assembly that it was their duty to establish white supremacy in the law.

After Roosevelt won election to a full term, he tried to sooth the damaged feelings of the white Southerners by touring the South and eulogizing General Robert E. Lee. Among his stops was a night at the old Bulloch homeplace at Roswell, Georgia. He made statements sugarcoating his thoughts about the South. When he went back to Washington, he left behind whites and blacks who were angry at his oversimplifications. In the next few years Roosevelt became so disillusioned with the South that when he broke away from the Republican party and organized the Progressive party in 1912, his Bull Moose national convention refused to seat black delegates elected from the South.

The Republican nominee in 1908, William Howard Taft, was the first from his party to take a presidential campaign into the South. Following the advice of his Southern strategists, William Garrott Brown and Walter Hines Page, who believed the Republicans could break up the Solid South by appealing to the outermost Southern states, Taft carried his campaign into Kentucky, Tennessee, North Carolina, and Virginia. When the votes were counted several weeks later, he had increased the Republican vote in these and several other Southern states. He came very close to winning Tennessee and North Carolina, and the Republicans picked up three congressional seats in North Carolina. Following the election, in a speech to the North Carolina Society of New York, Taft predicted (wrongly) that in the next presidential election the Republicans would carry three or four Southern states, and the President-elect stated that his party and his administration would not interfere with Negro disfranchisement in the South. In 1909 President Taft toured every Southern state but Florida. Like McKinley, he told each audience what he considered it wished to hear. Like Roosevelt, he praised Southern military heroes. Taft named a number of prominent white Democrats to federal offices in the South, and he appointed fewer blacks than any of his Republican predecessors. At various stops he called upon Southern businessmen to support Republican economic policies and openly endorsed white supremacy. Nevertheless, the Republicans were trounced throughout the South in the midterm elections, and in 1912 the Democrats with comfortable majorities in every Southern state swept the nation, and Woodrow Wilson became the first Democratic president of the twentieth century.

After Wilson's two terms a Southern Republican vote began to solidify in the cities, and in 1920 Warren G. Harding won Tennessee as well as a respectable vote in most of the urban areas of the South. Some political analysts of the time credited the party's strength in Tennessee with the Republican support for the state's ratification of woman suffrage. However, Harding and party bosses were stuck with the dilemma of how to combine the traditional black vote with the growing white vote in the South. At the semicentennial celebration in Birmingham, Alabama, in 1921, President Harding told the crowd that he would "stand uncomprisingly against every suggestion of social equality," but he argued that the black man should vote "when he is fit to vote" and should have equal opportunities "in precisely the same way and to the same extent."[15]

During the late 1800s and early 1900s the regular Republican party in the South was predominantly black, and became known as the Black and Tan Republican party, while the country club white elitists, transplanted Northern businessmen, industrialists, and wealthy Southern urban-dwellers split off to form a party known as the Lily-White Republican party. For instance, in 1920 Mississippi sent two delegations to the Republican national convention in Chicago. Attorney Perry Howard and Dr. S. D. Redmond, a dentist, led the Black and Tans, while the state party chairman, M. J. Muldihill, a national committeeman from Vicksburg, led the Lily-Whites. Both delegations were seated, and each delegate was given half a vote. When Dr. Redmond discovered that the other delegation, which had been supporting General Leonard Wood for the presidential nomination, had decided to switch their support and even their hotels in order to prove they had been with Harding all the while, Redmond obtained a certified copy of the hotel register to prove the Lily-Whites had indeed not been there from the beginning. The Lily-Whites moved their support to Warren G. Harding on the fourth day of balloting, and after his victory in November and inauguration in March, Dr. Redmond took his certified proof to the Republican bosses in Washington. Angered at the Lily-Whites, who had misrepresented themselves, the national leaders gave Dr. Redmond the support he needed to have President Harding give one-third of all Mississippi patronage to the Black and Tans. As a result the Lily-Whites became angry at their own leadership, and in 1924 some of the whites voted with the Black and Tan faction to elect Perry Howard national committeeman over Muldihill.

After Harding's death Calvin Coolidge let the subject drop. Like Harding, he supported strong federal antilynching laws. But, also like Harding, Coolidge did not restore black patronage in the South.

The Democrats claimed the former governor of Massachusetts had the support of the Ku Klux Klan, and posters dotted the North reading, "Kool Klammy Kal Koolidge Kant Kondemn the Ku Klux Klan. You Kan Kill the Kruel Ku Klux by Kanning Kwiet Kal."[16] In 1924 Democratic nominee John W. Davis carried the Solid South, but Coolidge beat him elsewhere, and Progressive candidate Robert M. LaFollette came in third.

The South never came to terms with Coolidge. It watched from a distance this Vermont native who was strangely remote to the natural openness and off-handed friendliness of Southerners.

In 1928 Stanford University-educated engineer Herbert Hoover used the South's Black and Tan delegations to help secure his nomination. He courted them throughout the region. After he was nominated, he created a separate campaign committee whose chairman, Colonel Horace A. Mann, was sent out to drum up the white Southern vote independent of the regular Black and Tan organizations.

In 1928, when the Democrats nominated Alfred E. Smith, a New York Catholic, the South generally turned away from its traditional Democratic allegiance. For the first time since Reconstruction a Republican candidate won a substantial portion of the South. Alabama, Arkansas, Georgia, Louisiana, Mississippi, and South Carolina stayed Democratic, but all the other states went to Hoover as well as the urban "New South" areas of Houston, Dallas, Birmingham, Atlanta, Chattanooga, and Richmond.

After he was inaugurated, Hoover praised the Lily-Whites of the South. He reached down and removed from office such Black and Tan leaders as Ben Davis of Georgia, William "Goose Neck Bill" McDonald of Texas, and Walter L. Cohen of Louisiana. In each case he gave the party positions to whites.

In Mississippi Hoover's people launched an investigation of Perry Howard, and while he was under indictment for bribery and the sale of federal offices, he was dismissed as committeeman and stripped of his party power. He was tried in Jackson by an all-white jury, which acquitted him.

In the meantime Hoover stated, "This is my golden opportunity to clean up the Republican party in the South. It is time for the cream to rise to the top."[17] And he put Southern patronage in the hands of his white country club supporters.

A New Division

When Hoover sought reelection in 1932, for the first time since they were enfranchised after the Civil War, the majority of the Southern blacks did not vote Republican. At the time it was more Hoover's dictatorial attitude toward them that turned the black voters off rather than Democratic candidate Franklin Delano Roosevelt's turning them on.

A widely circulated cartoon of the time showed an elephant walking along proudly on its hind legs. The caption read, "It's an elephant's job to keep the U.S. economy on the right track. It's no time for donkey business."[1]

But the Great Depression had hog-tied the economy, more people were unemployed than ever before in the history of the U.S., and Roosevelt won with his promise of the New Deal.

With his Work Projects Administration, Civilian Conservation Corps, Social Security, and soak-the-rich taxes, Roosevelt managed to out-liberal the Republicans, put poor people to work, and embrace the Southern black political organizations. By the time of his reelection bid in 1936, when his opponent, Alfred Mossman Landon, the Kansas Coolidge, emphasized, "I believe a man can be a liberal without being a spendthrift,"[2] Roosevelt had a tight grip on the Solid South. At the Democratic national convention in Philadelphia that year South Carolina Senator "Cotton Ed" Smith walked out in a rage when he saw that many black delegates were being seated. Later, in a speech on courthouse steps in his native state, Smith recalled:

> When I came out on the floor of that great hall, bless God, it looked like a checkerboard: a spot of white here, a spot of black there. But I kept going down that long aisle, and finally I found the great standard of South Carolina. And, praise God, it was a spot of white! I had no sooner taken my seat when a newspaperman came down the aisle and squatted by me and said, "Senator, do you know a nigger is going to come out up yonder in a minute an offer the invocation?" I told him, I said, "Now don't be joking me, I'm upset enough the way it is." But then, bless God, out on that platform walked a slew-footed, blue-gummed, kinky-headed Senegambian! And he started praying and I started walking. And as I pushed through those great doors and walked across that vast rotunda, it seemed to me that old John Calhoun leaned down from his mansion in the sky and whispered in my ear, "You did right, Ed."[3]

The former governor and U.S. senator from Louisiana, Huey P. Long, spoke out loudly not only in the South for his own candidacy in 1936. "With Napoleonic audacity, this egotist hoped to supplant Franklin D. Roosevelt as the presidential candidate of the Democratic Party, or at least cause Roosevelt's defeat at the hands of a Republican rival,"[4] wrote historian Francis Butler Simkins. "Long devised a scheme for federal spending far more lavish than that of Roosevelt and his New Deal—the Share-Our-Wealth Plan. Under it, the great fortunes of the United States would be confiscated, so that each family might enjoy a home, an automobile, a radio, and a minimum income of two-thousand-five-hundred dollars annually, and every promising child might receive an education. The popular response to this scheme took the form of mountains of mail and huge audiences for its originator."[5] But in September 1936 Long was assassinated in his home state, and no one took up his banner.

In the minds of many white Southerners who believed in the white supremacy that had been in their state constitutions since the turn of the century, 1936 was the beginning of the end of the Solid Democratic South. And in 1937, after Roosevelt was inaugurated for his second term and he pushed through Congress the Farm Tenant and Housing acts and then started his reform of the court system, which Republicans called court-stacking legislation, Southern congressmen generally rebelled. While the president was not successful in his maneuver, he irretrievably damaged his standing with the Southerners. Both senators and representatives stood firmly against almost every attempt to liberalize the laws. They voted adamantly against discriminatory freight rates, just as their predecessors had sixty-five years earlier. The Farm Bureau's conservative influence with its Southern strength lambasted the administration's tenant program. These same congressmen criticized FDR's stand for organized labor. And the Southerners even filibustered Democratic-supported antilynching bills. Only a handful stood in support of the president.

In the congressional midterm elections of 1938 Roosevelt attempted to persuade Georgia voters to go against incumbent Walter George and South Carolina voters to elect Cotton Ed Smith's opposition. Both attempts failed and Roosevelt's power waned further among some of the Southern delegations.

But in 1940 the Southern voters could hardly accept the one-world liberalism of Wendell Willkie, whom the Republicans picked to try and unseat Roosevelt. In South Carolina the Democrats backed a ticket pledged to Senator Harry F. Byrd. In Mississippi and Texas voters chose unpledged electors. However, Roosevelt still carried the Southland.

Through World War II, the South remained steadfastly attached to the Democratic party. It was the party in power, dedicated to winning for the United States a great victory over Germany, Italy, and Japan, and institutions such as The Citadel in Charleston and Virginia Military Institute kept alive the esprit de corps Southerners had felt deeply since the first shots were fired in the Revolutionary War.

Roosevelt carried the South for the fourth time in 1944 against New York Governor Thomas E. Dewey. Then, in 1948, following more than three years of Harry Truman after FDR's death in the spring of 1945, the South's rebellious nature surfaced again at the Democratic national convention. Of course, it had been seething for at least twelve years, but it boiled over when Mayor Hubert Horatio Humphrey of Minneapolis, in an attempt to fuse the black support for the Democrats, spoke out for a strong civil rights platform. Thirty-five delegates from Alabama and Mississippi walked out. Amid boos from Southerners Humphrey heaped praise on President Truman, who "had the courage to issue a new emancipation proclamation." The boos heightened when Humphrey stated, "It is time for the Democratic party to get out of the shadow of states' rights and walk forthrightly in the bright sunshine of human rights."[6] Declaring that "the South is no longer going to be the whipping boy of the Democratic party," half of the Alabama delegation and all from Mississippi stomped out of Philadelphia.

Three days later more than 6,000 Southern Democrats, not believing they could support Dewey and the Republicans, met in Birmingham, Alabama, and chose Governor J. Strom Thurmond of South Carolina as their candidate for the presidency. Forming the States' Rights party, the convention issued a four-page declaration of principles, calling "upon all Democrats and upon all other loyal Americans who are opposed to totalitarianism at home and abroad to unite with us in ignominously defeating Harry S Truman and Thomas E. Dewey, and every other candidate who would establish a police state in the United States of America." One speaker told the group, "We have no choice between the little man with the sickening smile and the little man with the little mustache." And the forty-five-year-old Thurmond said, "We have just begun to fight. If the South should vote for Truman this year we might just as well petition the Government to give us colonial status. President Truman has betrayed the South, and we Southerners are going to cast our votes for candidates who are true believers in states' rights principles. For our loyalty to the party we have been stabbed in the back by a president who has betrayed every principle of the Democratic party in his desire to win at any cost." Thurmond's running mate, Governor Fielding L. Wright of Mississippi, reiterated, "We will not turn back. This is the South's big opportunity to show that we are the real Democratic party. Those who believe we would never be able to carry this fight on to a successful conclusion are beginning to tremble."[7]

The two campaigned hard throughout the South and seemed to be a strong symbol of rebellion, but in November the ticket won only in Alabama, Mississippi, Louisiana, and South Carolina, where the Dixiecrat delegates ran under the regular Democratic rooster emblem and where voters could not have pulled the lever for Truman if they had wished. The regular Democrats won the rest of the South with Senator Alben W. Barkley of Kentucky the vice-presidential nominee. When the Dixiecrats met a year later in an attempt to solidify their efforts, forming the National States' Rights Committee, their leader, Thurmond, was engaged in the only losing battle of what was to become one of the longest and most successful Southern political careers; he was attempting to unseat Democratic Senator Olin D. Johnston.

Still smarting from the defeat of the Dixiecrats, three Southern governors—James F. Byrnes of South Carolina, Robert F. Kennon of Louisiana, and Allan Shivers of Texas—endorsed Republican nominee Dwight D. Eisenhower in 1952. Although Adlai Stevenson, former governor of Illinois, picked Senator John Sparkman of Alabama as his running mate, many leaders in the South, including white supremacist Leander Perez of Louisiana's Plaquemines Parish, waved the GOP banner for Eisenhower. As far back as early 1950, Alabama Democratic executive committee chairman Gessner T. McCorvey had proposed that Southern political bosses promise their electoral college votes to a man like Eisenhower so the region could claim more power within a major political party, but States' Rights leaders turned him down at the time. Later, in 1950, the Republicans sought support in the South and began spreading their election motto of "Liberty Versus Socialism," likening Truman's Fair Deal to communism or fascism. With the help of Southern Republican delegates Eisenhower forces ran roughshod over Ohio Senator Robert A. Taft and nominated their man on the first ballot; youthful Senator Richard M. Nixon of California was picked as his running mate.

The big story in early September of 1952 was the Southern support for Eisenhower. In Texas, where the traditionally dominant Democratic party organization officially endorsed the Republican ticket at a state convention, trouble had long been brewing. The 2,000 delegates called for an end to "Trumanism." The state, which accounted for twenty-four electoral votes or ten percent of the 266 needed to win the presidency, divided its vote three ways in 1948: 66.4 percent Democratic, 24.4 Republican, and 9.2 percent States' Rights. Indeed, two months later the Republicans won Texas as they did several other Southern states—with more votes than they had gotten since 1928, when the last GOP ticket had won. Florida, Tennessee, and Virginia joined Texas in moving to the Republican ranks.

William S. White, reporting in the *New York Times*, stated, "A century-old Democratic tradition in the Old South has been broken, for the first time in a fundamental sense, and there now are the beginnings at least of a two-party system below the Potomac." Pointing out that Eisenhower won 57 of the South's 128 electoral votes, he added:

> He lost in Alabama, Arkansas, Georgia, Louisiana, Mississippi, North Carolina and South Carolina, with a total of seventy-one electoral votes, but in some cases only by an eyelash. He polled about double the highest popular vote ever before given a Republican candidate in the South—two-and-one-half million given in 1928 to Herbert Hoover. Here and there the Eisenhower vote approached three times that polled by Mr. Hoover. Moreover, General

Eisenhower's enormous personal victory had carried with it the loss to the Democrats of four Southern seats in the U.S. House of Representatives.[8]

It was emphasized by Southern political observers that the strong vote, particularly in the urban areas throughout the South, showed a growing change among the dominant white groups of political leaders toward a Republican way of thinking.

After the *Brown* vs. *Board of Education* decision in the U.S. Supreme Court in 1954, making the separate-but-equal school system illegal, Strom Thurmond cried out his old segregationist shouts in South Carolina. When the Democratic state committee refused to call a new primary after the death of Senator Burnet Maybank, in order to chose its own nominee to fill the unexpired term, Thurmond staged his political comeback by campaigning on the issues of too much federal control and the need for more competent leadership in Washington, saying that he would stand up for the rights of Southerners in the capital city. He won an unprecedented write-in vote to fill the vacancy.

Two years after the school desegregation decision Thurmond again attempted to muster a Southern rebellion similar to the one he had orchestrated in 1948. He sponsored a Southern Manifesto, or Declaration of Constitutional Principles, in which 101 Southern members of Congress pronounced the Supreme Court's school desegregation ruling "a clear abuse of judicial power."[9]

After a loyalty battle at the 1956 Democratic national convention yielded a small handful of Dixiecratic splinter candidates, the rebellion was more or less doused. Five Southern states independently endorsed T. Coleman Andrews of Virginia. A right-wing opponent of income tax, Andrews gathered only a scattering of votes. And a small percentage of South Carolina and Mississippi voted for Senator Harry Byrd for president.

When in 1956 the Democrats tried again with Adlai Stevenson, the South rumbled slightly, like an earthquake waiting for its time to break loose. Out in Texas Senator Lyndon Baines Johnson steamrollered over Governor Allan Shivers for control of the Democratic party. At the same time, under the leadership of Undersecretary of Labor Arthur Larson of South Dakota, Republicans were shaking the bushes across the Southern landscape, trying to make the earthquake happen. The GOPers warned that the Democratic party would bring civil rights chaos to a countryside that was already visibly shaken. The men and women of Dixie nodded but said little, waiting until the Democratic national convention in Chicago, where the presiding officer, Speaker of the House Sam Rayburn of Texas, gaveled through a compromise civil rights platform that at least temporarily soothed the South. Again the region voted Democratic, but it was by that slim margin the party had witnessed in 1952. Eisenhower took the four states he had won four years earlier, and for the first time since the disputed Hayes-Tilden election of 1876, Louisiana went Republican.

By 1960 the Democratic national convention meeting in Los Angeles no longer accommodated the racism of conservative Southern Democrats. As Anthony Lewis wrote in the *New York Times*:

> The astonishing civil rights plank in the Democratic platform signifies a major shift in controlling forces of the party in the last four years. At the 1956 convention the advocates of accommodation with the South were in the saddle. The nominee, Adlai E. Stevenson, had strong Southern support and was personally quite restrained on the civil rights issue. The Platform Committee was under control of these same believers in mollifying the South. The chairman, Representative John W. McCormack of Massachusetts, literally locked the drafters of the civil rights plank in a hotel room until they finished so that civil liberties lobbyists could not reach their friends on the committee.[10]

The result, Lewis reported, was a pallid six paragraphs with little weight. But four years later, "younger men, more liberal on the civil rights issue, have taken charge," he wrote, and the dominant forces were those directed by Kennedy men, who "believe that most Southern states will stay with the ticket despite this forceful civil rights plank." With Senator Johnson on the ticket as vice-presidential nominee, running against Richard Nixon and Henry Cabot Lodge, they were proven right. When the earthquake started to rumble again, it gave off a small squeak from supersegregationist Governor Ross Barnett of Mississippi, who was joined by a few Old South rebel-rousers. Kennedy received significant black support throughout the South as well as the North. This was the first show of dramatic vote-shifting by the blacks. In Houston, where twenty-three predominantly black districts went for Stevenson in 1956 by 11,592 to 6,006, in 1960 Kennedy won 22,156 to 3,393 for Nixon. In three similar districts in Tampa, Florida, where Stevenson barely won in 1956 by the paper-thin margin of 1,011 to 995, in 1960 Kennedy won by 1,980 to 558. And in strongly black districts in Richmond, Virginia, where blacks were still voting Republican in 1956, Kennedy won by a two-to-one margin over Nixon. All other Southern black areas showed similar trends. And before the votes were counted, Senator Barry Goldwater of Arizona, a leader of the conservative forces in the Republican party, began criticizing the liberal wing of his party, which had been represented in the race by vice-presidential candidate Lodge, who he said "gambled the industrial North by losing the South."[11]

By early 1961 Goldwater was wooing the South with his conservative approach, shaking his finger in the face of Kennedy liberalism. While the Democrats racked up impressive wins in Congress in the midterm election of 1962, at least one old-time Southern Democrat had a tough time holding his seat. Senator Lister Hill of Alabama, who had practiced progressive populism for years, was challenged by James D. Martin, a Republican who roamed the state quoting his hero Goldwater and criticizing the Democratic administration's use of federal troops while integrating the University of Mississippi. Martin had been assisted, as were other right-wing Republican candidates, by Virginia Republican chairman I. Lee Potter's Operation Dixie. After Potter helped Martin and picked up five congressional seats in the South, his efforts were attacked by *Advance* magazine, published by a group of young Republicans, which stated that outsegging Dixiecrats and renouncing Abraham Lincoln was betraying Republican heritage and would continue to alienate the annually growing Negro vote in the South. But the magazine's criticism went unheard, and at the end of 1962 the Republican National Committee met in Washington, D.C., and praised Potter's work in bringing about 1,400,000 more votes than the Republicans had ever counted in congressional races in the South.

The earthquake shook the ground from Richmond to El Paso and from Louisville to Miami. After President Kennedy was assassinated and Lyndon Johnson accelerated the Democrats' liberal programs, Goldwater spoke out for conservatism. For the most part Southerners liked what he was saying. In Texas, Gladwin Hill wrote in the *New York Times* in 1963, the people were saying, "Revolution." It was heard spoken by a professor in Austin, a lawyer in San Antonio, and a labor leader in the Rio Grande Valley.

> What they are talking about is a bloodless, but acrimonious, upheaval in politics—with important implications for the 1964 presidential campaign, and for race relations over a wide area. The revolution has two aspects. One is the emphatic burgeoning of Texas—where for generations practically everybody has been some kind of Democrat—into a two-party state. The other aspect is a clearly defined threat by long eclipsed "minority" groups—liberal, labor, Negroes, and Mexican-Americans—to play a decisive, if not dominant, role in a radically revamped Texas Democratic party. What is at stake in this ferment can be seen by looking back at the 1960 presidential election.

John F. Kennedy eked out a victory over Richard M. Nixon in 1960 in Texas by a scant 40,000 votes out of two million. And Texas's twenty-four electoral votes were an important block in the Kennedy victory.[12]

While the Democratic leadership had dropped in popularity, Barry Goldwater's score in the polls had jumped from twenty-two to thirty-nine points. "And Texas is abuzz with Goldwater enthusiasm," Hill stated. It had only been two years earlier that Texas' first Republican senator since Reconstruction, John G. Tower, had been elected. While no precise figures were available to show membership in the Republican party in Texas or in most of the South, political analysts displayed persuasive statistical breakdowns of voting in successive Democratic primaries, runoff primaries, and general elections that indicated steady erosion of conservative loyalty to the Democratic party.

When Goldwater won the Republican nomination on the first ballot in San Francisco in July, the die was cast for a Republican sweep in the South for the first time ever. Goldwater took virtually every Southern delegate's vote. Naming Representative William E. Miller of New York as his running mate, Goldwater, while not mentioning civil rights directly, used all the right-wing code words in his nomination speech. "We do not seek to live anyone's life for him. We seek only to secure his rights and guarantee him opportunity to strive, with government performing only those needed and constitutionally sanctioned tasks which cannot otherwise be performed," he told his cheering GOP audience. "We seek a government that attends to its inherent responsibilities of maintaining a stable monetary and fiscal climate, encouraging a free and competitive economy, and enforcing law and order." And in his most fiery moment he said, "The sanctity of private property is the only durable foundation for constitutional government in a free society. Extremism in the defense of liberty is no vice . . . moderation in the pursuit of justice is no virtue." The words echoed across the Southland to cheers from the new middle-class white people who had grown up with the peace and prosperity of the Eisenhower years and despised the uprising of the blacks that was taking place in their homeland. And they cheered louder when he said, "The Good Lord raised this mighty Republic to be a home for the brave and to flourish as the land of the free— not to stagnate in the swampland of collectivism, not to cringe before the bullying of communism."[13] This new Southern society had been children when the United States won World War II. They had forgotten the solid, true belief in Franklin Delano Roosevelt because in the middle of the Great Depression he had turned on electric lights across the South and had given people jobs to take the place of starvation. They remembered the proud stance of Ike, the military hero who led their land to wealth by advocating a political philosophy of quiet and doing little.

The Goldwater-owned Southern delegates were no accident. The winning of the delegates, a continuation of Operation Dixie, was designed and captained by a young Birmingham attorney, John Grenier, who had been beating the bushes for his favorite conservative for several years. Grenier and his team covered the South with a fine-tooth-comb approach, letting no Republican stone go unturned. "We were aware not only of the liberal attitudes on race that Lyndon Johnson had promoted that were foreign to Southerners, but his liberal economic scheme of giving away everything to appease the small black minority was ridiculous in the minds of most Southerners," Grenier remembered. "We offered a level-headed conservative approach from a statesmanlike individual."[14] And after Goldwater secured the nomination, Grenier's people went back to the South to try and drum up support in the November election—not only for Goldwater but for the many Republicans on the ballot in local elections from mayoralties to congressional seats.

In the meantime Governor George C. Wallace of Alabama, who had carried a message of racism and defiance of federal court orders to the nation in a swing through the East and Midwest and had promised to run as a third-party candidate in at least sixteen Southern states, withdrew from the race in a move the *New York Times* reported held "great political significance."[15] Wallace, the *Times* stated, would remove an expected deep cut into Goldwater strength in the South. Wallace told a national television audience that he was the instrument through which "the high councils of both major political parties have been conservatized. Today we hear more states' rights talk than we have heard in the last quarter century."[16]

In the week prior to the Democratic national convention Wallace and fellow dissident Southern governors Orval E. Faubus of Arkansas and Paul B. Johnson of Mississippi came out in the open with their support of Goldwater.

At the Democratic convention in Atlantic City, New Jersey, the credentials committee heard a chilling story from the wife of a black sharecropper, Mrs. Fannie Lou Hamer of Rulesville, Mississippi, who said that after she had helped twenty-six other blacks to register to vote, the owner of the plantation on which they lived and her husband worked warned, "If you don't go down and withdraw your registration, you will have to go." On other occasions, she said, she and others were arrested when they attempted to help black people to register. After ordering her to lie down on a bunk a white officer told her, "You're going to wish you was dead," she said, and then two black men were ordered to beat her with blackjacks. Leaning forward in her chair, testifying before the committee, she said, "Is this America, the land of the free and the home of the brave, where we are threatened daily because we want to live as decent human beings?"[17] After listening to this tale of the old Black Codes still alive in the South, the convention seated only two members of Mrs. Hamer's delegation and allowed the others to remain in the hall but not as voting delegates. Watching these events on television was a white South that became even more attached to the Republican party. People said to themselves, the Republican party is more refined than this: It does not have the troubles that the Democratic party has, and it is not plagued with this kind of racism because it does not allow blacks to control it.

President Johnson was nominated in a roaring hall into which he walked, breaking precedent, to name his choice for vice president, Senator Hubert Humphrey, whom the South still remembered as an outspoken champion of civil rights.

As the fever of the campaign became hotter, several incidents occurred that helped to put the final, crumbling blow on traditional Southern politics. The old warhorse from Columbia, South Carolina, Senator Strom Thurmond, the former leader of the Dixiecrat National States' Rights party, appeared on television and stated that he was again quitting the Democratic party. Not facing reelection in 1964, Thurmond asserted, "The Democratic party has abandoned the people. It has repudiated the Constitution of the United States. It is leading the evolution of our nation to a socialistic dictatorship." He asked all Southerners to join him "in my move to a party which supports freedom, justice, and constitutional government."[18]

Along with the added support of three Southern governors and other high-ranking Southern Democratic politicians, "these forces now seem certain to bring the final emergence of a two-party system in the South this year no matter what the result of the election November 3," wrote political reporter Claude Sitton in the *New York Times*.

Even if President Johnson manages to hold a majority of the 128 electoral votes of the 11 Southern states for the Democrats, many students of the region's politics believe that deep divisions among voters will remain. Political forces being what they are, the old alliances that are being shattered now can never be restored.

There have been other defections to Mr. Goldwater's camp. C. C. Aycock, the Democratic lieutenant governor of Louisiana, had endorsed the Senator. Governor Paul B. Johnson Jr. has declared that he and most other Mississippi Democrats will vote Republican.

Politicians are frequently followers rather than leaders of public opinion, and this principle may apply here. J. Drake Edens, South Carolina's Republican chairman, said of Mr. Thurmond's switch: "We had most of his supporters in the party already. He was just following his people. Many of these new converts to Republicanism have long been Democrats in name only."[19]

The prize-winning *Times* reporter, who would later become editor of the *Raleigh News and Observer*, concluded that the polarization in Southern politics was reflected in the willingness of Thurmond and other Democratic officeholders in the South to switch to Goldwater Republicanism. He pointed out that the effects of the political polarization had been felt by other Democratic leaders, who had shunned the presidential race. The Democratic nominee for governor of North Carolina, Dan K. Moore, had drawn fire from Democratic loyalists because of his refusal to help in Johnson's campaign. Likewise, Republican candidates for state and local offices throughout the South called for party loyalty. Claude Sitton reached back to World War II in his reasoning of the breakup of the one-party South. He stated that the disenchantment began with the Democratic administration's efforts to improve the rights of black people. "It increased even under the Republican Administration of President Eisenhower, as a result of the progressively stronger civil rights planks written into the Democratic presidential platforms by Northern liberals. President Kennedy, who did more than any of his predecessors to put these platform principles into practice, proved to be more than many Southern white Democrats could take. The final impetus, if any were needed, was provided by President Johnson's support of the Civil Rights Act of 1964." Sitton added that civil rights was not the only issue in the South, but that it was generally agreed to be the most important issue. He quoted Thurmond as stating, "The party of our fathers is dead," and concluded that "in accepting these Democratic dissidents, the Republicans may find that they will inevitably be forced to accept some of their views as well."

It was of no little significance for the future that during the 1964 race Southern voters were captured by the nationwide appeals made by a man they had watched on the television screen and had admired from a distance. The sincere plea of Hollywood actor and TV personality Ronald Reagan for the candidacy of Barry Goldwater placed his name in political prominence. Previously his name had only been whispered as a possible candidate of the future. But his open endorsement for the conservatism of Barry Goldwater put him out front as far as Southern Republicans were concerned. Listening to his well-chosen words for "my friend, Barry Goldwater" made the Southerners sit up and take notice. It was the first time many of them began to think of Reagan as a possible national candidate of the future.

But Lyndon Johnson was no lackluster politician. He covered the territories outside the South, and he rode through the Southland on a whistle-stop train trip reminiscent of FDR. But for the Southerners Johnson lacked the appeal of Roosevelt: he had already turned his back on radical conservatism; and he had proven beyond a shadow of a doubt that he was not a racist. Many white Southerners felt that his signing into law the Voting Rights Act of 1964 was equal to, if it did not surpass, the Radical Reconstruction Acts of ninety-eight years earlier.

Johnson swept the nation in one of the greatest landslide victories in American history. But Goldwater won big in five Deep South states. For the first time in history Georgia voted Republican in a presidential election. Alabama, Louisiana, Mississippi, and South Carolina all went heavily for Goldwater. Republicans gained a handful of Southern congressmen for a total of seventeen in the House of Representatives, and in all five of the Goldwater states as well as in closely contested Tennessee, Virginia, and Florida, the Republicans won a scattering of seats in the legislatures, majorities of many county commissions, and even some city council seats. In most of the five states he won, Goldwater, had huge margins. In Mississippi, where Johnson's stand for civil rights was strongly attacked by white leaders, Goldwater won by more that eighty percent.

Much publicity was given to the heavy black vote across the United States for the Democrats. The Columbia Broadcasting System estimated that more than ninety percent of the blacks voted Democratic, most of them voting that way for the first time ever. In Tennessee, where about 200,000 blacks were registered, it was estimated that about 63 percent voted in the election and that about 99.5 percent voted Democratic. In the same state in 1960 only about 60 percent voted for John Kennedy. Of Georgia's 270,000 registered black voters, about 80 percent voted with about 99.5 percent voting Democratic, yet Goldwater won. For the first time black voting strength was felt strongly in favor of the Democrats. Whitney Young, Jr., executive director of the Urban League, called the Democratic vote "a milestone. Thanks to the combined efforts of the responsible civil rights leadership across the nation, their unprecedented turnout is growing evidence of their desire to share the responsibilities as well as the privileges of citizenship." And James Farmer, national director of the Congress of Racial Equality, said, "I think it means the beginning of genuine and effective political action."[20] However, in the South, George C. Wallace declared:

> The Democrats have won with their new Negro friends. But this will be a lasting day in their memory. While they begin to force-feed welfare-giveaway programs that reek of communism down the throats of the white South, the rest of the nation will look at us and it will know that the time will not be long coming before they too will face the same type of treatment. The time will come when all responsible Americans will want to join with the South in standing up against the tyranny of an unresponsive and overpowering federal government. They will at last realize that while on one hand you have a giveaway program, on the other hand you have a takeaway program.[21]

In the aftermath of the election an editorial cartoon in the *Syracuse* (N.Y.) *Herald-Journal* showed an angry Uncle Sam spanking an elephant who was quivering and bawling. The caption read: "I love you but don't ever do that again!"[22] Former Vice President Richard Nixon, who had been defeated two years earlier in his bid for the governorship of California, blamed New York Governor Nelson Rockefeller, who he said "dragged his feet, was a spoilsport, and a party divider."[23] In return Rockefeller said, "This kind of peevish post-election utterance has unfortunately become typical of Mr. Nixon. It is neither factual nor constructive." Rockefeller was making reference to Nixon's statement to the press after his California defeat, "You won't have Nixon to kick around any more." Rockefeller continued, "My differences and those of other moderate Republicans with Senator Goldwater were not personal but were matters of principle. Senator Goldwater had advocated making Social Security voluntary, withdrawal from the United Nations, giving control of the use of nuclear power to field commanders, leaving the problems of civil rights to the states, including such states as Mississippi and Alabama, selling the T.V.A., and the immediate termination of farm price supports. This is a time for constructive rebuilding of the Republican Party as a vital force in the mainstream of American political life. Mr. Nixon's latest maneuver is hardly calculated to advance [the Republican party]." Nixon continued the bickering: "I won't comment on what the Governor says. I would only suggest that it's now time for him to quit his criticism of Senator Goldwater and other Republicans and start putting his shoulder to the wheel to get the Republicans to win in 1966. He brought on this split in the party. Now I think he should try to heal it. He's continuing his vendetta against Senator Goldwater, and he should knock it off."[24]

While other Republican leaders, including former President Dwight Eisenhower, Michigan Governor George Romney, Pennsylvania Governor William Scranton, Kansas Governor John Anderson, and former Republican National Chairman Meade Alcorn, interjected their two-cents' worth of comment into the argument, one of the most conspicuous abstainers from the discussion was the man who had spoken out so eloquently for Goldwater during the campaign. Ronald Reagan had already made one unpublicized tour through the Southland, touching places in Tennessee, Alabama, Mississippi, and Louisiana. He told small gatherings about the qualities of this man Goldwater, and he showed off his own quiet qualities as far as they were concerned. Then he went back to California, where he sat down with a roundtable of Republican businessmen and started planning his debut as a candidate.

Others in the party quieted, but Richard Nixon seized upon the opportunity to begin anew his bid for national party leadership.

> We need a period of cooling off. The blood is still too hot and we're too close to disaster. We have to begin to take steps in 1965 to bring the Republican party nearer to center. The center does not try to read anybody out of the party. But the farther you go in either direction, the greater the inclination to read others out—to say, "It's my way or nothing." That is not the way we should be. On the other hand, the election will be badly interpreted if it is interpreted as a rejection of conservatism. It was a rejection of reaction, a rejection of racism, a rejection of extremism.[25]

He added quickly that the election did not show that the new Southern strategy was wrong, but the party had "lost votes in some Southern states in which it had been gaining strength," such as North Carolina, Virginia, Florida, and Tennessee. "In Tennessee we would have elected two senators if we had had some Negro votes," he added.

Nixon declared that he saw only himself as the leader to bring about a coalition of all the wounded factions in the party. "There is a strong conservative wing of the Republican party. It deserves a major voice in party councils, and the liberal wing deserves a party voice, but neither can dominate or dictate—the center must lead." And where was Richard Nixon? "I'm perhaps at dead center," he answered.

Enter: The Good Guy

While Richard Nixon talked about taking control of the Republican party from the center, the youthful-looking fifty-five-year-old former president of the Screen Actors Guild, Ronald Reagan, entered the California gubernatorial primary. A man who had started his political career by opposing Nixon in 1952 by supporting the liberal Democratic candidate for U.S. senator, Helen Gahagan Douglas, who was accused during her campaign of being pro-communist, Reagan was in 1966 a spokesman for the party's right-wing conservatives. When he announced early in 1966, Reagan stood before a fireplace in his cozy den, just as he had on the "Death Valley Days" television show, and he spoke out to all the people of California, whether born in the state or just arrived or lived there for thirty years, like himself: "California's problems are our problems."[1] And that was the way his campaign developed in its personal style, bringing the people into his man's home, making them believe in him personally, and when he said, "A Great Society must be a free society. It must be a Creative Society calling on the genius and power of its people,"[2] those Southerners who had just arrived from Baton Rouge, Midwesterners from Columbus, and many others believed him.

To the professional politicians of the Republican party, here was obviously a prospect for the national scene. If he could appeal to the wide spectrum of voters in California, he had a future throughout the United States.

He told the people, "I think we have to have a moral crusade. The legislature should hold public hearings on the charges of communism and blatant sexual misbehavior on the campus. We have to find out who is responsible for the degradation of a great university."[3] They cheered him because the average citizen in the middle class knew deep down that the University of California at Berkeley was being disrupted by outside agitators. They *knew* the good children of California would not riot against a war in Vietnam, nor would they march against the government that was sending young men to Southeast Asia to fight, nor would they burn their draft cards and bras on the campus quadrangle. When the people voted, the professionals knew that he was a better demagogue than George Wallace, who had been stirring people up down South for years. Reagan stirred them up, and they voted right.

First he whipped his Republican-primary opponent, George Christopher, former mayor of San Francisco, by a two-to-one margin—shocking even the Republican pollsters, who had predicted he might win by five percent in a state where two years earlier Goldwater had beaten Rockefeller by less than two percent.

Again, Reagan had been working. He stayed up in his big fine mansion overlooking the Pacific Ocean even after most of the lights in his upper-middle-class community had been darkened. He studied. He went out among the people. He learned their ways. He was an actor, wasn't he? He knew how they talked, what they said, why they were worried, and he had always been a fast learner. As he later wrote in his autobiography, *Where's the Rest of Me?* he only needed to be kicked in the head once by a mule before he learned to move out of the critter's way. As Nick Thimmesch wrote:

> The political success of Ronald Wilson Reagan is what happens when a clean-cut man spends a lifetime fretting. Eventually, and if he has the opportunity, he will burst onto stage and blurt his story. And if he has the qualities of Ronald Reagan, he becomes the hero of all the Joe and Mary Doakeses, the people who form the backbone of the nation though they might be scoffed at by pseudo-sophisticates. "Credence" is the key word here, and Reagan has drawn it from several constituencies in his lifetime, only one of them the ballot-box electorate.[4]

People had always liked "Dutch" Reagan. He was a good boy. The son of an alcoholic, he got kicked around when he was a kid.

On the streets of Dixon, Illinois, population 8,191, he learned to take care of himself with his one consuming talent: being humbly sweet, while his father kicked up a fuss in the midst of a stupor and his mother did dramatic recitals for whoever would pay her. It was a melodramatic childhood, like some of the films in which he would play. Ronald and his brother Neil lost themselves in sports, football, and swimming, and later at Eureka College he earned a scholarship for his swimming ability. At the small college about twenty miles from his hometown he boxed, became president of the Booster Club, and was captain of the freshman debate squad.

Outgoing in a bashful sort of way, Reagan kept himself busy, made good grades, edited the features in the yearbook, and served in the school senate. In his senior year he was elected president of the student governing body. "He liked everybody, and everybody liked him," recalled a classmate. "He was best in the privacy of our dormitory, or in the fraternity house, where a group of us would sit around after hours and talk about problems of our times. He was never at a loss for words. He wouldn't push himself on people. He would sit back and give other people their time to say whatever they wished to say. Finally, he would come into the conversation and tell it the way he saw it. Usually he cut right straight to the bone."[5]

Leaving college in the middle of the Great Depression, armed with a bachelor's degree in economics and sociology, Reagan became a resourceful youth, made the rounds of the business world of Chicago, and found it lacking in enthusiasm for a fresh-faced young good-looker from downstate. But in Davenport, Iowa, he discovered that Doctor B.J. Palmer, who owned and operated the Palmer School of Chiropractic Medicine, was looking for a clear voice to broadcast play-by-play accounts of the University of Iowa's home football games. For $5 a game Reagan put forth his best effort over WOC—Wonders of Chiropractic—and within a few months he was promoted to the WOC's staff announcer's position at $100 a month. Before the year was out, Reagan was sent to Des Moines, where he became a top-billed sportscaster and entertainment-oriented announcer. A fellow employee was later quoted as saying, "He was a fast-mover. He had nice, easy-going ways, but beneath his lackadaisical exterior was a guy who had to get on top, with his sweet smile or his kind words, and he never let anybody get through Station WHO without shaking hands and talking and saying he would like to find out more about the world."[6]

And before the other people around the station knew it, Reagan had read a scene for Warner Brothers motion picture company and was on his way to Hollywood with a contract giving him $200 a week. He drove into the flashy town in a convertible wearing his hair crewcut style.

By his own account he was placed in eight B-grade movies with little time in between, finishing them in eleven months.

> I played a radio special events and news announcer, punished by the boss for brashness, and the punishment was assignment to the kiddies' program. Sound familiar? It was a rewrite of *Hi, Nellie*, the great Broadway newspaper stage success in which the star reporter was assigned to the lovelorn column. Brynie [Warner Brothers' executive producer Brynie Foy, son of comedian Eddie Foy] had made it about six times, but this was the first time in radio. Of course, like the original hero, I would outsmart the police and solve the crime. I've often described those first eight pictures, or most of them, as the kind in which you could count on me rushing into the room, hat on the back of my head, grabbing a phone, and yelling, "Give me the city desk—I've got a story that will crack this town wide open!"[7]

He whizzed through some forty-six more motion pictures during his career, the best of which were overenthusiastic melodramas such as *Knute Rockne*, in which he played the ill-fated and lovable Notre Dame football star, George Gipp, "the Gipper," who would die before the big game. He was a rich young playboy whose legs had to be amputated in *King's Row*, the movie in which, after he looked down at his body, he uttered, "Where's the rest of me?" He hit the big time, made $3,500 a week, married star Jane Wyman, whose career outshined his in role after role, and served in the army, making documentary films at Culver City studios during World War II.

After the war he made several rah-rah pictures, in 1947 became president of the labor union of his trade, the Screen Actors Guild, and supported Harry S Truman for President. An archliberal who joined the Hollywood Independent Citizens Committee of Arts, Sciences and Professions and later was appointed to its board before it was alleged to be a communist front, he called himself "a near hopeless hemophiliac liberal."[8]

"Maybe it was just the lifestyle of Hollywood that changed Ronnie Reagan, I don't know," said his old friend, B-grade actor Myron Douglas. "He was suddenly no longer the little Midwestern kid who came to town wearing a crewcut. He was now a high-paid star. He made picture after picture, lined his pockets real good, joined up with some actors who were buying land in southern California, and he was doing better than he had ever done before. Or maybe it was guilt-feelings for not having gone overseas and fought with the other American servicemen. A lot of guys back in those days were called draft-dodgers for much less."[9]

In 1948, as president of the union, he was one of the liberal Democrats who tried to push General Dwight Eisenhower into running for president on their ticket. The same year he and Miss Wyman were divorced. Two years later he campaigned vigorously for Mrs. Helen Gahagan Douglas against Nixon. But throughout these days Reagan was seeing what he believed to be the errors of his ways. He winced when he remembered the days when he would speak out against communism and met silence in Screen Actors Guild meetings. But he was still president of that organization through the fifties. At that time he was urged to run for Congress, but a young man who was on Senator Joseph McCarthy's staff, Robert F. Kennedy, later said, "Ronald Reagan was too liberal to be run as a Democratic candidate in those days."[10]

It didn't take a great deal of soul-searching in 1952 for Reagan to become a Democrat for Eisenhower. And the campaign that year made him start thinking about his own position within the Democratic party. With his stand for Ike, he said, he began "picking and choosing on the basis of my own belief, of right or wrong."[11] He became what he termed a "one-man battalion" against communism, breaking up meetings of what he determined were subversive groups at the homes of prominent actors and actresses in Hollywood. And in 1954, after he had married actress Nancy Davis, he took the big-money bait dangled by General Electric Corporation to be host and program supervisor of the industry's television series, "General Electric Theatre." He swallowed the bait hook, line, and sinker, becoming company spokesman at conventions throughout the country while insisting that GE "never once suggested what I should or should not say."[12]

Again in 1956, he supported Eisenhower for the presidency. Public relations executive William J. Mooney of Atlanta, Georgia, remembered:

That was the first time I ever saw Ronald Reagan in person. Here was this tall, nice-looking man smiling down on me, speaking in his quiet Western-Midwestern drawl, telling me it was time America shaped up. I had to think about it a long time afterwards. He really didn't say anything. His words were like cotton candy. He had everybody in his audience smiling with him, nodding their heads, saying to themselves, "Yes, sir, I need to go home and do right and make sure this country really does shape up." But that's all there was to it. I guess it was a lot, considering 1956 and 1957, when we had peace and prosperity, and not much was happening. He gave us public relations food for thought, and it was easy on everybody's palate, and it wouldn't get in your way even if you had an ulcer. I knew all the way back then that Ronald Reagan could be a great politician if he wanted to be. A friend and I talked about it two or three days after his speech, and we both agreed that he was not really selling GE. Not really! He was selling good old Ronald Reagan, all-American guy, somebody who would always be there if we needed him, only forty-four or forty-five years old then, but tough and strong and capable of the long haul."[13]

He stayed with the Actors Guild until 1959, leading it on a six-month strike, dealing with management, but at the same time speaking out for the General Electric front office. It was a paradox he rationalized as easily as he spoke the lines in his B-grade movies.

By 1962 Reagan signed his name to the dotted line on a Republican party register, came out in favor of conservative Republican Loyd Wright in the U. S. Senate race, and spoke out for Richard Nixon in his unsuccessful bid for the governor's chair. Seeing the kind of spokesman they had in the wings, a group of ultraconservative California businessmen and attorneys called Reagan and set up a clandestine meeting at a resort hotel north of Los Angeles. The group, including New England Brahmin William French Smith—educated at Harvard College, where his great-great-great-grandfather had been president, a highly respected member of the law firm of Gibson, Dunn, and Crutcher—and several other top-drawer industrialists sat down with Reagan and asked where he intended to take his new brand of conservatism. He began the same way he had spoken to the audiences in Atlanta and Dallas and Fort Worth and Miami for General Electric; he tilted his head to one side, grinned widely, looked them blue eye for blue eye, and said he wanted to do what was right. Who could argue with that? As Nick Thimmesch later wrote, "credence" was his key word, and even the multimillionaire attorneys, land dealers, and businessmen listened with interest to his easy words. After they heard him out, they asked if he still harbored any of his labor union sentiments. It was straight out, point-blank, without beating around the bush, and he tilted his head just a little farther, grinned wider, and spoke the words that made them nod their heads. They had found themselves a boy, and when the time was right, they would let him move out in front. For the time being, however, he just needed to keep himself out of trouble, sit back, make the GE speeches, be smooth and natural on television, and they would let him know when to make his move. Not unlike when he was the hired gun for the Wonders of Chiropractic or Warner Brothers' eight movies in eleven months or the Screen Actors Guild spokesman or GE's laid-back new image, Ronald Reagan had found a new set of masters. He was comfortable with them and held back on his six-shooters until they gave the high sign. He didn't have to wait long.

Late in Barry Goldwater's campaign for the presidency in 1964, after Ronald Reagan's speech, "A Time for Choosing," was polished and repolished, his new bosses said okay, let 'er go, and he ambled onto the stage in front of the camera and was as natural as a cow in a pasture. He fixed his eyes on the millions of average everyday citizens out there in televisionland who had watched him so many times before. He leaned his head to the side and grinned, and he told the folks that they should choose the way he had chosen: Barry Goldwater and the Republican party were good for America. He sold those people who sent in hundreds of thousands of letters, many with small bills attached to heart-throbbing letters. The contributions which amounted to more than $8 million, helped out the Goldwater ticket but mainly gave Republican political credence to the name of Ronald Reagan as a viable candidate for *anything*; he was salable.

Reagan's benefactors, including Justin Dart of Dart Industries; Holmes Tuttle, a Los Angeles Ford dealer; William A. Wilson, land dealer, rancher, and real estate entrepreneur; Earl Jorgensen, steel company executive; William French Smith, and others, recognized the fact that they had a hot political item in Ronald Reagan. He didn't need the kind of grooming California political machines had experienced with some of their other candidates, like Richard Nixon. While they were still putting much stock in Nixon, now operating from a New York base, they began expending more and more time and energy with their latest prospect.

When Reagan stepped into the ring with George Christopher, a veteran Republican politico from northern California, they were neck and neck. Reagan surprised everybody but himself and his backers with his two-to-one victory on June 8, 1966.

He launched into a two-fisted campaign against old-timer Edmund G. "Pat" Brown, the incumbent governor who was attempting a precedent-setting third term. "It's time we put the government of this state back into the hands of the people," he said in low-key television speeches. "It is time we got away from the intellectual clique in Sacramento."[14] He pushed forward his Creative Society while taking swipes at President Johnson's Great Society, with which he identified Brown. And in return Brown called Reagan "the crown prince of the extreme right who embraces the John Birch Society. He was a so-so actor who at best would be a so-so governor."[15]

Reagan spoke softly, saying, "I strongly support welfare programs designed to provide the permanently disabled, the aged, and the infirm with not only the necessities of life but also some of the comforts, but too often our purpose gets confused. We too frequently perpetuate poverty by making welfare a way of life," as Brown's people were put into a tailspin by the polls that showed them behind. One of Brown's advertisements showed the governor squatting next to a small black youth. Brown was telling the boy, "You know about Abraham Lincoln, our great president." Then the governor chuckled. "You mustn't forget," he said, "it was an *actor* who shot President Lincoln."[16] The scene faded away to the card: "Vote For Pat Brown." The viewers saw it and cringed; they recognized it as political advertisement at its worst. And in the state where there were more than twice as many Democrats registered, Reagan won by a landslide.

The headlines flashed across the nation: REAGAN WINS, REPUBLICAN CONSERVATISM SOARS! The man whom political columnist David S. Broder called "a polished, plausible new face" became "the brightest hope the conservatives have seen since they left the Cow Palace [when Goldwater was nominated in 1964]."[17]

Dixie Republicans Rise Again

All the way across the country, down in the pork chop of Florida, at the same time the conservative Republicans were celebrating for Ronald Reagan, a Southern state elected a Republican governor for the first time since Reconstruction.

A huge chunk of a man, six-foot-two-inch, 200-and some-odd-pound Claude Roy Kirk, Jr., was forty years old when he squeaked by city-oriented liberal Tennessee-born Robert King High, a teetotaler who had upset incumbent Governor Haydon Burns in the Democratic primary by hollering that there was too much crime in the cities and towns of the state.

Awakened the morning after his victory in his Hollywood-by-the-Sea hotel, Kirk's first answer to his first question as governor-elect was, "Us Republicans have done beaten the shoes off the Democrats!" His baritone voice was not whisperlike. "I'm hungover, and I'm proud of it," he added.

The Oklahoma-born investment banker who had sold insurance in George Wallace's backyard in Montgomery, Alabama, said, "It was a Claude Kirk sweep. Not a Barry Goldwater sweep, mind you. I'm a Republican and I'm proud of it. And right this minute, Florida is a Republican state, and it's proud of it."[1]

Jowly, jaunty, a millionaire at least three times over by his own estimation, Kirk was soon to be called Governor A Go-Go by the Florida press. The state that prognosticators in the mid-1960s said was a GOP voter in national elections because "more and more Midwesterners keep moving in around Tampa and St. Petersburg,"[2] had gone out-and-out Republican in a midterm year at the same time Governor George Wallace was electing his first wife, Lurleen Burns Wallace, governor up in Alabama.

"They said it couldn't be done," Kirk told this reporter. "But we showed them. All it takes is a strong fiscal program and day-and-night campaigning, and any good conservative Republican can win Florida."[3] He pointed out that the state had gone for the GOP in 1952, 1956, and 1960, and Goldwater had lost by only 43,000 votes in 1964.

"My economics are excellent," Kirk said right off the bat. He had promised to increase Florida's revenues by $1.3 billion during his first two years by luring new industry into the Sunshine State. "We will get the industry by the truckloads by giving them tax incentives and the best place anywhere for them and their families to live," he bragged. Within two years, while he wooed and won a German-born ex-wife of a Brazilian businessman, industry did relocate in Florida, but not by the billions of dollars' worth that he had estimated.

And when it was pointed out that he and his lovely blonde wife, Erika Mattfield, had had their honeymoon flight to Germany paid for by a tax-supported state agency, Governor Kirk denied nothing, repaid the money, and complimented the press for a job well done. "I like headlines," he added. "Any politician who doesn't is a goddam liar."[4] And he grinned from ear to ear while he and his bride went off on a cruise on the yacht owned by George A. Wackenhut.

Within a year Kirk hired Wackenhut's private detective agency to take care of the rising crime that his Democratic opponent had harangued about during his campaign.

After a series of rapes and murders in Orlando beauty parlors, motels, and private apartments, handgun sales soared to between 200 and 300 a week. Policemen were shocked when they were stopped by miniskirted housewives asking them how to load and fire the pistols their husbands had given them to protect themselves.

The cry went up over South Florida for Governor Kirk to do something, and he hired Wackenhut, a former FBI agent, and his squad of professional private eyes.

Wackenhut, a wealthy, gray-crewcut conservative, didn't flinch when the accusing shouts of "Nazism!" and "Dictatorship!" went up from the liberals and the Democrats. And he was backed totally by the governor, who proudly announced a month after the Wackenhut Agency was hired that twenty-three indictments had been handed down.

Before the end of 1968, however, Wackenhut was out of a job, and the Florida Legislature had created a statewide law enforcement bureau. "That's what I wanted all the time," Kirk said proudly. "It just takes action to get action sometimes."[5]

Hosting the Republican Governors Conference in Palm Beach, Kirk gave interview after interview to visiting newsmen. "This is Claude Kirk," he introduced himself, offering his ham-sized palm for a hearty shake. "I'm the governor of Florida. Do you read my press? Then you know I'm a tree-shaking sonofabitch!" And he grinned widely and glanced around to catch the approving eye of his wife. "I like the idea that I'm Governor A Go-Go. I am too. I'm selling orange juice. I'm selling Kirk. And I'm selling Florida. People pay attention when Claude Kirk comes around."[6]

Riding from Miami to the capital in Tallahassee in a new extra-long shiny black limousine with a television and a bar, Kirk pushed a button and watched the orange juice stream onto his vodka and ice cubes. "This is what I call living," he said. "We ought to have a scene like this in our television ad that goes out all over the country to tell people how great Florida is. This would sell our state." He leaned back and stretched his ham-hock legs out in front of him and tasted the drink. "Ahhh! Pure Florida orange juice! Nothing like it!"[7]

While out in California Ronald Reagan was selling the state airplane, Governor Pat Brown's beloved Grizzly, because he said it cost too much to operate, Claude Kirk and his wife and other members of his entourage traveled more than 10,000 miles a month in a Lear jet he had purchased from the governor's office funds. He explained, "This is the way a governor is supposed to travel. If the people of Florida hadn't wanted a first-class governor, they wouldn't have voted for Claude Kirk."[8]

In the meantime the *Miami Herald* dubbed him "Claudius Maximus," while he took over the tax-supported Florida Development Commission, which he used to promote his own politics. Its appropriated funds paid for much of Kirk's travel expenses, reprinted brochures that contained not only the contents of his speeches but his handsome three-color portrait, footed the bills for publicity and photography, and kicked off his campaign to run for president on the next Republican ticket. His critics said that Kirk's enthusiasm had run to "egomania," and he agreed, smiling and nodding and shaking hands.

When Senator Everett Dirksen telephoned former President Dwight Eisenhower during the Republican Governors Conference at which Kirk was host, a loudspeaker was set up so that everyone could hear the conversation.

Dirksen began by telling Eisenhower, who was at his vacation home at Palm Desert, California, "The weather couldn't be better if Claude Kirk had ordered it from Mt. Olympus with ambrosia and nectar."

Ike replied, "That shows the power of a Republican governor in a Democratic state."

While the governors laughed lightly, Kirk clasped his hands over his barrel chest and leaned back and looked very pleased.

"Look at him," said a gubernatorial onlooker. "He believes every word of it!"[9]

Kirk proved to be an excellent host, however, and when the GOP went looking for a site for its 1968 national convention, Claude Kirk was there before anyone else had a chance to put in a bid.

And after he faced the first statewide teachers' strike in Florida's history with the offhanded remark, "So, close the schools for a year, two years from now you'll never know the difference,"[10] he described himself as the conservative Republican alternative to George C. Wallace.

He grabbed headlines again in August 1967 when black militant H. Rap Brown, chairman of the Student Nonviolent Coordinating Committee, arrived at a baseball park in Jacksonville to find the governor standing in the midst of a crowd of 200 blacks.

Kirk walked up to Brown, snatched the portable microphone from his hand, and said, "Welcome to Florida."

Speechless, Brown stared blank-eyed at the governor through dark glasses.

Kirk offered his big hand and said, "You are welcome if you come here in faith and in spirit. We don't want any talk about guns."

Brown ignored Kirk's hand and snapped, "Let me have the microphone! I didn't ask you to come here!"

"Mr. Brown, we welcome you to Florida," Kirk said into the microphone. "If you are here in good spirits, I'm glad you are here. Are you here in good spirits?" His face formed a smirk after he spoke.

Brown insisted, "I'll speak without the mike then."

The crowd chanted, "We want Rap! We want Rap!"

The governor said, "Quiet! Quiet! May I have your attention?" as the chants grew louder and louder.

Taking the microphone from the bemused governor's hand, Brown said, "If this honkie wants to campaign, let him pay for it." To Kirk he said, "Don't come here and run no game on me."

Kirk grinned and walked away several feet.

Brown hollered into the microphone, "If you are gonna loot, brother, loot a gun store."

The crowd screamed, "Yeah! Right on, brother!"

"Don't be running around here looting no liquor store, 'cause liquor's just for celebrating—and we ain't got nothing to celebrate about. You better get yourselves some guns, baby!"

Standing on the edge of the crowd next to his bodyguard and several reporters, Claude Kirk sighed. "Nobody wants to hear me talk. It's a shame. I can give dandy speeches at the drop of a hat." And he grinned again.

When a local reporter asked if Rap Brown wasn't breaking a state law against inciting a crowd to riot, the governor said, "No, not at all. We had a little debate, that's all. Debate is our way of life. If Mr. Fidel Castro, who is only ninety miles away, comes to Florida, I'll debate with him too."

Asked if he thought Brown was a communist, like Castro, Kirk said, "If it looks like a duck and walks like a duck, it must be a duck."

Moments later, hesitating before sliding back into his limo, Kirk said of Brown, "You know, he's got a lot to learn about demagoguery. If that's the way to start a riot, he's not much at it. I'd advise our leaders in Washington to give him about three hours on national TV, and then forget about it."[11]

Kirk read the polls like his fellow Republicans, and in November 1967 he saw that, according to Gallup, most of the voters in the United States preferred to see Republicans rather than Democrats at work on the nation's problems. The four percentage points' difference reflected the midterm gains the Republicans had made nearly a year earlier. And it looked as though 1968 would be a banner Republican year.

When George Wallace said he would "run to win" on a third-party ticket, Kirk knew that this would be his chance to take at least the vice-presidential nomination.

Kirk teamed up with Nelson Rockefeller, deciding that it was the New Yorker's time to win the nomination. Kirk flew from one primary to another to appear with Rockefeller. Not only was Rockefeller's a sinking ship, the taint of the Northerner's liberal philosophy was too much for the Florida Republicans to swallow. Well-heeled through his business and political dealings, Kirk became a one-term governor. He moved out of the spotlight and back into the world of business.

The Southern Strategist

After President Johnson withdrew from the running in 1968 and Senator Robert Kennedy was assassinated in California, Vice President Hubert Humphrey was an easy winner of the Democratic nomination.

Former Vice President Richard Nixon carried his middle-of-the-road philosophy to Miami, where he won the Republican nomination on the first ballot. On paper the Nixon nomination looked simple. He won 692 to Rockefeller's 277 and Reagan's 182, while several favorite sons totaled another 182 delegate votes. As he campaigned on the floor of the convention hall, Reagan did a great deal of winning friends and influencing old acquaintances from the Southern states. And when the nominating process started and Alabama was called first, the state yielded to California, which meant the Reagan forces would be able to nominate their man first. Mrs. Ivy Baker Priest Stevens, former treasurer of the U.S., became the first woman ever to nominate a major presidential candidate. She said that Reagan was "a man who will confront the radicals on our campuses and the looters on our streets and say: The laws will be obeyed!" After three others, including Representative James C. Gardner, Republican candidate for governor of North Carolina, also nominated Reagan, banners mostly from the South and West waved to the tunes of "California, Here I

Come" and "Dixie." Later, after the first ballot, convention chairman Gerald R. Ford, Representative from Michigan, suspended the rules in a motion made by Virginia, and Reagan was allowed to speak. Declaring that "this nation cannot survive four more years of the kind of policies that have been guiding us," he asked the convention to support Nixon unanimously.[1]

To appease the South, Nixon chose outspoken conservative Maryland Governor Spiro Agnew as his vice presidential running mate. With the Northern liberals nipping at his heels with sharp criticism, Nixon insisted that Agnew was the best man for the job. Besides, he said, he was after a new coalition of traditional Republicans, the New South, black business people, and new liberals who were disenchanted with Democratic do-nothingism.

Amid violence on the streets of Chicago when police confronted anti-Vietnam War demonstrators, Humphrey picked Senator Edmund S. Muskie of Maine to share the Democratic ticket.

Saying there wasn't "a dime's worth of difference between the two major party tickets," George Wallace became the candidate of the American Independent party and named retired Air Force General Curtis LeMay as his running mate. On the ballot in all states Wallace spoke out for "the good little people who need representation as much as the elite folks who run the major parties in this country and look down their noses at you and me."[2]

George Wallace was a Southerner. He talked about standing up for Alabama, sending the rest of the nation a message, and working for law and order like all good Southern people. But Richard Nixon didn't take it for granted that the South was lost in 1968. He had Senator Strom Thurmond of South Carolina on his side, and Strom sent Nixon to the man whom *Time* magazine called his Rasputin, Harry Dent, a Columbia attorney who knew how to play the political game with the best of them. He had been Senator Thurmond's man back home and had shown him how to slow desegregation and keep black children out of public schools, and he knew Southern politics inside and out. "When you talk about the guy who could slip and slide out of dark alleys, steal votes here, grab votes there, and generally be a nuisance to his man's opponent, you're talking about Harry Dent," stated one South Carolina journalist who had covered the statehouse for a number of years.[3]

A man who would later repent, become a born-again Christian, and serve in the lay ministry, Harry Dent back in 1968 was "the original dirty trickster," as he was dubbed by at least one national politician. As administrative assistant to Thurmond through the early and mid-sixties, Dent developed the reputation as a hard-nosed pragmatist who knew instinctively and consciously how to win the Southern vote. He was very much in his element in that dog-eat-dog world of down-home grass-roots politics. He charged onto the political battlefield, his game plan always new and different, surprising the enemy with his superior knowledge.

In working the South for Nixon Dent discovered a twenty-seven-year-old youngster who had already suffered the pangs of outrageous defeat at the hands of the Democrats back in 1964. Bronx-born and Harvard-educated Kevin P. Phillips showed Dent a mass of charts and graphs and statistical data that, he said, showed beyond a reasonable doubt that the Republicans could win the Outer South if they gave it half of a chance.

"It's in the charts," Phillips declared. If the Republicans followed the old populist line and concentrated on politicking in the South and West, Phillips predicted, the GOP "will continue to control the political spectrum past the year 2000."[4]

In 1966, when he was twenty-five and an administrative assistant to U.S. Representative Paul Fino, Kevin Phillips knew that the time for the Republicans had arrived. He *knew* it. Nobody could tell him differently. History was changing. People in the East, South, and West voted out of gut feelings, no longer for historical reasons. They were looking at Now; they were reacting out of resentment and discontent; they were unhappy about high-and-mighty Democrats dealing out welfare to blacks and chicanos—the new boys on the block of the poor. The Irish and Italians and Poles and Greeks and other European immigrants of the East resented the new poor; they had made it on their own during hard times—why couldn't the blacks and the Latins? In the South the low-class and middle-class whites were already shaking their heads and joining the country clubbers who had been traditional Republicans, all of them uttering in unison, "It took a Texan to give away the South." And in the West the leather-tanned cowboys and the oil rig workers and the small-business people were meeting with the big ranchers and the new oil rich and shaking their fists at the Mexicans who were given handouts from a benevolent administration.

From his days as John Mitchell's right-hand man during the presidential campaign of 1968 and later in the Department of Justice to his holier-than-anyone position as head of the Conservative Caucus, Kevin Phillips saw his Republican party emerging as the majority.

He predicted it in his testament, *The Emerging Republican Majority*.[5] Carrying the New Right banner high on his six-foot frame, the bespectacled Phillips wrote that "the great political upheaval of the Nineteen-Sixties is not that of Senator Eugene McCarthy's relatively small group of upper-middle-class and intellectual supporters, but a populist revolt of the American masses who have been elevated by prosperity to middle-class status and conservatism. Their revolt is against the caste, policies and taxation of the mandarins of Establishment liberalism." Although he dedicated his chart-spotted diatribe to "the new majority and its two principal architects: President Richard M. Nixon and Attorney General John N. Mitchell," he was well aware that Nixon and Mitchell and the Republicans had won in spite of themselves. "It was not unlike the Democrats picked up the silver platter and handed it across the table to them. And the Republican leadership almost stumbled and almost dropped it," he reasoned. But in his book he did not "feel free to criticize the Republican party." It was in character for him to watch, make judgments, and keep them to himself until the right moment. He was by nature *right*.

The son of a career bureaucrat, William Phillips, who later became a top official of the New York State Liquor Commission, Kevin Phillips peered into books as well as the life around him with thought toward political advancement from the age of thirteen. He was part of the ethnic mishmash of the Bronx. Born part Irish, English, and Scotch, his father a Catholic and his mother a Protestant, he was aware of the community made up of Jews, Irish, Italians, and other immigrants. At an early age he began to study the makeup of the community and how the various groups voted.

When he was twenty he became the youngest legislative assistant on Capitol Hill. Two years later he became known as the ethnic expert with the Republican National Committee. And at twenty-three, when Congressman Fino made him his administrative assistant, he became the youngest in the House of Representatives.

While with Fino, in 1965, at the age of twenty-four, Phillips drew a new State Senate district in the Bronx so skillfully that it withstood a court challenge. A new Republican senator was added to the statehouse because this political Picasso knew what he was doing and made sure the local Republicans understood as well.

His tongue-in-cheek attitude to some of the most serious political questions bore down hard on the rolling-stone Democrats who had felt the stomp of his conservative foot. He *knew* the Catholics were changing, and he pointed out to *New York Times* reporter James Boyd more than fifty congressional districts "where working-class Catholics were leaving the Democratic Party in droves." And in his 1975 book, *Mediacracy: American Parties and Politics in the Communications Age*, he wrote that "in New York City, the blue-collar workers and bus drivers of Queens keynote conservative animosity toward the liberal post-industrial upper-middle-class of midtown Manhattan, a reversal of industrial era ideological conflict."[6]

After he left the employ of Congressman Fino, he traveled back to the Ivy League and pushed himself handily through Harvard Law School. Shortly before graduating he won the Bureau of National Affairs Award for a dissertation predicting that civil rights progress through the courts would vanish as soon as the burden shifted from the South to de facto segregation in the North.

During the next two years, while working diligently for the election of Richard Nixon, he put together his own version of the Apostles' Creed in *The Emerging Republican Majority*, which became, if not the bible, at least the new testament for the Nixon strategists. His condensed version was circulated among the chiefs, and it was adhered to by most; they saw expertise as well as audacity in this young man, who stated emphatically, "You ask me about any congressional district in the country, and I will tell you its ethnic composition, its voting history and the issues that would appeal to its electorate."[7]

While he had several successes—particularly in his Outer South strategy—he felt Nixon was going too far with the Madison Avenue approach that was later criticized sharply in Joe McGinnis's book *The Selling of the President 1968*. "The public relations people were muddying the water, clouding the issues," he told a group of journalists in 1972. "Nixon knew his campaign stunk. He wanted to be himself and he knew he should have fought the campaign on the issues Middle America was ready for—the simple, straightforward, no-nonsense strong issues that George Wallace was expressing. But he had this big lead in August and didn't want to change a winning game plan. It was October 28 before he found out from the polls that he was blowing it. And it was too late then to do anything but hang in there and hope."[8]

In the meantime Kevin Phillips carried his Outer South strategy to the behind-the-scenes leaders. It was his idea that the border states such as Florida, Tennessee, North Carolina, and Virginia could be carried more easily than the Deep South, Wallace-controlled states that Goldwater had swept in 1964.

My argument was this: Your outer Southerners who live in the Ozarks and Appalachian mountain ranges and in the Piedmont upcountry—and now in urban-suburban Florida and Texas—have always had different interests than the Negrophobe plantation owners of the Black Belt. This is a less extreme conservative group. It adheres with other Republican constituencies across the country and can be appealed to without fragmenting the coalition. When you are after political converts, start with the less extreme and wait for the extremists to come into line when their alternatives collapse.[9]

Loaded with statistics, graphs, and charts, he bore into the why as well as the what. He took the South apart section by section, analyzing the voters. His selling of the Outer South strategy became the most verbose in dealing with the Dixie upcountry.

Not all of Louisiana, Mississippi, Alabama, Georgia, and South Carolina is agriculturally rich, flat, Black Belt Dixiecrat country. A small section of northern Alabama and Georgia belongs to the Appalachian highlands and a much larger area of the Deep South is "upcountry"—the archetypal red hills, clay hills, and Piedmont home terrain of the poor white or "peckerwood" Deep South. Although many Appalachian counties are at least as impoverished, the upcountry operates in a different cultural and political pattern; since Civil War days, it has been institutionally Democratic in the Black Belt manner rather than traditionally Republican like the mountains. For this reason, it was as Democrats rather than Republicans that the dirt farmers of Mississippi, Alabama, Georgia, and South Carolina upcountry became camp followers of populists and demagogues—Democrats all—like "Pitchfork" Ben Tillman, Gene Talmadge, Theodore Bilbo, James K. Vardaman, "Kissin' Jim" Folsom, Tom Watson, and J. Thomas Heflin. The Deep South upcountry is a land of dirt farms, textile mills, relatively few Negroes, multifunctional gas stations, "Yes, We'll gather at the River" Protestantism, Coca-Cola advertisements and a deep-seated Snopesian dislike for both white plantation owners and black field hands. Atlanta, a world apart from its rural environs, is the only major city.[10]

While making such listings, Phillips seemed flip in his pop political generalizations. It was this kind of blind blanketing of some areas that wrinkled the fabric of some critics and caused Senate Republican leader Hugh Scott to call it baloney and others to say he was a quack. Journalist McGinnis in *The Selling of the President 1968* characterized Phillips as a misprogrammed computer filled with sawdust and turned loose on the political world. In his Lamar Lectures on "The Disruption of the Solid South" Professor George Brown Tindall of the University of North Carolina stated:

The Emerging Republican Majority, widely celebrated as the manifesto of the Southern strategy, proved to be a nine-days' wonder that perfectly illustrated the hazards of prophecy. Its author predicted that the true majority in the United States for the remainder of the twentieth century would be conservative and Republican, with its bastions in the South and in the "heartland" of the plains and Rocky Mountains. A new era had begun, Phillips told the reader: "The long-range meaning of the political upheaval of 1968 rests on the Republican opportunity to fashion a majority among the fifty-seven percent of the American electorate which voted to eject the Democratic Party from national power"—that is, the fifty-seven percent who voted for Richard Nixon or George Wallace. A fitting epigraph for the book, one reviewer thought, would be George Wallace's rallying cry: "They's more of us than they is of them."[11]

Arguing in favor of his Outer South strategy, Phillips traced the presidential voting trend starting with the economic boom in Florida and Texas in 1920. However, he disregarded some Republican strength in the Memphis area, where Democratic Boss Crump had held the strings for many years, and dismissed Dwight Eisenhower's immense personal popularity as a military leader—something that has always appeared clear to the majority of Southerners. He failed to mention Truman's civil rights stand while stating " the 1948 Dixiecrat upheaval was an essential prerequisite of Republican success; it shook loose the partisanship of a large number of conservative Democrats whose support proved essential to Eisenhower."

Phillips' study emphasized that "the deep roots of the new Republican position in the Outer South became somewhat more obvious after Richard Nixon held Florida, Virginia, and Tennessee in 1960, becoming the first losing GOP presidential candidate to carry a Southern state. But while the 1960 election spotlighted Republican strength in the mountains, ranch counties, suburbs, and cities of the Outer South, it also underscored continuing party weakness in the local Black Belts."[12]

Phillips maintained that four years later Goldwater reversed the traditional Republican mold in the South. But others argued that Phillips was again showing "elaborate ways in which he can justify his overwhelmingly conservative point-of-view and conclusions," as Southern political watcher and Washington attorney Charles Morgan, Jr., saw it. "There are two things that win elections in the South. One is race. The other is military. Dwight Eisenhower had both going for him, and he won substantial victories in some parts of the South. If a candidate is for the white race and strong military while his opponent is a moderate on race and so-so on military strength, the former will win every time through two-thirds of the South—and that's all you need to win. It's as simple as that. All of Kevin Phillips' maps and charts will not change that."[13]

Still believing in his Republican strategy, especially after seeing it work for all practical purposes in 1968, Kevin Phillips moved into the Justice Department as Attorney General John Mitchell's special assistant. Not long afterward he felt the walls closing in and left to have more time for his own writing. He produced a syndicated column, made speeches espousing his political philosophy, and worked for several conservative organizations in Washington. He called for the abolishment of the Electoral College because it impeded new parties and thereby hindered the neopopulist revolt he saw on the horizon. He backed strict restrictions on the press's First Amendment rights and said that too much federal money was being spent on the poor and not enough to aid the middle-class, hard-working consumer. In a "My Turn" column in *Newsweek* Phillips proposed a presidential ticket of Ronald Reagan and George Wallace, a proposal he repeated in a number of speeches.

Kevin Phillips lived through Watergate, saw his hero Richard Nixon disappear into the West and watched his old boss John Mitchell shipped off to federal prison, and felt the crumbling of his emerging Republican party. But he still *knew* that the *right* combination of South and West would make the Republicans click. He latched onto former Texas Governor John Connally, whom he praised as "America's potential Matt Dillon, Washington's putative Wyatt Earp,"[14] but it was not long before Connally's stand against outlawing abortions soured Phillips' right-to-life associates and Connally's lukewarm approach to gun control turned off other New Right conservatives. Phillips came back to the Reagan-Wallace ticket, knowing that such a combination would score a solid uppercut to the Democratic foes, but few in the Republican party listened seriously to his "Right Deal."

Phillips then situated himself solidly on Ronald Reagan's bandwagon. He saw in Reagan the savior of all sacred to loyal conservatives. Here at last was a chance for the New Right to succeed. His prophecies of more than a decade earlier would at last come true. Reagan was the man who could fuse the South with the West. He had all the credentials for putting the Republican party together again.

As the party fused and became successful, Richard J. Barnet, spokesman for the Institute of Policy Studies, a Washington, D.C., think tank, said that he believed Phillips might have been right in his analysis of voting patterns, how to weld the South and the West, and the conservative government that would come to pass.

The forces he writes about, together with the national security-military institution, may well produce the nightmare he describes. He uses the key figure in his plan as Thomas Jefferson. But the analogy is not with Jefferson; it is with Adolf Hitler. The elements are all there—deep-rooted social cleavage, insoluble problems, rhetoric which attempts to legitimize and encourage hate, a phony genetic and geographical underpinning, a despised minority to blame for everything. It all adds up to scapegoat politics, which is a tactic of fascism."[15]

Phillips dismissed such critics as "crybaby liberals" and added, "The people have now found their answers in the Republican party of Ronald Reagan, who talks to them about *real* issues. He does not hide behind pseudo beliefs. He speaks out for everyday realities."

Speaking in a quiet, deliberate tone, he said:

Liberalism has turned away from the common people and has become institutionalized into an establishment. Its spokesmen are driven around in limousines and supported by rich foundations, the television networks and publishing houses, the knowledge industry, the billion-dollar universities and the urban consulting firms which profiteer from poverty. Liberalism is dominant only in parts of the Northeast, which is always the last bastion of a dying order of privilege. The Northeast resists the populist surge of our day just as it fought the revolution of Jefferson, Jackson, Bryan, and Roosevelt. The states that Humphrey carried in 1968 were roughly the states that Hoover carried in 1932.

His predictions continued:

Southern politics, like those of the rest of the nation, cleave along distinct ethnic—racial, in this case—lines. Whereas in New York City the Irish are lined up against the Jews, in the South it is principally a division between Negroes and whites. Every year, Negroes constitute a smaller percentage of the population in most Southern states. This is not just because Negroes are being chased out of the South by the mechanization of agriculture or lured away by Northern welfare dollars. Even as Negroes are leaving Dixie, middle-class whites are flooding in, drawn by the climate, expanding commercial opportunities—and perhaps even by the sociopolitical climate.[16]

It was primarily through this development across the Sun Belt that Kevin Phillips saw his private political utopia becoming a reality.

And in November 1980, when the Solid South—with the exception of Jimmy Carter's home state of Georgia—pulled the levers in the ballot boxes for Ronald Reagan, Phillips' charts and graphs and maps glowed like neon.

A Conversion to Republicanism

Nixon won in 1968 by a razor-thin popular margin—43.4 to 42.7—the lowest percentage of any president elected since 1912. The election was barely kept from being thrown into the House of Representatives by the presence of George Wallace, who carried Alabama, Georgia, Louisiana, Mississippi, and Arkansas while amassing little more than nine million votes, or 13.3 percent of the total. Nixon's victory "established the Republican Party as a formidable and probably permanent political factor in the South and Southern border states," wrote Max Frankel in the *New York Times*.[1] The Democratic ticket lost everything south of West Virginia and east of Texas to the Republicans or Wallace. As Kevin Phillips had predicted, Nixon won the Outer South: Kentucky, Virginia, Tennessee, the Carolinas, and Florida.

Nixon's vice president, Spiro Agnew, helped to solidify the South in the next four years. While Eastern intellectuals poked fun at Agnew's bumbling manner, his speaking-without-thinking modus operandi, such as when he referred to an official from Japan as "a fat little Jap," in the South bumper stickers reading "Spiro Is My Hero" began appearing on pickup trucks. In red, white, and blue splendor the stickers dotted the hinterlands.

By 1970, three of the original eleven Confederate states had Republican governors: Winthrop Rockefeller in Arkansas, Claude Kirk in Florida, and Linwood Holton in Virginia. The Republicans held four seats in the U.S. Senate, and twenty-six of the region's 148 congressmen were Republicans. Locally, the party had more than 250 members of state legislatures and hundreds of city and county officials.

New York Times reporter Roy Reed found, "In state after state the Republicans were found to be better organized than the Democrats and about as well-heeled. From El Paso to Richmond, there is hardly a Southern district left where the disorganized and dispirited Democrats are a match for the Republicans in partisan enthusiasm."

Late in 1969 Reed discovered at a Southern Republican conference in New Orleans that "President Nixon's failure to persuade the Senate to confirm Judge Clement F. Haynsworth of South Carolina for the Supreme Court might have been expected to depress some Southerners, especially Republicans. But the Republicans here seem to feel that Mr. Nixon's heart was in the right place and that he should be praised for trying. After Haynsworth received a two-minute standing ovation in appreciation of his "overwhelming abilities," the man who had brought his name to Nixon in the beginning, Harry Dent, told the group that there really had been no Southern strategy but that "we are just like any other part of the country."

Roy Reed wrote that the Republican party in the South was "not basing its expansion solely or even primarily on the Wallace brand of race exploitation. The party is diverse as Dixie, and Dixie has always been more complex than some Northerners thought. If the new Southern GOP were searching for a human symbol, it would be hard put to choose between Senator Strom Thurmond, the South Carolina conservative, and Representative George Bush, the young moderate from Texas."[2]

At the time Southern Republicans were adding almost daily to their organized strength. They were concentrating on the urban areas and the growing middle class, allowing the traditionally Republican hill country to hold its own. In North Carolina Republican party registration increased from 344,700 in 1966 to 448,637 in 1970, while Democratic party registration fell from 1,540,499 to 1,415,432 in the same period. Republican strength picked up primarily in the Piedmont cities of Charlotte, Winston-Salem, and Greensboro.

Differing from their fellow party members in the Black Belt of Alabama, Mississippi, and the Carolinas, Texas Republicans actively worked for the support of blacks and other minorities. In the other

Deep South states GOP leadership took a hands-off attitude toward the predominantly black regions. But in Texas Norman Newton, director of the state Republican executive committee, remarked, "We are making for the first time a real effort with the Negro voter, with the idea that we will get the percentage of their vote moved up to twenty-five to thirty percent over a period of ten years."[3]

The problem with most of the Southern states' Democratic organizations during this period was that they were divided into separate factions. There were Dixiecrat-leaning Wallaceites vying for state party positions while more moderate regular Democrats were working for national party unity. After some lifelong Democrats watched the bickering among their own party officials in the South, they converted to out-and-out Republicanism. In the last few months of 1969 five state officials in Georgia and five legislators in Mississippi publicly declared, as Strom Thurmond had before them, that they were Republicans. And Southern Republican leaders preached that conversion would be a way of life in the modern South. "Nobody is comfortable when they don't know from one day to the next how their party stands on a particular issue: whether it's the race issue or taxes or a Supreme Court decision. In the Republican party, one knows," said Jake Lattimer of Tennessee.[4] However, of the ten conversions in Georgia and Mississippi, only two remained in office for the next term; seven were defeated at the polls, one retired halfway through his race, and two in Mississippi won reelection.

By mid-February of 1970 the Louis Harris poll showed that "for the first time in the modern political era, the Democratic party has lost its position as the majority political party." In a sampling of the national electorate, Harris wrote in the *New York Post*, "those who call themselves Democrats have slipped to forty-eight percent, down from fifty-two percent in 1968. Although those who think of themselves as Republicans come to only thirty-three percent, the nineteen percent who classify themselves as independent now make it impossible for a new Democratic victory along straight party lines."[5] Those who considered themselves Republican in 1968 amounted to thirty-one percent, and independents seventeen percent.

Among the Southern officeholders who converted to Republicanism was an Alabamian of medium height, prematurely gray hair, smoothly tanned country club complexion, and a pair of sparkling blue eyes. His name was Don Collins. He talked in a soft voice, ready, willing, and able to meet the qualifications to run for governor of a state that had not had a Republican governor since Reconstruction. But he was not sure he wanted to run. He had changed from Democrat to Republican, and as a Republican he had suffered several defeats. In the mind of the author he became representative of the many conversions to Republicanism in the sixties.

"I thought Republican for a long time before I made the decision to come out of the closet and state publicly that I was a Republican," Don Collins said. "A lot of people all over Alabama and all over the South started to think this way in the sixties and seventies. I believe in the eighties more and more Southerners will step forward and state without a doubt, 'I am a Republican.' And they won't be ashamed of it. They will be proud."

Over many cups of coffee, talking fast and fine, like a debatemaster making his point, the former legislator continued:

> The Republican party has become something different in the last thirty or forty years. It's not the same party it was when Mark Hanna had control and he and his leadership were corrupt, showing the American public the bad side of big business controlling the Republican party. It's no good to look back at that, the way some Democrats do, and say, "That's the Republican party." That's nonsense. The parties have reversed position since that time in the 1930s. It was an example of the old adage: Absolute power corrupts absolutely; that's what Hanna and his crowd did. And I think that's what's happened to the Democratic party today; Edward Kennedy and his liberal crowd have a strong hold on it; they are controlling it absolutely. Today the leadership of the Democratic party is not supplying the people with what they want or need. It's the same thing that happened back in the 1930s with the Republicans. When Roosevelt came in, he did something; desperate times called for desperate measures; something had to be done, and he did it. He might not have been right. As a lawyer, I don't think a lot of it was right. But he did it when something had to be done. Today, Ronald Reagan and the Republicans are doing something; again, after the lack of leadership from Jimmy Carter and the Democrats, something had to be done.[6]

A native of Etowah County in northeast Alabama near industrial Gadsden, Don Collins is the youngest of nine children and the only one who finished high school.

> My people are ingenious, independent, hard-working, strong people. But my family was poor because of the time in which they lived. They learned to live and survive. That was the name of the game. We didn't sit around the fire on cold nights and talk about politics. At night, everybody was too tired to talk politics. My family's politics was whatever they had to choose from. Back when I was growing up, and until very very recently, Alabama was a no-party state.

I grew up tough, worked hard, made my way to college, attended the University of Alabama, and I asked myself: What kind of politics do I want to grow into? What will bring the best future? What will the dream be like under this, that, or the other? I got very interested in politics, became president of the student government, was associate editor of the *Alabama Law Review*, and won several scholastic awards in law school.

It was during college that I first saw that Alabama was really a no-party state. There were different shades of philosophy. You asked, "Where does he stand on this issue or that issue?" When you found out where a person stood, then you knew something about him; not whether he was a Democrat or a Republican. There were no Republicans to speak of, just different shades of Democrat. You stood back and said, "He's a conservative," or "He's a liberal."[7]

After clerking for a justice on the State Supreme Court in Montgomery, Collins worked for a law firm in Birmingham for a year and then became a partner in a large firm in that city.

"In 1960, I worked for Richard Nixon for president. I was a Nixon admirer. I thought he was a very good vice president. I thought he knew more about the political system and how to work within that system than John Kennedy," he said.

Several years later, when Collins decided to run for a seat in the Alabama House of Representatives from Jefferson County, he stood before the probate judge who asked him to sign the oath of loyalty to the Democratic party. "Nobody who seriously wanted to win ran on the Republican ticket in Alabama back then," he explained.

I told the probate judge that I had supported Nixon, that I thought he was a fine man and an excellent politician, and I said I would probably support him if he ran again.

The probate judge said, "Oh, never mind that, go ahead and sign it," and I signed it. But I never forgot that moment of being dishonest, reading the oath and signing my name to it, and I even dreamed about it.

I campaigned, I won, and I went to the Legislature. But I never forgot that moment of hypocrisy in signing the oath. I went down to Montgomery and sat in the hallowed halls of the capitol, and I didn't feel too good about my situation: acting and voting as a Democrat.

I kidded myself for a while, telling myself that I was a George Wallace Democrat, that I didn't believe in the national party, but that didn't really matter. I was a good friend of George Wallace, and I did believe in what he was trying to do, trying to keep the federal government from infringing upon the state's authority and dictating to us exactly what we had to do in any matter.

But I discovered that I was a thread in a large piece of cloth that I disapproved of. I asked myself: "How can a person be an Alabama Democrat and not intellectually believe in the national party?"

After thinking about it, talking to my wife about it, and dreaming about it, I stood up in the Legislature on the morning of January 12, 1966, and read my statement of principle.[8]

With his voice ringing through the high rafters of the old building, Collins stated:

What I have to say comes from many hours, days, and months of soul-searching. For many months my heart and conscience have been troubled by the signs of decay in our political and social system. Over three years ago the good people of Jefferson County elected me to represent them in the State Legislature. I will always be grateful to these people for their expression of confidence. In serving them I have tried to exercise this public trust with dignity—using the energy and whatever ability God gave me to do my best for our state.

Like most people who sought to serve their state in an elected office, I entered politics at a time when there was but one active party in Alabama. In that party there were liberals and conservatives. I campaigned as a conservative or Southern Democrat; or, as some call it, an old-fashioned Democrat. My thinking was accepted, and my thinking has not changed; I have not changed. While I have not changed, and while the people of Alabama have not changed, the political philosophy of the national Democratic party has changed and has left me an orphan. We all watched the last national Democratic convention and witnessed the disgraceful treatment of our legally elected delegates to that convention. The national Democratic party has swapped the people of Alabama with their voice of reason and their honest opinions for the votes of the unreasonable mobs.

At a recent point in time, the Republican party philosophy became that of the Southern Democrat. And the national Democratic party swung far to the left, throwing conservative Alabama aside for the greater number of votes in the big cities of the North and East. Not content with casting us aside, the national Democratic party holds us up to ridicule for our respect for constitutional authority and religious traditions. Perhaps the national Democrats are in fact represented by Bobby Kennedy who was reported as saying in Berkeley, California, that he would give his blood to our enemy, the Viet Cong—the same Viet Cong bandits who are murdering our Alabama boys by the hundreds.

Today the theoretical dictates of the LBJ's, the HHH's, and such are unproven, unsound, and corrupting. They are leaving America and its children a legacy of financial, spiritual, and moral bankruptcy. I believe this action and philosophy is unacceptable to Alabamians today and in the foreseeable future. My conscience, weighed with the responsibility of the futures of my children and your children, will not allow me to support a party whose philosophy, in my humble opinion, is destroying this nation with the speed of a grass fire. It is for these reasons that I must state to my constituents that I can no longer be a part of a national party that stands for and daily promotes disrespect for lawful authority, unsound fiscal policies, and frequent, disastrous wars which they apparently do not intend to win. I cannot, according to my own philosophical political dictates, and will not, stay any longer in the ranks of the national Democratic party. I want to become a part of the solution, instead of being a part of the problem.

I offer my services to, and join hands with, the new Republican movement in Alabama. In my opinion, they offer something constructive to Alabama.[9]

Later, three legislators from other Southern states reiterated Collins' sentiments. They too switched parties with similar statements. Like Collins, they would be defeated in subsequent elections.

In giving further reasons for his switch Collins said that the Republican platform was one

Alabamians can be proud to stand on and leadership they can be proud to follow. Long . . . too long . . . many of us have masqueraded under the Alabama Democratic banner in the now desperate hope that somehow, some way, sanity would return to the party of our fathers. But simple honesty requires me to say that the term Alabama Democrat no longer has meaning. No longer can we campaign as individuals on a personality basis and hope to accomplish anything constructive for our state. It is time to stand up and be counted. The lines are drawn. I ask all the people of Alabama, great, proud, and outnumbered as they are, be they Republican, Democrat, ex-Democrat or Independent, to join hands with us toward a new freedom for all. In my way of thinking, and contrary to the vicious northern liberal press, Alabamians do have a strong sense of fair play and justice. With the proper leadership we will approach our problems with reason, common sense, and justice. Alabamians definitely will solve our social, economic, and political problems with greater sincerity and success than the phony, South-baiting liberals who hate us openly and who do not have our best interests at heart. The voice of reason is alive in the hearts of Alabamians *today*! We know it is useless to oil old harness because we are not living in horse-and-buggy days. Alabamians are living in the very shadow of the rocket that will soon carry man to the moon—for that rocket is being manufactured in Huntsville, Alabama [at NASA's Redstone Arsenal].[10]

The new day of modern responsibilities was on the state, Collins warned in his best populist fashion. And if the people of the state were to face the new day, "it will be brought about by leadership which is willing to admit on which side it stands. In this way, we can start afresh, this year, to develop this richly blessed state into its rightful place in the United States."

Collins went on to predict that the Democratic control in Washington would bring about in 1966 "the most massive and brutal display of centralized federal power that this country has seen since the reconstruction days." He criticized Johnson's Great Society, his "captive Congress," and his use of the robed Supreme Court justices who applauded the president's programs on nationwide television. "In order to stem this tide of heavy-handed federal intervention, which is deliberately designed to crush the conservatism of the South, we must have dedicated and unselfish leadership which is attuned to the philosophy of Alabamians today. In order to achieve this and bring forth this leadership, I say we not only need a clean sweep—*we need a new broom*! This broom, I believe, is embodied in the Republican philosophy. I intend to become a part of this by using my sweat, muscle, and energy to move this broom across the state of Alabama."

Collins ended his speech with the announcement that he intended to run for the nomination to the office of attorney general. He won the uncontested nomination but was defeated soundly by McDonald Gallion, the Democratic nominee who had already served one term as Alabama attorney general.

"After that speech," Collins recalled, "most of my Democrat friends criticized me, saying I was being expedient at their expense. And my Republican friends criticized me, saying I was being expedient at their expense. A lot of people came up to me and said, 'Don, I always liked you. You would have had a wonderful career in politics if you hadn't changed over to the Republicans.'" Collins grinned like a good old boy who saw the truth within himself. "But, you know, I say right back to them, 'What would you want me to be the rest of my life: a successful hypocrite?'"[11]

After his unsuccessful campaign for attorney general, Don Collins went back to his home town of Gadsden and opened his own law office. He ran for lieutenant governor on the Republican ticket but was beaten badly. "For all practical purposes," he pointed out, "the two-party system has just been thrown around in Alabama. It has no meaning without competition, and there has been no definable competition between parties." On the other hand, however, there remained the stubborn streak of his pioneer forefathers when he insisted, "I do believe that Alabama and the South are changing and that we will see a new day for Republicanism and that day is *now*."

He looked back at his wife Hannah's grandfather, Byron A. Case, an Ohio farmer and writer who moved south after the turn of the century. Old Byron Case was a lawyer and an inventor, and he left his heirs a magnificent country place where the Collinses lived until 1981. Don Collins backtracked to Birmingham and laid designs to run again some day for a state office on the Republican ticket. He believed that after Watergate, about which he would not talk because "it is over and done with, and everybody has already talked about it too much," and after retired Admiral Jeremiah Denton became the first Republican U.S. senator from Alabama in 101 years, and after Ronald Reagan started "doing what had to be done, because something had to be done," Alabama and the South were ready for widespread Republican victories on the local scene.

> It is time for good politicians, good men and women, all Republicans, to dispel the myth that Republicans cannot win local elections in the South. For all practical purposes, it has already been put down as being nothing but a myth. But the Democrats try to keep the folklore alive. In this day and time, I see the acceptance of the Republican party socially. People have started looking at Democrats in the South as welfare cheats; that's the way they are characterized. Republicans have to create new images constantly. That's one reason why we are in the business of converting people toward accepting the name Republican. We are the modern evangelists among our own families and friends. We must convince our people who call themselves Democrats that they are such in *name only*.[12]

Shortly after his own conversion he mapped the way for many other newly turned Southern Republicans all over the South. For the next decade and a half they would proselytize from Louisville to Miami and Charleston to El Paso; they would preach out the gospel of Republicanism, attempting to change a people who had been hardcore Democrats for more than a century. He talked about it to his new Republican friends, and he continued to polish his speech every chance he got. "It is the semantical, or name-only, conversion of our friends who think and act Republican, yet, from habit, call themselves Democrats. This is our mission. We will not have to ask them to turn away from established habits, actions, and customs. That would be difficult to achieve. Ask any minister. We only have to convert our friends in name only from the title of Democrat to Republican. Most Southerners are *already* Republican—but they don't know it!"[13]

He preached to the converted. He tried to churn up the GOP juices, even said that that was what the party was: The GO party! The Republicans cheered. They clapped their hands and stomped their feet. But many of them had heard the same words before with just a little twist. "The problem was, he was preaching to the already saved," commented a long-time GOP member of the audience. "We were ready, had been ready for years, and we knew a lot of the problems. But it was good to hear the words from a new convert."[14]

But Don Collins didn't let up.

A political conversion should not be a difficult task for dedicated people, such as yourselves, especially when the goals are clearly defined, as I believe they are. Certain juices start to flow in the soul when certain bells are rung. What are these bells? We hear the politicians using such symbolic bell-ringing phrases as "freedom of the individual," "states' rights," "local government," and "freedom of religion." These are all good Republican principles. But the Southern Democrats have in the past and are still trying to appropriate these bell-ringing phrases to their exclusive use. For they know that these are concepts accepted by Southerners today. Let us go forth today—together—and ring these bells. Let's make sure when the juices start flowing, they are flowing for the right cause—constructive Republican conservatism. We will be working for and with people who are wonderfully individualistic—a people who sprang from the world's hardiest stocks, and who fled to this country to escape the persecution of state religions backed by strong central government. Our forebears came to the South seeking only freedom and a chance to succeed. They were, as I said, strongly individualistic, self-reliant, stubborn, and tough as horseshoes. They believed in thrift, industry, and as much education as they could afford for their children. They had strong family ties, were devoutly religious in their own way, and wanted the right to govern themselves through local government at the lowest level. They ripped the state of Alabama from a virgin wilderness by their own strong individualistic actions, and never for a minute thought of subscribing to a principle that power was the goal of government. The only power they wanted was their own power, and the power of their religion. The power to swing an axe and to aim a gun, devoutly hoping they would have to aim this gun only to feed their families, but standing ever ready to use it against their enemies when necessary.

We must remind our friends that freedom—political, religious, economic, and social freedom—has always been the very cornerstone of the Republican philosophy. They will understand. Ask them to compare the two parties nationally on that basis, and see which matches Alabama's spirit. Tell your friends that the Republican party wrote and passed the Homestead Act, under which our forefathers settled Alabama and the rest of the South. Tell your friends that the Republican party also wrote and passed the national banking systems laws to secure your hard-earned money. It also wrote and passed the Sherman Anti-Trust Act to control big business—and the Taft-Hartley law to help keep labor and management in line with the public interest. Tell them the Republican party wrote and passed the Pure Food and Drug Act . . . and the Child Labor Laws . . . and the Railway Labor Mediation Act. Aren't these facts a matter of pride for *any* political party?

And, by the way, you can also tell them the Republican party wrote and passed the Civil Service Act, protecting millions of people from the evils of the Jackson Democrats' spoils system, and that your party passed the Parcel Post and Savings System. Heard enough? Does that sound like forward and constructive conservatism? And that is only a small part of the record—building a *Solid Society*.[15]

Responding during an interview years later, George Wallace said,

I've always liked my friend Don Collins. He was with me from the beginning. He turned Republican. I was sorry to see that. He didn't need to do that. He should have understood that we in the Democratic party can differ with each other but we're still Democrats. It sounds like to me, when I hear all of this talk about our basic freedoms, that the Republicans have stolen a lot of their thoughts and their words and their principles from George Wallace. You know, I should have copyrighted all of my speeches. If I had, the Republicans in Alabama, throughout the South, and all over the nation would be paying me hundreds of thousands of dollars. They owe everything they have to my kind of Democratic thinking. I have rung some bells in my time, and they know it; they know where the votes are in Alabama and in the South and in other parts of the country too. You can sure tell they've listened to me, can't you?[16]

But Don Collins didn't agree. "George Wallace was on the right track in the beginning, back in 1962 and 1963 and 1964. But later he got greedy. He let his old principles fall to the wayside because he wanted the national Democratic party to pay attention to him. If he had gone all the way, become a Republican and run on an honest Republican ticket, I think he would have *really* stood for something solid."[17]

In 1981 Collins praised the Republican strength that he said was

continuing to grow around the South. It's a strong growth from within, as solid as it ever was. But today we are more organized than we were back in 1966, when I preached to my newfound Republican friends. The Republican organization is sweeping across the Southland with renewed vigor, because it knows and believes in a Ronald Reagan style of government. It hits home to the Southerners. I'm not talking about the New Right and its piousness, although that too is building in strength. I'm talking more about good solid strong principles of conservatism. Ronald Reagan and his people are putting these principles truly into operation. The South cannot help but see it. The region is in the midst of it. Within a short time we in the South will experience a Republican generation.[18]

Mississippi by a Mile

During the early years of the 1970s the homespun, down-to-earth philosophy talked about by Don Collins and other Southern converts to the Republican party was basically lived up to by Richard Nixon and his administration. Late in 1971 George Wallace told *New York Times* reporter James T. Wooten, "The only thing that would keep me out [of the 1972 race for president] would be a meaningful change of direction in the Nixon administration or the Democratic party. I have no realistic hopes that such miracles will come to pass," he stated, and added, "I will be running to win."[1] And after a strong Wallace victory in the Florida presidential primary the right-wing Alabama governor's stock went up, only to fall abruptly when he was gunned down by an assassin in May 1972. Wallace was campaigning in Maryland on the eve of his greatest achievements in national politics when an assailant pumped six bullets into his stomach. Wallace was hospitalized, paralyzed from the waist down. The next day he won Democratic primaries in Maryland and Michigan. Unable to campaign in the remaining primaries, the wheelchair-ridden politician was later invited to address the Democratic convention. In his speech he urged the party toward conservatism in its platform. Regardless of his pleas, the Democrats nominated Senator George McGovern of South Dakota on the first ballot. He named Senator Thomas F. Eagleton of Missouri as his running mate. However, Eagleton withdrew his name several days later after it was revealed that he had not disclosed the fact that he had undergone psychiatric treatment. He became the first vice presidential nominee ever to withdraw from candidacy for any reason other than death. McGovern chose Sargent Shriver, brother-in-law of the late President John Kennedy and the first director of the Peace Corps, as his new running mate. In late August President Nixon was given a near-unanimous vote for renomination. With Spiro Agnew again by his side, Nixon swept the South and the country.

Mississippi gave Nixon his strongest margin as he broke several records. He became the first vice president since Thomas Jefferson to be elected to two terms as president, and he became the first two-term vice president to be elected to two terms as president.

In that same election a tall, trim, chestnut-haired, handsome, country-club-fashionable thirty-one-year-old who had served four years under Democratic Representative William Colmer, chairman of the House Rules Committee through most of the sixties, rode Nixon's coattails in Mississippi's Fifth District, where Nixon beat McGovern with 87 percent of the vote.

Like so many Southerners of his day Trent Lott had been raised a Democrat. But he ran as a Republican. He was born in Grenada, Mississippi, on October 9, 1941; his father was a farmer and his mother a schoolteacher. "My grandfather was a supervisor in Carroll County, Mississippi, as a Democrat for twelve years. My father, until his death in 1969, thought of himself as a Democrat. When I came to Washington, I considered myself a Democrat," he recalled.

> When I first came up here to Washington I was working for Bill Colmer, my predecessor and a really great guy and sort of the last breed. He was a leader of the Southern Democrats, as we knew them back in those days when they had eighty or ninety they could count on for just about any vote. They had power back then, and Colmer was a real gentleman, a fiscal conservative; so many of the things he advocated back then—financial reform measures, a tight national budget, fewer welfare handouts, tax cuts—are now the fad. It was a great experience working for him. I learned right quick after I got up here, though, that philosophically I just was not a Democrat—and neither was Mr. Colmer. In fact, the last several years he was up here, he had an eighty-nine percent Republican voting record.[2]

His voice tingled with excitement as he leaned forward and glanced down at the porcelain magnolia bloom on the sidetable and then behind it at the large photograph of himself standing proudly next to Barry

Goldwater, whom he supported for president in 1964, although at the University of Mississippi campus he still regarded himself a Democrat. "Senator Goldwater is one of the all-time great men of our nation," he stated. "He surpasses party politics. I consider him a statesman."

Still a child when his family moved to Pascagoula, which he continued to call home and where his father worked at the Ingalls Shipyard, Lott worked as a field representative for his alma mater for a year before he went back to Oxford and earned his law degree. He practiced law for a year before becoming Colmer's administrative assistant.

We worked hard in that office, we knew what was happening, *had* to know, Mr. Colmer was that important then. I could see the workings of the Democratic party all around me, and I didn't like what I saw.

I can remember just like it was yesterday *the* moment when I said to myself and to the person who was with me: "I am not a Democrat."

I was with a friend, Gene Ainsworth, who was administrative assistant to Congressman Sonny Montgomery, and we went to a luncheon one day at the Capitol Hill Burroughs Club, a club for staff members of Democratic congressmen, and our speakers were Larry O'Brien, chairman of the national Democratic party, and Ray Blanton, then a congressman from Tennessee, and they remarked about how the government had to grow and take care of the citizens and that government had to be the end-all and do-all for the people, and after everything they had to say was revealed and I realized what they were saying, I nudged my friend and said, "I don't agree with a damn thing either one of these fellows have said. I am not a Democrat." And I think from that moment on I thought of myself as a Republican.

The biggest part of what they said was that they just looked for government solutions to everything, and I came from a poor family in Mississippi. Like most of us across the South, when I was born my mama and my daddy lived so far out in the country—I mean, when you got there, it was the end of the road. My mother taught school, my daddy drove a school bus and raised cotton. It was a traditional hard-working, Baptist churchgoing family. We are right now in Mississippi only one generation removed from that end-of-the-road lifestyle. After we moved down to Pascagoula, my father worked in the shipyard and my mother taught school. Everything I heard that day from these Democratic leaders was contrary to everything I had been taught by my family. My mother and my father worked hard. It was hard for them to even get me through four years of college. And then I was on my own in law school. Everything I heard that day in Washington went against the grain for me and went against everything I had been raised to believe in and the way I had been taught to seek solutions. To me and my folks, the government was just not the answer to everything. What these guys were saying was the government should do this and the government should do that, and we should pay no attention to what we were doing to the deficit, what that was doing to inflation, what it was doing to interest rates, and the fact that the chickens would come home to roost some day. And now they are here.[3]

His Colgate smile underlined his political self-righteousness as he nodded knowingly. In the private office he enjoyed as Republican whip in the House of Representatives in 1981, he sat back with his wavy dark hair coiffured to perfection.

His walnut-brown eyes staring from behind stylish gold-rimmed glasses, he spoke in a college boy manner about "this great new day for the South and for America. I'm getting calls nowadays from small businessmen, small plant people who produce easy chairs, from officers in savings and loan companies, and they're saying, 'Hey, help! We're sinking!' And you know what? I can't give 'em much hope. We're going to cure their problems, but it's a year off or two years off before our programs and our solutions will do any good. What are they going to do in the meantime? They're going to hurt, and that's because of the programs Larry O'Brien and Ray Blanton were advocating back in the summer of 1968; that's why we are where we're at today."

After he became disillusioned with the Democrats, he met conservatives Paul Weyrich and George Will. With other conservative staffers of the House and Senate, they organized the Conservative Luncheon Club of Capitol Hill, where they could hear their kind of speakers. They set up a communications system through which they could tell what other conservatives were doing, when they were doing it, and how they could benefit each other.

When Colmer, who had served forty years in Congress, decided to retire, it wasn't difficult for Trent Lott to make up his mind to seek the congressional seat. It seemed to be in the stars, the natural order of things political, "but I did think and think about *how* I was going to run for office. And when the time came, I just could not bring myself to run as a Democrat. I could not be a hypocrite like that. I talked it over with Mr. Colmer, and he didn't say, 'Do it!' but he didn't discourage me either. I did run as a Republican, and in the last week of my campaign Mr. Colmer endorsed me," the congressman remembered.

In the Fifth District of Mississippi Republican strength had been developing through the years with work by the state executive committee and with the influx of white blue-collar workers who tended more and more to vote Republican because they believed blacks had taken over the Mississippi Democratic party. The district spanned the Gulf

Coast area with more than half of the inhabitants living in or around Biloxi, Gulfport, and Pascagoula. The only area in the state that has such an urban population outside the capital city of Jackson, the remainder of Lott's district stretched northward to Laurel and Hattiesburg, the rural piney woods dotted with papermills. With one of the smallest black populations in the Deep South, which dropped from about nineteen percent to around sixteen percent in a decade, the district is home to many people who are not unlike Lott. Most of the Mississippi natives came from a poor background and gained an education, many of them becoming the first in their families to receive a high school diploma or a college degree, and many have gained a comfortable prosperity. With the work of Colmer, U.S. Senator John Stennis (chairman of the Senate Armed Services Committee), and most recently Representative Lott, more than half a billion dollars annually has been paid by the Defense Department to the Ingalls Shipyards in Pascagoula, where Lott's father worked when Lott was growing up.

It was no wonder that when a year later Litton Industries, Ingalls' parent company, asked, it received one of the largest contracts to be let by the Defense Department. Litton claimed it simply bid low and assumed the Pentagon paymasters would fill in the cost-overrun payments later. As it turned out, Litton did receive the payments, but the controversy died only temporarily while newshawks on the national level continued to delve into the books. As far as Lott was concerned, he let it slip past him like water off a duck's back, and he talked about how proud he was of the industrial development, new jobs, and higher salaries that he helped to bring into his district. With Chevron Oil Company's refinery near Ocean Springs, already one of the largest in the world, making a billion-dollar expansion, Lott said, "This kind of growth means a great deal to the people who vote and put me in Congress."

He shook his head as though thinking of fantasy when he outlined the events in recent history through which he served in the House of Representatives. "Boy, we've had Watergate [in which he stood staunchly as a Nixon defender during the House Judiciary impeachment hearings], Vietnam [which he opposed as a no-win war but supported with appropriations to strengthen the military], Jimmy Carter [whom he would talk about at the drop of a mention], and now Reagan [whom he supported as strongly as he defended Nixon]. We now have a Republican Senate and a working majority in the House. We've come a long way from a very low ebb to the brink of a new majority in politics in America. And I think this is based to a large degree in the growth of the party in the South.

"Recent polls show that nationwide the Republicans are gaining on the Democrats, and the parties are in a dead heat as far as national public opinion is concerned. To me, that is phenomenal. And I feel kind of like I've been right in the middle of the transition as it has developed. And now to be the whip in the House makes it even more fun. It's a real thrill for me," he added with his characteristic underplayed Sigma Nu fraternity boy excitement.

To win the position of minority whip at the beginning of the Ninety-seventh Congress, Lott surmised, "I had to get all of the votes in the South, all of the votes in the West, and just enough votes in the Midwest to offset the losses in the Midwest and Northeast. It wasn't really a regional battle, but my opponent was from the Northeast and I was from the South—so it just shaped up that way."[4]

His opponent, Bud Shuster of Pennsylvania's Ninth District, a self-made millionaire businessman who had the reputation of voting his Allegheny Mountain constituents' powerfully conservative beliefs, was already chairman of the Republican Policy Committee when he went against Lott.

But, Lott simply outpoliticked Shuster. He had his ducks in a row, had the confidence of the president, and had all of his people ready to vote for him. Then Lott became the first Southern member of Congress to be elected Republican whip since the office was created in 1897, according to the Library of Congress.

"Having this job is important—it's nice to have this office," Lott said as he looked around at the high-ceilinged, plush quarters and offered his visitor a Coke from a hidden refrigerator. "I have to work on every issue. You don't get a chance to pick and choose," he added, keeping an eye peeled on the screen of a television set monitoring the House vote. "When you are having to work on every amendment and every bill, it keeps you hopping, and you also know you're going to lose some," he said, before ducking out to register his vote on an issue and returning five minutes later. "We had a bill down there this morning. It was this infant formula thing [resolution to stop U.S. manufacturers from sending prepared baby formula to foreign countries], and it had no party or philosophical or regional overtones. The administration did not want us to pass that resolution. I was down on the floor for several hours trying to round up votes for our side. It was tough. It's always tough."[5]

During his first season as whip Lott not only worked on the Reagan administration's massive package of legislation reform bills, he cradled his own baby in the shape of House committee improvement amendments. Writing on the op-ed page of the *Washington Post*, he articulated his philosophy concerning a "Blueprint for a House That Works."

The recent revolt against increased committee staffing requests in the House of Representatives reflects not only the new budget-cutting mood of members but also a growing consensus that the institution itself is becoming unwieldy and unworkable.

The House reform revolution of the last decade has replaced the centralized committee system with a sprawling and decentralized subcommittee system that had dispersed powers so much that today the institution is nearly powerless. As House Judiciary Committee Chairman Peter Rodino recently observed, "If the trend is not reversed, the day is not far off when every majority member will head a subcommittee. Then we will have no leadership and no 'fellowship.' Everybody will be a boss."[6]

Lott went on to outline a specific proposal to streamline the committee and subcommittee staffing, cutting down instead of ballooning. The exactness of his proposal was not necessarily important. But he believed in his conservative stand, wrote about it, had it published in *the* newspaper in Washington, and was proud of his stance.

He showed his intense fiscal conservatism, saying that he believed in

the mandate that the people of the United States gave to the Republican party and to Ronald Reagan in November of 1980, and it is for that reason—as well as a personal belief in my own political responsibility to my constituents—that I would like to streamline the national government.

And I don't mean taking food out of the mouths of the poor, starving children the way some liberals paint the picture. I don't mean that at all. In my politics, although I am from the southernmost portion of Mississippi, I have systematically avoided race as an issue. I have had black support. In 1980 I got more than fifty percent of the black vote in my district. In 1976 I ran against a Democrat who was much more liberal than I and who should have appealed more to the blacks of the district, but I got a majority of the blacks then too.[7]

A newsman in Lott's district agreed that the congressman received a "fair number of black votes during the last race," but insisted that the Democratic candidate, Jimmy McVeay, was "only a token candidate," receiving twenty-six percent of the votes compared to seventy-four percent by Lott. And in the 1978 general election Lott was unopposed.

He is about as conservative as a politician can be, even in Mississippi. He has never had to be racist in his campaigns, but he has never been for free lunches in schools, has always been against Legal Services, is for cutting out all welfare, and is absolutely opposed to abortion and federally supported funding for abortions for those who cannot afford such medical treatment. Lott has gotten the highest marks possible from the National Associated Businessmen, the U.S. Chamber of Commerce, the Committee for the Survival of a Free Congress, the Christian Voters' Victory Fund, and the American Conservative Union. He's smart, crafty, and totally ruthless. I would say he has never and would never vote for a piece of humanistic legislation.[8]

But Lott saw himself differently. While proud of his Watchdog of the Treasury Award from the National Associated Businessmen and Guardian of Small Business Award from the National Federation of Independent Business as well as other plaques from other conservative groups, Lott stated flatly:

I am not a racist. I would never use racism in a campaign. I don't operate like that.

I think there's a big difference in the modes of political thinking. You've got your old-line Democrat; he was a social conservative, a military hawk, and a populist. Then you've got your moderate Democrat who is a social liberal, a little more on the dove side of military, and slightly more economically liberal; there is still a streak of populism in him but not as pure as the old-line Democrat.

You've got what was your traditional Republican who was economically conservative, socially moderate to liberal, and moderate on the military. The modern Republican, however, is moderate to conservative on social issues, uniformly conservative on economic issues, and strong on military.[9]

Talking in a soft but energetic Southern drawl that had become well-known and listened to on the floor of the House by late spring of 1981, Trent Lott continued,

The binding force between the Republican forces, and the greatest appeal we have in the South, are economic issues: balancing the budget, reducing regulations, getting federal government out of people's lives, pulling the federal government out of Washington, and cutting taxes which should in the long run produce jobs. With these issues, we make an appeal to the blue-collar worker, the black worker, because we get out and produce jobs. I work aggressively in my district with elected officials to pursue industry. Although I can't take credit for having gotten all the industry, I've worked hard at getting it, and in the past five years we've gotten General Motors, United Technologies, DuPont, and Chevron is now undergoing a one-billion-dollar expansion. What I'm talking about is jobs. And so, I'm a Republican more because of economic issues than anything else. And that's not populism either.

We have the industry. We have the jobs. People in my district are very well off. I think economics has no race, sees no color; I want everybody to thrive. And, you know, blacks respond well to that. You can show them some way you can attract industry where they can get a job and make ten dollars and fifty cents an hour as a semiskilled or skilled laborer, you show them where they can get training and go to a junior college or a vocational education program, where they can get a job—hey, they're ready to try it! It's like Jack Kemp [of the Kemp-Roth tax cut plan] says: good economics starts with good jobs! Hey, the blacks in Mississippi and throughout this country have strived for so long to get a ticket to get on the train—they finally prevailed; they've got a ticket and they're on the train. They've got a right to vote, they've got civil rights guarantees, they've got a right to own a home where they want to. But back a year or two ago, just as they get on the economic train, it stops! Interest rates are too high, homebuilders are not building homes, savings and loans are going busted, plants are not expanding, and the blacks are the last hired, first fired, and they're saying: "Hey, something's not right here." And I think that's what Republicans should address, and I think we're addressing it. If we attack that problem: getting the economy moving, providing jobs for people regardless of race or sex or anything else, we'll become the dominant party in this country.[10]

But, still, he insisted that he was in favor of some type of "workfare" program whereby the poor would not be given welfare but allowed to work for their food stamps, commodities, or federal check. "Some people might say that's a racist thing, but it's not a question of whether somebody is black or white, able-bodied or unable to work; there's no reason why somebody who is able should not perform some task for what they get. And maybe I'm wrong, but if I committed a crime right now, and I was put in jail, I think I would rather be out planting bushes or trees along the roadside in Pascagoula or raking the parks than being shut up inside a building. I don't understand that that's supposed to be degrading: it's work! I would rather be out doing something constructive than cooped up inside a building. I think that I would consider that a reward," he added with enthusiastic emphasis.

And, too, Trent Lott saw absolutely nothing racist about his being opposed to extending the Voting Rights Act. He still winced at the South's mistreatment in the aftermath of the Civil War.

One of the things I feel strongly about as a Republican is that I am a part of the national Republican party. I'm not described as Trent Lott, a Southern Republican; I'm Trent Lott, Republican. Period. I happen to be from Mississippi. There's no Southern Republican thing. People think of Democrats as Southern Democrats or national Democrats. The national guys won't speak to the Southern guys and won't invite them to their meetings; it's all a regional thing. I like being a part of the national party. I'm not an outcast of my own party. I'm not in a small faction within my own party. I'm in the mainstream of the Republican party. That has always given me great pride; in the Republican party the South has been readmitted to the Union.

Now, as an Illinois congressman said, one of the worst parts of the 1965 Voting Rights Act is Section Five preclearance provision. It doesn't give nine Southern states and parts of thirteen other Southern states any way to rejoin the Union. There is no real trigger mechanism in it. Even if a municipality is all white and has no history of discrimination, if the state is still under the 1965 Voting Rights Act, under a Supreme Court decision, the municipality cannot get out from under it. This is just patently unfair. I have to agree with Mr. Justice [Hugo] Black's dissent in South Carolina versus Katzenbach that this is clearly contrary to the constitutional intent of our forefathers. This sort of preclearing of state law by federal government was discussed and consciously ruled out by our forefathers when they wrote the Constitution. The only defense of this type of legislation is in an era like the Reconstruction period, but now we even have an opportunity to end Reconstruction. I'm just saying: Until the Voting Rights Act is made totally nationwide, or at least Section Five is made nationwide, we are still undergoing Reconstruction.[11]

He also pointed out that if any area in the South wished to be relieved from jurisdiction under the act, it had to appeal to U.S. District Court in the District of Columbia, which he found "totally unfair because the Mississippi courts have a (civil rights) record that would compare fairly to the D.C. courts." The act has been effective in improving the representation of minorities in the South, he said, but "I see no reason why the state and local governments should be required to continue to come up here and kiss the ring of the attorney general for any changes in voting precincts, districts, and other requirements they might seek."

And because he believed that Republican congressmen throughout the South have been working toward similar goals

I think it's a great possibility that within the next few years we will see a Solid Republican South. We will become the dominant party in all likelihood. In the next ten years there will be a steady growth of the Republican party in the South like we have never seen before. We've given the Democratic party more than enough time to right its ways, and it has only gotten worse; it is completely dominated by the liberal forces in this country. That is unacceptable to me, and I think it's unacceptable to the majority of Southerners. And Ronald Reagan, of course, has been a very major factor in the movement in the right direction.

I can honestly see the day in the not too distant future when the Democratic party in the South will be the equivalent of the so-called Black and Tan Republican party that lasted until the 1950s in Mississippi—and at that time the Republican party will be the majority party of the South.

The Republicans in Mississippi have a man right now who will make a great candidate for governor. He could be the first Republican elected governor of Mississippi since Reconstruction. He's not a lawyer, not a politician, he's a successful businessman, successful farmer, a graduate of Annapolis, where he was an All-American in football and boxing and where he was commander of the brigade. He's a great guy and wants to be governor so he could run the government in a businesslike manner. If we do get a Republican governor and he shows that Republicans really do have a business approach to government, then it can make a difference. It would cinch it for us in Mississippi.[12]

However, in 1979, Democrat William F. Winter defeated Republican Gil Carmichael sixty-one to thirty-nine percent in the Mississippi governor's race. Carmichael had fared better four years earlier, when Democrat Cliff Finch beat him with fifty-four percent to Carmichael's forty-six percent.

Asked if his prize candidate did not sound similar in background to Jimmy Carter of Georgia, Lott visibly stiffened. He shook his handsome head.

No, no, no, no, no, no! Jimmy Carter never could cut the mustard. He went to Annapolis and was a businessman and a farmer, but that's where the similarity ends. He didn't know how to work with the legislature when he was governor of Georgia, and he didn't know how to work with Congress in Washington. He never got a handle on how to deal with the issues, how to present his programs, and he had a Democratic Senate and a Democratic House; you would have thought he could have taken the bull by the horns and gotten whatever he wanted. But he simply didn't know how to do that. If he told you one thing, he might waver on it. You never knew how he stood on anything.

Ronald Reagan is altogether different. We were all naturally concerned about how President Reagan would work with the Congress. We knew we would have trouble in a Democratic-controlled house. But he has been fantastic. President Reagan is open, he listens, he meets with us regularly—both Democrats and Republicans. He is so persuasive one-on-one, he really surprises you. You get into a small meeting with him, he's dynamite!

Ronald Reagan is helping Southern Republicans more than anything else that has happened in the party in a long, long while. Right now, I think we have completely recovered from the Watergate fiasco. When you look at purely numbers, the party has gotten back to the point where it was before Watergate. When I came into the House in 1973 we had 189 members. Now we've not only got back to that point, we have passed it. We now have a majority in the Senate and a president in the White House again. So I think 1980 was a watershed year, an election for the Republican party, and that meant a lot of things including the final closing of the Watergate chapter in our party.

In Mississippi, there was a long-lasting support for President Nixon. As much as anything else, the state had a feeling for him as an underdog. The people down there felt that he had been hit on pretty hard by the press, and Mississippi as a state had been through that for years and years. I guess that's true of the entire South.

And then, in the past few years, Jimmy Carter had been a very positive factor for the Republicans in the South. The South had gone for him solidly in 1976, stuck by their guns and gave him their okay, and then he turned on them when they needed him. And, you know, in the South we have a lot of pride—especially in a Southerner being elected president. But if there is anything that has more wrath than a woman scorned, it's a Southerner betrayed. And I think the South felt absolutely betrayed by Jimmy Carter.[13]

The man who was keeping his future political goals to himself in the summer of 1981 maintained, "We are making more and more progress every day in the South. In my lifetime I believe we will see a Solid Republican South." And late in 1981 some of his friends in conservative Capitol Hill organizations claimed that there were movements afoot to have him elected Speaker of the House "when Republicans take control of the House in 1982." But the congressman himself kept his mouth closed and his options open.

A Kinetic Chaos

A whirlwind of hellfire engulfed the Republican party during Richard Nixon's second term. First, two determined young reporters, Bob Woodward and Carl Bernstein, unraveled the news story of the century on the pages of the *Washington Post*, telling the sordid details of Watergate, the burglary of the Democratic national headquarters at the luxurious complex of buildings on the banks of the Potomac River, the subsequent coverup that went through the GOP ranks from little big guys who watched over millions of dollars in cash to the attorney general to the president's office. In October 1973 Vice President Spiro Agnew became the first to resign from that office. In early December veteran Representative Gerald R. Ford took the oath of office, and the tightrope on which President Nixon had been walking seemed to give way with the realization that a man declared honest by his peers in Congress was now vice president. Sentiment in favor of impeachment proceedings heightened with that realization. Nine months and two days later Nixon resigned the presidency rather than face impeachment. Ford became the thirty-eighth president. Gallup showed in his poll that the Republican party's twenty-four percent rating was the lowest since the first poll had been taken in 1940. In that first poll, when people were asked the same question, "In politics, as of today, do you consider yourself a Republican, Democrat, or Independent?" thirty-eight percent identified with the GOP.

The Democrats wooed not only the South but the nation. Houston attorney Robert Strauss was elected chairman of the Democratic National Committee. After midterm elections in 1974, R. W. Apple, Jr., of the *New York Times* wrote, "The American electorate vented its wrath on Republican candidates across the nation Tuesday, striking hardest at state legislators and United States Representatives—those theoretically most responsive to the public will. The Democrats made marked gains in state legislatures, posting triumphs in states as diverse as New York, Tennessee, Illinois, and Wisconsin."[1]

At the same time, as Congressman Trent Lott stated, the South was the last region to turn its back on former President Nixon. They considered him an underdog. He had been beaten by the all-powerful Eastern establishment press, which included the television networks; that's the way the South saw it. The average Southerner didn't like the press, felt as though the region had been the whippingpost for the press for a long time, and would have still voted for Nixon for president.

Four years after he winged away from the White House teary-eyed and visibly shaken, he was invited back to the mountains of Kentucky, where Bowling Green resident Al D. Johnson said, "We love seeing the statesman-like Nixon holding his head high and speaking out loud and clearly for the conservative businessman of the community."

In an interview by correspondence, Nixon staffer Kenneth L. Khachigian, who helped put together the former president's memoirs, answered questions concerning Nixon and the South.

While he conceded that the former president had been offered a Southern strategy, Khachigian wrote that

> the term Southern strategy did not originate with President Nixon's 1968 campaign and is somewhat a misnomer for that election. Because of Governor Wallace's presence on the ballot, the more effective approach personally devised by President Nixon was a "rimland strategy." The goal was to concentrate on those border states in the Southeast which had to be won and in which the Wallace candidacy was not as strong. States such as Missouri, Kentucky, Tennessee, Virginia, Maryland, North Carolina, South Carolina, Florida, and Texas ringed the heart of the Deep South and were winable. Combined with President Nixon's great strength in the midwestern, mountain, and far Western states, sufficient electoral votes could be strung

together to overcome the split caused by three candidates on the ballot. The strategy worked. All but Texas and Maryland were won, and those were lost by the combined total of less than 60,000 votes."[2]

Nixon began to gather his Southern strength in the late 1960s, according to Khachigian, "when the Republican party began strengthening its position in the South. It was during that period that Southerners recognized that the national Democratic party was failing to represent faithfully their hopes and beliefs. As the parties and personalities of the Democratic party turned more to the left and away from the more traditional positions forged by the old Roosevelt coalition, more and more Southern voters turned to the Republican alternative."

Nixon himself stated in writing:

I was first exposed to Southern customs, traditions, and attitudes during the three years I attended Duke University, from 1934 to 1937. I gained great respect for my Southern classmates—for their intelligence, their sense of history, and their nonparochial view with regard to the United States' role in the world.

During the four years I served in the House and two years in the Senate, I had a number of contacts and developed friendships with many Southern members of both bodies. I often said at that time that the Southerners were the best politicians in the Congress. In 1952 Senator Dick Russell ran for the Democratic presidential nomination. I recall talking to him after he had defeated Estes Kefauver in the Florida primary. I told him what I believed to be true then, and believe now, that of all the candidates, including Eisenhower, Taft, and Stevenson, who were being seriously considered for the presidency, he was the best qualified from the standpoint of background, experience, and judgment. He may have lacked the mystique which is essential for winning a national election, but had he won, I believe he would have been a great president. The insurmountable problem which confronted him was that at that time no Southerner had a chance either to be nominated or elected president of the United States—a situation which had existed since the war between the states.[3]

Speaking about his 1960 campaign decision to go into all fifty states, Nixon said it was "unprecedented."

Many of my advisers felt that going into the South was a waste of time from a political standpoint. I agreed with them, but I felt at that time that it was essential to begin the long process which would bring the South back into the nation so that we would not in the future automatically rule out a third of some of the ablest potential candidates for the presidency simply because of the accident of their birth in the South.

Ironically, one of the states I visited, Mississippi, gave me a very warm welcome when I spoke from the capitol steps in Jackson, and voted overwhelmingly against me. Twelve years later, Mississippi gave me the biggest majority of any state in the union.[4]

He had met U.S. Senators James Eastland and John Stennis "during his years as vice president," wrote Khachigian. "They were strong supporters of the bipartisan coalition [fashioned by then Majority Leader Lyndon Johnson], which supported President Eisenhower's foreign policy. President Nixon came to respect these men for their integrity; for keeping their word; and for putting America's interests above their own. This naturally developed into a strong political relationship when he became president in 1969 and continued to depend upon these two patriots for their unwavering support on essential national defense and foreign policy matters."[5]

Nixon reiterated the answer by replying, "During my presidency, I would not have been able to have achieved the foreign policy successes in our relationships with China and the Soviet Union, ending the war in Vietnam, and starting the process of building a lasting peace in the Mideast, had it not been for the support I received from Southern Democrats in the House and Senate. I also benefited not only from that support but from the very wise counsel I received from leading House and Senate Democrats on major foreign policy issues."

Nixon continued:

I consider that one of my major domestic achievements was the peaceful desegregation of Southern schools. After the Supreme Court decision of 1969 ordering immediate desegregation, I was determined that we should resort to legal sanctions which might even have included a Little Rock episode only if all other attempts to resolve the situation failed.

That was why I set up the advisory committees of blacks and whites in each of the Southern states, met with them personally and eventually persuaded them to comply with the law voluntarily even though many of them disagreed totally with the court's edict. Ironically, it might be said that my refusal to demagogue the race issue and make the South a whipping boy where school desegregation was concerned, paved the way for a Southerner finally to be elected president in 1976. But putting all partisanship aside, and regardless of how one evaluates the current incumbent, I am gratified by the fact that just as the 1960 elections effectively removed the barrier which prevented a Catholic from being elected president, the actions we took during our administration removed the barrier to a Southerner from being elected to the highest office in the land. One of my favorite statements was that "this is one nation, and no individual who is qualified for a position should be barred from obtaining that position because of his religion, race, or his geographical background." Our success in achieving this goal was dramatically demonstrated during my visit to Atlanta in the 1972 campaign. A young college student ran up to me in the motorcade and shouted, "Thank you for making the South part of America again."[6]

Back in mid-1974, after Senator Edward M. Kennedy dropped out of the race of the Democratic nomination, a number of New South politicians climbed to the forefront in national politics. The *Wall Street Journal* pointed out that the only Republican among the Southland's new crop, Howard H. Baker, Jr., had an excellent chance at winning the vice-presidential slot on the GOP ticket, although Ford had already named Nelson Rockefeller as his vice president. And in the meantime former Texas Governor John Connally, who had switched from Democrat to Republican, was indicted for bribery in a milk fund scandal. Although he was later acquitted, Connally's political future was damaged beyond repair by the indictment. Among the Southern Democrats seen as hopefuls were Governors Reubin Askew of Florida, Dale Bumpers of Arkansas, Jimmy Carter of Georgia, Edwin E. Edwards of Louisiana, and George Wallace of Alabama. Little known to the national press at the time, Jimmy Carter and his small band of followers from Georgia had been quietly toiling in the vineyards, in a manner not unlike the behind-the-scenes work of Ronald Reagan at the same moment. Carter's number-one assistant, Hamilton Jordan, stalked the small towns of the Midwest, telling the people about the goodness of Jimmy Carter. His press secretary, Jody Powell, shook hands and spoke out about the man from the little village of Plains and what he could do for this country. And when they returned home, they began feeding bright young college people into Florida, where Carter politics was discussed from Pensacola to Key West. Reagan workers had been down there, too, but not in the droves like Carter's caravan. Carter outpolled the crippled Wallace, who broke one of his paralyzed legs while boarding a plane in Pensacola during the primary. Ford defeated Reagan in Florida in March, but the Reagan people didn't leave. They stayed behind to look toward another day in the future. Carter defeated Wallace in primary after primary in the South, and he went on to win the Democratic nomination by an overwhelming margin.

Two moves on the eve of the Republican convention in Kansas City were pointedly interesting in retrospect. First, after President Ford and Vice President Rockefeller called for the GOP to broaden its base to include moderates and liberals, Reagan firmly rejected the plea, stating, "A political party cannot be all things to all people. It cannot compromise its fundamental beliefs for political expediency, or simply to swell its numbers. It is not a social club or fraternity engaged in intramural contests to accumulate trophies on its mantel over the fireplace." The Republican defeat at the midterm polls was due partly to Watergate, the former California governor said, but it was also due to the lack of basic differences in the two parties. "No one can quarrel with the idea that a political party hopes it can attract a wide following, but does it do this by forsaking its basic beliefs? By blurring its own image so as to be indistinguishable from the opposition party?" he asked the more than 2,000 participants in the Republican Leadership Conference. "Does any Republican seriously believe that any Democrats who subscribe to the profligacy, the big government policies of the present Democratic leadership will be won over to our side if we say these are our policies, too?" Quoting the late Senator Robert A. Taft, Reagan said, "The only parties that have died are those which have forgotten or abandoned the principles upon which they were founded. A party kills itself and removes any excuse for its existence when it adopts the principles of its opponents."[7] He received a standing ovation, then went on to meet with various groups. He paid particular attention to Southerners, many of whom vowed to work on his behalf for any future candidacy. Then, days before the convention, Vice President Rockefeller withdrew from the race for the nomination. After Ford edged past Reagan for the presidential nomination, winning with 1,187 delegates to Reagan's 1,070, the former movie star declared he would not have his name put into nomination for the vice presidency.

Ronald Reagan had waged the most powerful intraparty campaign of the century against an incumbent president, and he was not about to accept the second chair. But Ford traveled across town to Reagan's hotel suite to ask him for full support. After the hour-long meeting behind closed doors, Ford described Reagan as "the most effective campaigner in America" and said the former governor had "one of the strongest organizations of any politician in America." Reagan did not respond. However, the man who had placed Reagan's name in nomination, his old friend Senator Paul Laxalt of Nevada, stated Reagan had challenged the entire Republican establishment, including the president, and "he has compiled a track record that proves without a doubt that he can win. I would dearly love to see Ronald Reagan debate Jimmy Carter. After one round of debating with Ronald Reagan he would have to go back to shucking peanuts—if that's what you do with peanuts."[8] And the man who gave Reagan's seconding speech, Senator Jesse A. Helms of North Carolina, who was given a fifteen-minute ovation when he stood before the convention, said, "I think it is in Ronald Reagan's best interest to hold off (from attempting the vice presidency). He is strong where others are weak. And his strength will grow and grow. His conservatism is a foundation, a bedrock of belief, and I do not believe that will ever go away."[9] In the end Ford chose Kansas Senator Robert J. Dole as his running mate, and Reagan said little during the campaign, which found the GOP team losing ground almost daily to Jimmy Carter and vice presidential nominee Senator Walter Mondale of Minnesota. Carter became the first man from the Deep South to be elected President in 124 years, Ford the first incumbent president to lose since Herbert Hoover. It marked not only a victory for Carter but a new start for Ronald Reagan. The polls had not closed before he was off and running. On January 15, 1977, Reagan's crowd suffered a minor defeat when forty-six-year-old conservative former Senator Bill Brock was elected chairman of the Republican National Committee over Richard Richards of Utah, whom they supported; but Ronald Reagan himself made fast friends with Brock and continued running out in the boondocks one on one, letting the people of his party know that he was ready, willing, and able to take the reins in 1980.

New Southern Strategist

When Ronald Reagan's gang marched out of the West and started looking for somebody to run their Southern operation, they were looking for the meanest, baddest, strongest, smartest, most capable, longest-winded, and fastest-thinking hombre below the Mason-Dixon. He needed to be a hard-nosed gunslinger who was accustomed to life in the fast lane. If Ronald Reagan could cut into Jimmy Carter's home strength, demonstrate his muscle in Dixie, and be able to stand and relax after some good tough quick-draw Republican primaries, he could emerge a victor from the whole shooting match in November.

They looked around and saw only a number of middle-aged conservatives, advertising executives in the glass-and-steel towers of Atlanta, a few oil-raised slogan-touters looking down onto the plains of Texas from Houston, a scattering of media people in Memphis and Louisville, and some campaign-worn speechwriters from Miami and Mobile. On top of the heap, having climbed up there while nobody was watching, was a twenty-nine-year-old, shaggy-haired, squint-eyed whippersnapper who didn't look like anybody's idea of a rough-and-tough, down-in-the-trenches political bareknuckle fighter. Besides his youth, his round face and modern-day Huckleberry Finn appearance, he grinned a lot.

And when he spoke, there was the hint of an evil giggle on the back edge of his voice.

In early 1980, Harvey Lee Atwater was already a veteran of ten years in big-league politics, having won a summer internship with his hero, U.S. Senator Strom Thurmond, all the way back when he was a freshman at Newberry College, a little school twenty-nine miles due west of Columbia in the South Carolina Piedmont. Lee Atwater spoke with a different kind of accent from that of his forerunner, Southern strategist Kevin Phillips, but he was just as outspoken and self-assured—if not as knowledgeable.

Back when he was bopping around central South Carolina, playing in a backroads rock-and-roll band, "I was just a hell-raiser type, you know; I thought politics was a vocation for duds. When I thought of politics, I saw these guys with big thick glasses, black ties, and pants that came up to their ankles. They sat around reading books, you know." And that little I-know-and-I-know-that-you-know-so-what-the-hell giggle eked from the edge of his voice. "But at Newberry College I got very interested in reading history, I wanted to know what had happened, what politics were all about back when, and then I wrote several essays about historical subjects and politics, and I won the internship with Senator Strom Thurmond. I went up to Washington. I was nineteen. It was just after my freshman year. I wound up being with him a lot. We talked. I got close to him, got to know him, and found out what kind of great man he was."[1]

While he was experiencing the growing-into-adulthood time of his life, feeling his mental and physical and spiritual maturation, "while most young people are reading Nietzsche or Ayn Rand, I happened to run into Strom Thurmond, and that's the direction I chose."

Atwater said that Strom Thurmond was "like a father to me in politics. Almost every trait I have that has any valor to it I picked up from Strom Thurmond. He is the supreme Southern politician. Of them all, he is the only guy who has made it through it all. He is the only guy who has been adept enough to get through all the land mines with the blasts going off all around him.

"And do you know why?" Atwater asked with dramatic flare, sitting up suddenly on the couch on which he liked to recline during interview sessions in his roomy office in the Old Executive Office Building, adjacent to the White House, after he became President Ronald Reagan's expert on Southern politics. "Strom Thurmond has always had a guy like me in on the act. It wasn't accidental that he picked me out of the group of guys who were working for him in

1970 and let me tag after him and talk with him and listen to him. Before me, there was Harry Dent [a Columbia, South Carolina, whiz kid who worked with Thurmond and later with President Richard Nixon as his Southern expert]. When Thurmond is about ninety-five and I'm forty-five, he'll get somebody else. He's always found the youngest sharpest political operator and let him handle the politics in South Carolina, and I think that's one of his secrets. I mean, I know I was totally in awe of him."

By the time Atwater went back to school at Newberry College, he had read Italian Renaissance political philosopher Niccolo Machiavelli's *The Prince* and for him it became practical how-to-win-elections-and-control-your-life poetry. He preached the word of Strom Thurmond on the campus at Newberry and traveled into the hill country and down onto the low country, and everywhere he went he enthusiastically spread the gospel of his mentor. Josh Landers, who was a cadet officer at The Citadel in Charleston in 1971, remembered Atwater from a conference of college students in Columbia that year.

> He was this short fellow with more energy than a team of fresh-woke-up mules, and he jumped up on stage like an evangelist leaping up there, and he took that microphone in his hand, and he started telling us about how Strom Thurmond was old in years but not in ideas. He said it was time we got up off our fannies and started working in politics and voting and being counted. He pointed toward the west and said, "Look out there! University students are rising up by the multitudes! They're saying, 'Ain't nobody worth nothing after they're thirty!' Are you going to stand for that? I don't believe it. I believe the young people of South Carolina are going to stand on their own two feet and be heard." Still pointing, he said, "They're saying, 'You ain't no good unless you smoke marijuana and run around with your hair down to your waist.' And what I say is: baloney!" I can hear him like it was yesterday, and all the kids jumped up and hollered and clapped and stomped their feet, and he stood up there and grinned from ear to ear. He was a ball of dynamite, and he knew just how strong his explosion was going to be.[2]

Keeping up a momentum that was tiring even for most college students, Atwater covered every campus in his state for Strom Thurmond. He graduated from Newberry and picked up his master's degree in journalism from the University of South Carolina in Columbia. He consumed two books a week—most of them political histories—a goal he continued even after he became ensconced in his massive office next door to the White House. And he ran fifty miles a week, never missing more than a day at a time, tallying more than 25,000 miles by the time he was thirty. "It is all a part of being a whole, complete person, understanding *The Prince* and maximizing the advantages in one's own favor and knowing what you want out of life and reaching out and getting it," he said.

As a junior at Newberry he reached out and practiced what he had been preaching. He got involved up to his freckled cheeks. He managed the candidacy of a man named William Edens who wanted to be mayor of a small town called Forest Acres. The first taste of that first victory was sweet, and "ever since I've been the head honcho cattle driver. That's just what I am. When the cattle are in the pen I ride into town and drink a sarsaparilla," he offered with his wide grin. And for the next ten years he amassed twenty-four wins in twenty-eight political matches.

In 1973 he set up his own media-buying advertising agency which he called Baker and Associates. "I found an antique picture in a garage sale of this old guy with a stiff neck and little strong piercing eyes and a string tie, and that was Baker." The hint of a giggle touched his voice. "We never had a Baker," he added. Sitting back, he said confidently:

> I was president and every other officer in the company. I would have to go down as one of the new breed of Southern politicos who finds alternative means of getting votes rather than going around to mayors and county pols and stuff like that.
>
> I'm a modern Southern operator. In retrospect, one of the reasons I believe I have been relatively successful in this business is because I didn't get involved before 1970.
>
> I view 1970 as a crucial year. It was a benchmark year. You had a totally new breed of people elected to office across the South. They were Dale Bumpers in Arkansas, Jimmy Carter in Georgia, John West in South Carolina, Bill Brock in Tennessee, Reubin Askew in Florida. It was a whole new ballgame, and I don't think it was accidental that you had that breed of modern, progressive young media types springing up all over the South. A lot of people in the political business who were in it before the 1970s are not able to leave behind a bunch of tools that were very useful and even mandatory prior to 1970. These guys still bring their old tools into the arena, and they don't necessarily enhance their causes; they actually hurt their causes with them.
>
> Look at what I think is the classic confrontation of the old and the new in Southern politics. I had been with Thurmond nine years, and I left him for the first and only time, I hope. I chose to go with Ronald Reagan and he went with John Connally in the Republican primaries. It was a classic confrontation of the old Southern style of political work versus the new style.

We used every new tool in the political arsenal. Thurmond and his group embarked upon the traditional Southern ploys of talking to mayors, seeing the highway patrol in the various areas, meeting with the old-school county coordinators who had been doing the same work since way back in the forties. You know, I'd go into these small towns to have my organizational meetings, the sheriff would come up to me and say, "Well, you little bastard, y'all ain't going to make it, Strom's already called everybody on the force and at the county courthouse; y'all are behind!" And I'd say, "Well, let me tell you something, I ain't even going to bother to call you any more, it's a waste of time. I ain't going to piss up a rope just to have it run back down on me where I stand."

And that giggle began to creep back into his voice as he talked with the same excited cadence he used to play to when he beat the keys of a portable electric piano in the rock bands. His chestnut eyes gleamed as he added, "Then I'd get my people together, set up a phone bank, get in touch with the people out there on the residential streets who know damn well they count for something, and I'd get my local direct-mail stuff going. It's quiet, but it's effective." And then he laughed. "A few months later, when the votes were counted, they knew old Lee Atwater had been to town." And the laugh grew louder.

Not only did he use the sophisticated tools of the modern political manager to build up the image of Ronald Reagan, who was already known as the conservative voice of the Republican party, but he also put into play what he called "my own one original theory about politics in America": the Negative Factor Theory.

He theorized that every candidate who walked upon the playing field entered with a negative factor. Any time a candidate's negative factor rose above thirty-five percent and his positive factor dropped within five percentage points of the negative, that candidate could be defeated. If his candidate's opponent did not have a strong negative factor, Atwater began building the negative into the opposition.

"With Connally we didn't have to worry too much," he recalled. "He already had a pretty strong negative factor. He had been through the trial in Washington where he was found not guilty, but he was still tainted. And we discovered that most of the voters in South Carolina equated him with LBJ. When they saw his name, they saw a connection between him and Lyndon Johnson, and it turned them off.

"Just by accident, a fellow by the name of J. Evetts Haley, who in 1964 had written a book called *A Texan Looks at Lyndon*, came on a swing through South Carolina for a tour called 'A Texan Looks at Connally.' " Atwater got tickled at his own words, and he stumbled over them, and he asked with a twinkle in his bright eyes, "You follow me?" And he added, "And that pretty well fixed that one." Baker and Associates arranged for Haley to appear on television talk shows, speak to groups throughout the rural countryside, and answer questions from callers on radio programs. When he was finished, Connally's negative factor had risen by leaps and bounds.

The campaign showed exactly how Atwater's Negative Factor Theory worked in real life. "From the very beginning I knew Ronald Reagan could win. I knew he could win against Connally in South Carolina. And for other reasons I knew he could win against President Jimmy Carter.

"American politics is a base game. A politician must have a base to be successful. Ronald Reagan had the Western states. He could go to other areas to campaign. Carter's base in 1976 was the South. This year, he didn't even get his own base."

To Atwater Reagan's win over Carter was "one of two critical elections of this century. The last was when Franklin Delano Roosevelt won in 1932. It was a critical election because in the South giant segments of the population who had consistently voted one party line altered their position and formed a new majority. Of course, this also happened in other parts of the country; but it was very significant when it happened in the South."

In 1932, he pointed out, FDR swept to victory by forging a new majority coalition of blue-collar workers, liberals, and Roman Catholics. Four years later many blacks who had previously voted solidly Republican joined in the Democratic majority and became strong across the South.

It was that basic coalition that stayed intact for the Democrats during most elections until 1980. In effect, with that election back in 1932, when the people turned away from Herbert Hoover and the Republican Party, Roosevelt created the America that we have come to know. He created big bureaucracy. He created big government spending. He created big government programs. This election in 1980 was a predictable, violent reaction to the New Deal. The cycle has now turned full force. The government, bureaucracy, spending, taxes, all of it has gotten so out of hand, so rampant, that across the board a new coalition has formed in the South and in the nation. This coalition is basically the producers—all of the people who work and pay taxes.

The win by Reagan signified a major breakdown in party politics across the South, Atwater stated. "People just aren't placing as much emphasis on party as they are on quality candidates. Party is disintegrating as a predominant reason for voting someone into office. The agenda is number one, and at the top of 1980's agenda was economics—inflation, big government, and taxes.

"One of the things that is very significant about this is the attitude of the people at the time of voting. In the South white people have voted historically with the Democratic party. Once that is broken down, the allegiances start to fall apart, and the Republicans will be able to make strong and lasting inroads with the voters," he surmised.

Before becoming totally committed to any given candidate, most of whom were Republican, Atwater moved out into the field and took polls on various aspects of the voting public. Calling the completed poll "my benchmark," he sat down with the heavy, legal-page-sized document and studied it to find the attitudes of the people, how they wished to vote, and which issues they were interested in. "The whole way to winning an election is by putting together enough chunks of voters to get fifty-one percent. You don't have time to waste in politics. In this business you go hunting where the ducks are. With my polls I know where the ducks are," he said.

Six months before election day he carried his benchmark off "where I can be cool, calm, and collected," he contemplated the statistics, and he began to dream up a strategy for winning. "He stays up later and wakes up earlier than anybody else," recalled close colleague Tucker Eskew who had worked with him on several campaigns. "He is always thinking about politics, he never lets up. He'll be standing up in the front row of a rock concert with somebody strong and jivy playing, and his head will be cocked back and his foot will be patting, and you think he's into the music one-hundred percent, and two minutes later he'll turn to you and say, 'We've got to show the people how candidate X hates dogs. Nobody likes a dog-hater.' He's that kind of thorough sonofabitch in politics."[3]

In setting his strategy nine times out of ten Atwater used his Negative Factor Theory. "It's good to have a candidate with a medium negative factor because any good candidate will establish a constituency that likes him and one that doesn't. When a candidate's negative factor is low, that usually means the people don't know much about him. Then we build his negative factor," he said. Of the eighty candidates he has studied since the time of Harry S Truman, only two have beaten his rating system, overcoming a negative factor of thirty-five with a positive factor less than five points above the negative.

Once a negative gets up to about thirty-five percent you can never erase it. It may hover at the same level for a while, but it's like a cancer. Eventually it'll grow and kill the patient. A candidate can't reduce it by campaigning, because when he has polarized that many people, it's self-reinforcing. The more they see him, the more they're reminded why they don't like him.

Once I set the strategy and the candidate has approved it, I never blink. The last month of a campaign is an existential existence. People get scared. They start hollering about this, that, and the other. They want to change things. The pressure is unreal. They get where they can't stand it another minute.

His voice, again tinged with a giggle, crescendoed as the cadence quickened.

In the last two weeks of the presidential campaign, a group of Republicans including a very prominent officeholder in South Carolina rushed up to Washington and met with our national people to try and get me off the job. They screamed and hollered. They said, "We're going to lose the state because Atwater doesn't know what he's doing." But really, who cares? I don't lose focus. You've got to be tough, and you've got to be mean sometimes if you're going to do this for a living. It ain't no easy life.

And the giggle bubbled out as he eased back onto the sofa and curled his shoeless feet beneath his body.

Other than handling the South successfully for the national forces, Baker and Associates worked six congressional elections in South and North Carolina and Georgia and won all six.

A repeat customer was incumbent Republican Congressman Floyd Spence, with whom he worked in Columbia before opening his media office. Spence, a fifty-two-year-old good old boy up for his sixth term in 1980, "didn't have a bit of reason to be scared," remarked Atwater.

He'll be elected forever, and he had a foolish guy for an opponent. Tom Turnipseed was an old-time Wallaceite who came to South Carolina, won a trip to the State Senate, and then tried to run for everything else in sight. From my benchmark, I could tell Tom would overreact to anything that might happen. But it showed Spence at fifty-four and Turnipseed at thirty-two, which isn't *that* bad; but to guys like Turnipseed who don't know their stuff, it *is* bad. And I *knew* he would overreact. I *knew* it! So I leaked my findings to the press, and they came out with big headlines and everything: SPENCE UNBEATABLE THIS YEAR, something like that. [And the giggle surfaced again, just this side of laughter]. I had also given them the verbatims; I had asked, "What do you not like about Turnipseed?" all that kind of stuff; and the people came back and said, "Big ego," "Maniac," "Crazy," blah blah this, blah blah that. And so the next day Turnipseed predictably calls a press conference to attack me, which is great with me because I'm not running for anything—and he totally explodes.

And the laughter gushed through his shiny, even teeth.

The next day I'm up talking to another client, Congressman Carroll Campbell, in Greenville, and my secretary calls and says, "Your mother just called the office and she's all upset about something," and so I call my mother, who never bothers me, and she says, "This guy Turnipseed just got on TV and attacked you," and I said, "What?" and she said, "Yeah, he was attacking your poll, said you had no credibility, you were a dirty trickster from way back, you learned everything you know from Haldeman and Ehrlichman, and every time he saw you you were running around with an impish grin laughing about that last dirty trick you pulled on someone," and I said, "Yeah, Mama, that's just what happens in politics. Frankly, that was my strategy. I wanted to get him all upset," and she said, "Yeah, son, but you shouldn't let these guys get to know you so well."

And the laughter overflowed while he bent double on the sofa and pulled his stocking feet tighter under his knees.

About six weeks later I did another poll that showed the gap between Spence and Turnipseed even farther apart. I found out a TV station had also done a poll, and their poll showed about the same as ours. I came out with mine on a Monday, he blew up on Tuesday, and on Tuesday night the TV station announced their poll, and that totally blew Turnipseed out of the water. He spent the rest of the campaign trying to sue the TV station.

And Atwater's laughter continued. Spence ultimately defeated Turnipseed fifty-six to forty-four percent.

Atwater has proven to be the nemesis of many a Southern politician. Twice his candidates have beaten millionaire businessman Charles "Pug" Ravenel, a button-down-collar, Ivy League-suit, big-city-polished candidate who at forty took on seventy-five-year-old Strom Thurmond. Four years earlier the former Harvard quarterback had entered the governor's race from nowhere and upset Lieutenant Governor Earle Morris and Congressman William Jennings Bryan Dorn in the Democratic primary. He was heading into the final stretch toward the general election when the courts reversed an earlier ruling and stated he could not run because he did not meet a constitutional residency requirement. Ravenel's name was stricken from the ballot, and the

Republican candidate became governor. In 1978 Ravenel looked like a super candidate to oppose Thurmond for the Senate.

In the Thurmond-Ravenel campaign the first survey I saw showed that Ravenel had a negative factor of ten percent. However, of that ten percent only fourteen percent knew about his New York connection—that he spent most of his adult life in New York, thought like a New Yorker, acted like a New Yorker, and would probably represent South Carolina like it was New York. So I said, "Lo and behold, let's make fifty percent of these people know about it and see what happens." Every time I'd push a speaker out of the gate, I'd tell him or her, "Now, don't forget to mention the New York connection, we've got to let the people know." And the next poll showed Ravenel with a negative rating of twenty-five percent.

Within two weeks things went completely haywire for Ravenel. Atwater said that a reporter overheard Ravenel say at a Manhattan cocktail party that he would make a great third senator from New York. "You can imagine," remembered Atwater. "I went crazy. God! We got the statement, leaked it to the papers, and they made a story of it. It splashed all over," he added.

But a political consultant to Ravenel, David L. Rawle, denied that his man ever made such a remark. "I know 'Pug' Ravenel. He's smart. He's quick. He wouldn't say anything like what they put into his mouth. It was ludicrous. When negative campaigning resorts to distortion and inaccuracies, and when it attributes aspects to a candidate that have no basis in fact, that kind of campaigning has no place in American politics."[4]

Atwater did not stop at leaking the so-called quote to the press. "Then we got us a Democratic state senator and put him on TV saying, 'I've been a Democrat all my life. I've always voted Democratic. But I can't vote for "Pug" Ravenel because I'm not going to vote for a third senator for New York.' Wham! Bam! That was it! The next poll showed Ravenel's negative rating up to forty-two. He collapses!" In 1980 it was a repeat performance; in the last three weeks of the congressional race Atwater was handling for Tommy Hartnett against Ravenel, a television blitz resurrected the old New York connection, and again Ravenel lost at the polls.

Among Atwater's other candidates were incumbent Carroll A. Campbell, Jr., from the heavily textile-industrialized Fourth District of South Carolina, where Atwater believed "he can be elected for the rest of his life if he doesn't try to run for a statewide office"; Larry McDonald, his only Democrat and only Georgian, a man who always voted with conservative Republicans on key issues; and John L. Napier "against Rita Jenrette . . ." The giggle seeped out again as he explained that he was not trying to be funny but meant John W. Jenrette, the Democratic incumbent from the Sixth District of South Carolina, where the Pee Dee and Santee rivers flow through tobacco, cotton, soybean, and textile country. Jenrette stood hardly a chance after being convicted in the Abscam scandals for taking a bribe and after his beautiful blonde wife Rita filed divorce papers and wrote a book about their lovemaking on the steps of the Capitol in Washington and posed nude for a layout in *Playboy* magazine. And then there was what he called "the most classic negative campaign of them all: Gene Johnston, a businessman from North Carolina's textile, tobacco, and furniture-making Piedmont, against Democratic Representative L. Richardson Preyer, who was going after his seventh term in Congress.

Armed with another of his theories "that in Congress an officeholder has a ninety-four to ninety-six percent chance of getting reelected," as well as a new benchmark poll for the area around Greensboro, High Point, and Burlington that showed an increasing interest in Republicanism, Atwater went to work for his wealthy businessman client, who had run and lost an earlier race for the State Senate.

At first glance the poll looked devastating. "Preyer was strong. He looked tough. The numbers showed Preyer with seventy-four and my guy with six. But I could also see that Preyer was a fuzzball. With his kind of background in twelve years in the U.S. House, Richardson Preyer was a liberal by all standards in that district," Atwater said.

Preyer was exactly what Atwater was looking for. Heir to a multimillion-dollar fortune in the Richardson-Merrell drug company, Preyer had gone north to undergraduate school at Princeton, graduated from Harvard Law School, returned home to become a local judge at age thirty-four, and was appointed to U.S. District Court in 1961 by President John Kennedy. After resigning the lifetime appointment, Preyer ran for governor in 1964 as a moderate but was defeated by a conservative in the primary runoff. After Democratic Congressman Horace Kornegay, a conservative, stepped aside in 1968, Preyer was nominated without opposition by his party and he won hands down over a well-known Republican in the general election. In 1978 Preyer had defeated Republican challenger George Bemus sixty-eight percent to thirty-two percent.

By all moderate Democratic measures Preyer had been a good and reliable and effective congressman. As a ranking member of the House Ethics Committee he worked with counsel Leon Jaworski to ensure a broad investigation of the Koreagate scandal. He was an advocate of tough financial disclosure for all congressmen. On the Health Subcommittee in the House he backed clean air legislation when automobile companies screamed that they were being squeezed out of the market by Japanese automobiles.

This experience, including a hot and bitter unsuccessful fight in 1979 to obtain the Health Subcommittee chairmanship, made Preyer a perfect target for Atwater-style politics.

We went into the race head-first. We painted Preyer into left field. What the hell, he'd gone to Princeton and Harvard, and he'd been a Kennedy appointee to the court, and he was this big rich drug-company heir, and he had gone against American industry! We crystalized his image way to the left. Then we came back and brought our guy in and put him right with the voters—blue-collar conservatives and white-collar management.

On Thanksgiving after Johnston beat Preyer, my aunt who lives in Greensboro came down and said, "We hate to tell anyone that you were involved in that campaign, it got so dirty." But it *really* wasn't dirty. It was just plain old politics.

And Atwater's laughter hit a high pitch; his slender chest vibrated with self-gratification. Like *The Prince*, he was in the game of life to win; if you are going to be a player, that's the only way to play.

Atwater returned to his pet tarantula, the Negative Factor Theory.

It is my whole theory that it can be used every time in a two-man race if one of the guys can't win. That's what happened to Preyer. He couldn't win. Of course, he had a little help. But he *couldn't* win. Then your guy comes out all right.

It is not totally foolproof. You have got to know when to use it and how to use it. When you can make it play, when you can find the salient type of issues to make it go your way, I think then it is foolproof. It can be manipulated in a thousand different ways, and it is definitely my own personal pet tarantula.

Unlike other candidates with strong negative factors, an incumbent president could, because of his superior office, erase negative percentages working against him, according to Atwater.

He can create the image of a strong, nonpartisan leader who is in control of the country; he has immediate access to the mass media; he can manipulate special interests and patronage; he can invite people to lunch at the White House and use the office as a platform for his issues and to raise funds; he can create staged events and nullify the events of others. Truman in 1948, Lyndon Johnson in 1964, and Richard Nixon in 1972 all utilized these advantages. If a president has any smarts at all, he's unbeatable. Look at Carter. In the fall of 1979 his negatives were in the thirties and his positives were in the forties.

But Carter began losing his toehold in a hurry.

His political people did not pay attention to the game plan they had set up from the beginning. The President started slipping way back in early 1980. It didn't take a genius to see that his Southern base was ruptured—particularly by late summer, when he discovered he had to face Ronald Reagan. In fact, he started bleeding like a stuck pig.

Our plan for the South was a resource game, just as it is with every candidate. We made Carter spend his two resources: time and money. Instead of spending his resources in Michigan, Florida, Ohio, and places where he needed to spend it, he had to do it down here in his own backyard. Making him do that, we were in pretty good shape. We *made* them fall apart.

"Basically, ours was a guerrilla operation," he continued. And with his ever-present grin that grated on the nerves of many opponents, he added, "You don't always hit the target by aiming at the bulls-eye."

He told a reporter in early October 1980, "I predict that Jimmy Carter will have to come back to South Carolina. He can't afford not to. If he loses South Carolina, he's no longer president of the United States. That means he's melted like an iceberg in the tropics and has lost thirty-seven, thirty-eight other states with it." In the same interview Atwater predicted that Carter could count on only Georgia and North Carolina and perhaps two or three other Southern states in the general election. Responding, Carter State Chairman James H. Quackenbush, Jr., said, "Lee Atwater is full of shit." With a large turnout of blacks, who comprised about thirty percent of the state's population, and with President Carter visiting milltowns such as Startex to win over the white blue-collar workers, whom Atwater labeled "the swing vote," and since Reagan had only the well-to-do country club whites who historically voted Republican, Quackenbush said that Carter would win. But Atwater said that the blue-collar whites were ready for a change "and besides, there's a little John Wayne left in Ronald Reagan, and I think the people are ready for some more John Wayne."[5]

It turned out that Atwater was right; Reagan won more than had been predicted, and the kid from the South Carolina Piedmont was offered a job under political adviser Lyn Nofziger. In the Reagan administration he rode herd on fifteen Southern states, taking care of the political angles, speaking fourteen hours a day to political folk from Oklahoma to West Virginia and from Miami to El Paso, thinking about ways to win votes and influence voters, and laughing all the while.

My other pet tarantula is that I never do anything twice. I *never* do it twice. I lay awake at night to think of new ways to use the old theory. My chief competition in South Carolina did campaigns over and over the same way. Most advertising agents who handle campaigns get branded with their fingerprints on races. That's just the way it is. You really have to work overtime to make sure you do things differently. It takes a lot of time and effort not to repeat yourself.

I'll use the old tools from Kevin Phillips and those old boys, the charts and maps and demographic layouts: they are useful tools. But most political operatives are mostly advertising people who are out to change opinions or are dealing with opinions. I'm out to deal with attitudes. An opinion is a verbalized response to any question. "What's your opinion about this or that?" Attitude is not verbalized, it's ingrained into the overall person. It's like a whole bunch of opinions affect someone's attitude. If I can get a hold on someone's attitude about some issue, the opinions will just wash away.

The problem with just using Kevin Phillips' voting studies, statistics, demographics, things like that, is that it's harder to be a renaissance man in politics by simply using these tools. I try to bring in another dimension in the use of these vital tools. I want to be a well-rounded person in politics.

I'm a totally devoted student of Machiavelli, and his writing probably has had the singlemost impact on my career in politics than anything else other than Strom Thurmond. Anyone who understands *The Prince* can understand how to proceed in politics; if you don't, it doesn't mean you can't get anything done, but you'll lose every time to the guy who does. Overall, the way I see it, when you get out there in the arena, you are competing; it's you—a man of virtue—with skill, cunning, this, that, and the other, versus fortune, which you can never overcome. Fortune can win at any time, but the man of virtue spends his entire life sitting down and figuring out how to build the odds up in his favor; he tries to dominate fortune the best he can by maximizing his own control against fortune. Rather than having a fifty-fifty chance to succeed, if you can get it up to fifty-one–forty-nine, in the long run you'll win; and if you can get it up to fifty-five–forty-five . . . hell, if you can get it up to sixty–forty, you're in good shape! But it all supposes a few things, the way I see it. Number one, you've got to be a long-term player; you've got to understand you're going to lose some time. Number two, you can't sit down, you can't let grass grow under your feet. What I do is five or six things that I feel will help build the odds up slightly. One of them is that I read two books every week on something; even if they are not good books, I've got to be physically awake and mentally awake, and by reading two books a week I keep up with something that has gone on or is going on.

On the table in front of his couch lay *Robespierre* by George Rudé. Atwater leaned forward, touched it, and laughed. "I'm on the French Revolution right now. I think this is a pretty good old boy. Robespierre knew what he was doing. He's all right." And then, he said, "I run my fifty miles a week, keeping me in shape physically, and I never miss more than one day a week no matter where I am or what I have to do." In the middle of campaigns he kept his shorts and Nikes nearby, ready to slip into them at nightfall and head out into the darkness for seven or eight miles.

Sitting on the soft sofa in the high-ceilinged office with Senator Strom Thurmond calling to ask his idea about an appointment to a judgeship, Lee Atwater appeared perfectly satisfied. Over his head were the portraits of his political heroes, Thurmond and Reagan, as well as soul singer James Brown and comedians The Three Stooges. Hanging up and shaking his head and grinning, he said, "That sure got my ass out of a crack," and he laughed again.

He leaned forward and blinked, bringing himself back to earlier thoughts. "You know what I am?" he said in his deeply rasping voice, while his aide Tucker Eskew sat at a nearby desk and smiled and nodded. "I'm a guy who in the academic world is considered a bastard. They say, 'He might be respected in the political world, but he's not a pure academic.' And in the political world people say, 'That's Atwater coming up with another one of his long drawn-out theories.' " And he laughed again. "I'm a man without a country because what I'm trying to do is extrapolate the best out of all of it."

Falling back onto the sofa, the cushion sinking in around him, the grin frozen onto his ruddy face, he said:

> Hell, I enjoy this stuff. I'm not in it to beat the world or anything like that. I don't take myself seriously. The guy who takes himself seriously in politics is the guy who will be dealt the death blow quickly. I'm not in it because I believe I can do anything other than make some small contribution and lead a good life.
>
> And it doesn't mean I'm going to run for any public office anywhere. My whole goal in life is to maximize my individual freedom. In short, in my estimation, anything less than that goal leads to unhappiness and despair. I can't think of a more desperate situation than to wake up every morning with the thought: "How does the public feel about me?" I think the most unfree person in America is the elected official. I admire 'em, love 'em to death, but I'm not qualified. And as Nietzsche said, "I don't want to go through the degradation of doing it in public."

Marching toward Victory

The sandy-haired young man in the bone-gray pinstriped suit had been a client of Lee Atwater, who had once worked with him in the South Carolina capital. In the Congress he was becoming well known as a man on the move. When he met a group of older congressmen in a wide hallway, he didn't slow his pace. His eyes surveyed the faces, recognizing each, nodding and speaking. But the soles of his dark shoes continued to click rhythmically against the parquet floor of the House office building.

In the twenty years since he first entered politics two years out of high school, Carroll Ashmore Campbell, Jr., knew who was who in a moment's glance. He had grown up a maverick in South Carolina political circles. He wasn't a beatnik of the late fifties or hippie of the late sixties or a yippie of the early seventies. Far from it. He was a pioneer Republican in that staunchly Democratic state. He was a true believer from the word GO, watching the Eisenhower-Stevenson race when he was a boy growing up in Greenville and wondering where all the Republicans were. "I knew the state Republican chairman because he was my Sunday school teacher, but he was about the only one I can recall," he said, but he knew deep down inside that Republicanism was the way of his convictions.[1]

In those days, before he became one of Ronald Reagan's first backers in the Congress of the United States, Carroll Campbell got involved in his only Democratic race.

It was 1960, and I wasn't even old enough to vote, and I helped a friend who was running in the Democratic primary for State House. The two of us paid a visit on an old Democrat ward heeler in an attempt to persuade him to support my friend's candidacy. The old pol, sitting with his feet on a desk and chewing tobacco, told us that he could assure us victory in five precincts—if we paid the price. Because my friend refused to be bought, he lost those five precincts badly, and he narrowly lost the primary. There were twenty-two candidates running for ten seats. My friend ran a good race. He was a good campaigner. But he got zeroed out in the areas the ward heeler controlled. He came in twelfth.

Because of that election, I became a pollwatcher for the Republican party. My friend who had run in that campaign joined me. And I saw some things I hated to see. I'll never forget. There was this fellow, his name was Chris Howell, he's dead now, he was a very active Republican, and he was watching the polls with us, and we kept our eye on this place where one of the ward heelers controlled what happened and didn't happen. Chris Howell went to report irregularities in that federal election in 1962. He got into a telephone booth and started dialing, and the people from there caught him in the booth and literally beat the phone booth in around him.

That was what I call a no-party system. The Democratic primary was the election. The Democrats ran against each other, and whichever one won was the winner. And I don't mean to imply that that kind of illegal violence went on all the time and was that widespread. It wasn't. But I happened to experience it. I had a taste of it coming up. And from that kind of situation I watched us build a two-party system.

What I'm trying to say is: we built a two-party system from nothing since 1960 in my state.

From the start Carroll Campbell knew where he was going. He was already a successful businessman back home in real estate and had a string of fast-food restaurants. And he also knew that afternoon early in 1980 when he took a quick turn and disappeared behind a tall oak double door. In the room he sat with fifteen other federal lawmakers who watched out the large window as the sun sank behind the Washington monument. They were not birdwatchers in pinstriped suits. (They all did indeed wear conservative dress; it is the uniform of Congress.) These backslappers felt particularly close on this wintry afternoon. Not only were they all congressmen and all Republicans, they had come together to form what they called the TNG. They were an elite group attempting to form strategy on behalf of their candidate for President of the United States. And that candidate, Ronald Reagan, had not only promised to listen to them, he had sent his man, Richard V. Allen, on whom he depended for foreign policy advice, to sit as chairman of the Thursday Night Group, as they called themselves. Co-chaired by the jovial Representative from Delaware, Thomas R. Evans, Jr., and Reagan's close friend, Senator Paul Laxalt of Nevada, the TNG took on the personality of these politicians who believed totally that Reagan was the only man who could run the United States as conservatively as they wished. They prided themselves on not being the New Right, although here was square-shouldered, Kennedy-haired Jack Kemp of New York's Thirty-eighth District sitting next to Campbell, the Greenville, South Carolina, businessman-congressman. Their philosophies jibed, although Kemp, the former pro football quarterback, was from the bedroom suburban areas of industrial Buffalo and Campbell represented the newly developed stretch of foothills of the Great Smoky Mountains running parallel to Interstate 85, where the textile industry had concentrated its irregular growth in the Piedmont. With them were the likes of bearded Mickey Edwards from Oklahoma's Fifth District, which included the oil-rich glass-steel towering skyscrapers of Oklahoma City, where President Gerald Ford had beaten Carter fifty-seven to forty-one percent in 1976 and where most of his constituents were as conservative and as Republican as Edwards. In essence the TNG was a solid body that agreed on its primary goal: Elect Reagan! As Campbell remembered:

In the beginning, we discussed the strategy our candidate needed to win in all the various parts of the country in the primaries. I talked about the South and what we needed to carry South Carolina and the other states. After New Hampshire, South Carolina was the fallback. There was no doubt about it. Our friends from the West talked about Iowa. But South Carolina was definitely the fallback after New Hampshire and Iowa. It was agreed that we were very important because we were the first Southern primary. Also, all of the focus would be on South Carolina since it was the only state where a primary would be held that particular week. And we knew that the press would concentrate on it because this was where John Connally would be made or would be broken. It was his big battle in the war for delegate strength. And, of course, we were also aware that if we didn't stop him in South Carolina, Connally could pick up momentum that might catapult him into the nomination. The odds were against it happening, but it could happen if we didn't win in South Carolina. And that's the kind of stuff we discussed in the TNG meetings. We got feedback from all over the country, and we made suggestions before it got cranked up and after, and we were able to get an awful lot of input that way. Dick Allen was our conduit. He sat in on nearly all of the meetings. He brought word from the candidate and from what was happening out there, and we let him know how we felt about how things were going.

On Mondays or Tuesdays or Wednesdays Carroll Campbell and some of the others from the TNG moved just as fast from office to office through the hallowed halls of their buildings in Washington to meet and plan Reagan positions. The Core Group was even older than the TNG, and it had no specific night for meetings; the fourteen congressmen led by Tom Evans and Campbell huddled over coffee in various cubbyholes on Capitol Hill as often as they got together at night. "This was before anybody else was on board. We were the original people who came out for Reagan. We did most of the legislative research for Reagan and the campaign. We wrote most of the position papers. We ran all over the country doing surrogate speaking. And eventually we ran the primary campaigns. We did a little bit of everything," Campbell said.

In the primary Campbell was the chairman for Reagan in South Carolina. Working closely with him was political behind-the-scenes professional Lee Atwater, with whom he had been closely attached since Campbell's days in the state legislature.

In 1972, after Lee had worked with Strom Thurmond one summer, he helped me all over the state on the issue to give eighteen-year-olds the right to vote. He was not much over eighteen himself. He was maybe twenty-one, and he spoke out in favor of my amendment to the state constitution, and he helped with the entire campaign, which carried. And he has been basically with me ever since in some degree. He came into my lieutenant governor's race in 1974 late. We were outspent better than three-to-one. It was a real heartbreaker. We carried about forty-eight and forty-four-one-hundredths percent of the vote. We just didn't have the money to keep up with the Democratic candidate. And after that race, that same year, Republican Jim Edwards won the governor's race, and he asked me to be his executive assistant, and Lee went to work for me in the capitol. And after that, Lee ran my 1976 campaign for the state senate. I can tell you this: he's smart as a whip, always thinking, never lets anything get past him. I told Lee that way back in the early seventies, after I'd run the campaigns in the sixties, Lee could learn something from me; but I know now that I could learn a great deal from him. He started off with us in the primary in South Carolina, then he took on Georgia and Alabama, and as the campaign progressed his authority expanded.

Campbell spoke in Illinois, Oregon, through the West, and down South. It was as a member of the Core Group that he began in-house criticism of the campaign leadership of Reagan manager John Sears. Campbell was already leery of Sears.

He had not acted and made decisions early enough back in the 1976 big push for the presidential nomination. Of course, it would have been difficult at best to unseat a sitting president, but we thought Ronald Reagan had a good chance to beat Gerald Ford out for the nomination. But John Sears spun his wheels too long. He and others didn't act in time. And then, when he made the desperate move of bringing Richard Schweikert of Pennsylvania into the picture as Reagan's choice of a vice presidential nominee, we viewed it as somehow ridiculous. Other people praised him for the move, but it seemed like an act of desperation to most of us. Then, in 1980, Sears wouldn't let his man out of the starting gate, and some of us started speaking out against his hard-line control of the campaign. One time, after I had flown out to Iowa to make several surrogate speeches for the candidate, Sears went out there and held a big press conference and explained why he was holding the reins so tight on Reagan. We got together back here on Capitol Hill and talked about it and sent out the message that we didn't want John Sears playing Ronald Reagan as a puppet in his hands. From our people very close to Reagan we learned that there was other dissension in the ranks. Sears and Ed Meese had been going at it; Meese wanted more control, and Sears wouldn't let him have it. Lyn Nofziger and Mike Deaver were in a pushing-and-pulling contest with Sears. We all knew something would have to give or the press would discover what was happening, and somebody might have a field day on national television or across every front page in the country. It wasn't long after that—I was back down in South Carolina with Lee, and we were putting together the campaign down there, and it didn't look good at all because our favorite politician in the world, Senator Strom Thurmond, was backing John Connally, and so was Jim Edwards, in whose governor's administration we had worked—I got a call to meet with Reagan and Sears. I drove out of Greenville, up I-85, and it was a miserable day, all overcast and dreary, and we met in a motel outside Spartanburg. Tom Evans had flown down with Reagan, and we had a head-on meeting with John Sears and told him he was making a mistake and the campaign had to open up. We talked to the candidate about it and told him what we thought; we didn't hold anything back; we emphasized the importance of this thing, how we had to move out and change our image right away. Just the day before I had been approached by some people at the University of South Carolina wanting Ronald Reagan to debate there. Prior to that Sears would not let him debate. He was keeping him under wraps. After we talked to Reagan, he nodded and said, "Yes, I'll do it." We walked out of that meeting, Tom Evans and myself and others, after leaning heavily on Sears, and we held a little news conference right there and accepted the debate for Reagan. That was the first debate he accepted. The first [debate] was not held in South Carolina, but that was the first time he accepted one. I believe that was a pretty good turning point in the campaign. It marked the time when he moved out as a candidate and quit being the guy behind the shelter. I think people started noticing him after that, he acted like a real leader, and people out over the country saw that he was a leader.

About one week after the meeting Campbell sat in his office in the Longworth Building in Greenville. His secretary rushed in and interrupted his concentration. "It's Ronald Reagan on the phone," she told him excitedly. The congressman didn't even look up from his reading. He said, "Tell his secretary I'll be right with him." And she said, "You don't understand, it's him!"

When I answered the phone, he said, "I just want to tell you, Carroll, I just fired John Sears." He was up in New Hampshire, and it was about mid-morning on the day of the primary up there, and he said, "Charlie Black's gone with him. We're going to be pretty short in the campaign. South Carolina's next, and you're running the show down there, and I want to know what you think we can do." I told him, "I think you've done what you had to do about Sears at this stage of the game. The fact that he wasn't amenable to changing his overall strategy would have hurt us down here. Now we'll be all right. I think we'll win South Carolina, although we still have Strom Thurmond and all of the rest of 'em out on the other side working against us." And he said, "All right, it's your show."

Carroll Campbell learned how to buckle down and fight early in life. He wasn't from a highfalutin rich family that could send money every time he turned around to keep him in the ball game. When he was a sophomore at the University of South Carolina, he dropped out and went to work, and after he watched his friend withstand the blows from within the telephone booth, administered by the goon squad of the Democratic powerbrokers, he learned politics in the most practical way. He lived through some tough defeats. But in the end he landed on his feet.

When he was thirty years old in 1970 he was elected to the State House of Representatives, and two years later he was given the largest number of votes ever received by a candidate in an election to the State House. Leaning over his crowded desk and anchoring his elbows on a pile of paper, Campbell said,

I don't want you to get me wrong. I don't dislike Democrats for being Democrats. That's their way. I just happen to be a Republican. I have a lot of Democrats in my district who vote for me and even form committees and go out and campaign for me. What I'm saying is: we've come a long way in the South since 1960, when Chris Howell was beaten up.

When I was growing up, I learned an awful lot from the old Democratic people like Solomon Blatt, who was speaker of the South Carolina House of Representatives. He had been speaker for years and years, since back in the late 1930s. He was very conservative. He was a power. He was one of the best State House politicians I've ever seen. And I learned a lot from him.

I plowed new ground with the few other Republicans in the State House, and I was fortunate enough to be able to negotiate with the Speaker fair representation for the Republicans on committees. That was one of our major things that we did, and we did it by holding our Republican votes together.

The Speaker wanted something. He wanted to defeat the clerk of the House. She hated him, and he hated her. So he was running his secretary against her. The clerk of the House was elected by the whole House, and he did not have enough votes to defeat her without the Republicans, and I held all of the Republican votes. We got all the votes together, and our chairman wasn't there for some reason, and as vice chairman of the minority party, I was sent to negotiate with him. I went to him and said, "Mr. Speaker, we have seventeen votes, and we'll vote your way, but we have to have fair representation on the committees." After little thought he agreed. He understood that kind of politics.

The next time when the committee appointments came due, I sat right by the Speaker's desk. He put a Republican on every committee, and we got several places on a couple. I learned a lot from him. I learned how to deal with him. He was honest, straightforward, and smart. He kept his word. It was one of those things that you learn if you're going to be in politics.

I was fortunate, because he and other Democrats were very fair to me. I was the first Republican elected to an office on a committee in the State House. In 1973 I was elected vice chairman of the Medical, Military, Public and Municipal Affairs Committee, and I'm very proud of that because it was a first; it took a lot of work to get there.

It was an interesting time. I'm glad I lived through it. It was a great transition. And I think we're still going through a transition. But that was the beginning.

In 1974 he was defeated in the race for lieutenant governor, and a year later he joined Republican Governor Jim Edwards, "and that was really a wonderful experience to be a part of putting together a progressive administration that looked toward a brighter and better future," Campbell said.

A political science professor at the University of South Carolina, where Campbell went back and took his degree by attending night school while he was working in the real political world, remembered;

He was a very good student. He worked hard. He wasn't a genius. But he knew what he wanted and where he was going. He was older than the other students, a successful man, but he never got in the way of the other students. He didn't try to run over them. He had a quiet chip on his shoulder and sort of dared us scholars to knock it off. I don't think he liked the way many of us taught our classes. But then, I didn't care too much for the way he ran the government; I don't think he kept the people in mind when he and James B. Edwards started building their "programs for the future." I guess what I'm saying is: They were too Republican.[2]

Another teacher who began teaching after Campbell earned his bachelor's degree said, "The trouble with Carroll Campbell is, he's too ambitious. Because of that, he's the most dangerous Republican in South Carolina. He is a true-believer in the conservative cause." [3] However, yet another school administrator from the low country of Charleston said, "I like him. He's smart. He doesn't talk unless he knows what he's going to say. In short, he's my kind of Republican." [4]

But Campbell never let the critical judgments from professors stand in his way. Even after he became a congressman in Washington he attended night classes at the American University to earn a master's degree in political science and government administration.

Campbell was elected to the South Carolina State Senate in 1976, served on the Banking and Insurance, Education, Medical Affairs, Judiciary and General committees, and two years later became the first Republican elected to the Congress from Greenville and Spartanburg counties in more than 100 years.

Like his political career, his activity in the national party grew consistently during the years. He was an alternate delegate to the 1972 Republican national convention, and four years later, as a delegate committed to Ronald Reagan, he served on the platform committee, where he got his feet wet dealing with such ultraconservatives as John East and Jesse Helms. And in 1980 he was chairman of the South Carolina delegation and assistant floor leader of the Reagan for President forces.

But back in the long days of the primary season in South Carolina Campbell and Lee Atwater did not find the pathway slicked for their candidate. He had the look of a winner, he had the first primaries behind him, and he was out in the open with a more-or-less new management team in the shape of Nofziger, Deaver, Meese, and Dick Wirthlin. But the local biggies were still backing Connally, and when Campbell and Atwater took their man into the small towns, they found that the schools where Reagan was to speak were ruled closed to the public by the county or city boards of education; then he would speak only to the students. It didn't take them long to schedule the speeches on the courthouse steps, whip up a rally with advance notice, and "nothing looked better than having our candidate arrive an hour late because he had to fight his way through crowds," Campbell recalled. And in the meantime Atwater did his negative-coating paint job on the former governor of Texas and, as one local observer stated later, "gave old John Connally a fitting and permanent farewell to the world of politics."[5]

Campbell followed Reagan to several more Southern states, becoming a surrogate speaker in Georgia, Alabama, and Mississippi. Between that time and the convention in Detroit, Campbell put together another strategy. While traveling through the Southern states and back home with Lee Atwater, the two sat down and came up with a plan.

> We knew that the South was the focal point away from which Jimmy Carter wanted to focus. This was his home base, his centerpiece, and without it he would be lost. The strategy we penned stated basically: make Carter come home and do battle on his own turf. If he has to defend the soil of the South, he will leave his flanks to the north and west wide open and vulnerable. It was very simple in concept, but we thought that we had a grip on his weaknesses. I presented the plan to Dick Wirthlin, and he took it from there.
>
> After the convention we organized loosely around our strategy. We got our little task force together and went around the South and hammered away here and there. We took 'em on on the issues, held press conferences in little towns, did all the grass-roots pushing, and they began to feel the rumblings up in Washington. They knew that things were coming apart on them down South.
>
> We scheduled Reagan into the South early, made a quick blitz, had a couple of big hoorah visits, and then we sent him along the way to the areas outside the South that he had to go to to win early. It gave us a fast reacquaintance with the people down here, it shook Carter's strength, and in that respect we forced Carter back into the South early in the game. And when he diverted his previous plans to go elsewhere, he looked especially vulnerable in his home. It was a reasonable move, and as it turned out, it gave us some narrow victories in Alabama and Mississippi, a good win in Louisiana, a virtual tie in Arkansas with Reagan actually winning by about five thousand votes, strong wins in Texas and Virginia, and victories in South and North Carolina as well as nearly two-to-one in Tennessee.

Even in Georgia Carter's 1976 final total of sixty-seven percent of the vote was whittled down to fifty-six percent in 1980, with Reagan carrying forty-one percent. "In the long run our strategy paid off," Campbell concluded.

In the primaries and general campaign Campbell spent a great deal of time with Reagan.

> We rode buses and airplanes to rallies all over the South. We were very close during a good bit of time between those places, and in traveling with him, I saw the qualities of him. He's a warm and extremely likeable individual. I was amazed at the depth of his own knowledge. He was able to discuss in depth much of the Old Testament, citing the different portions and stories and all. In many instances he displayed a great deal of human warmth and concern for other people. All of the rest of us may get frustrated, but he's the kind of fellow who can calm the waters and get things done. He is the kind of fellow who epitomizes something wonderful. Southerners can relate to him easily.

After becoming the first South Carolina congressman to be invited to join the Chowder and Marching Club, with an exclusive membership of top GOP leaders in the House, the thirty-second-degree Mason, Shriner, and member of Sertoma International civics club was appointed to the House Appropriations Committee in the Ninety-seventh Congress. He served on subcommittees on Commerce, Justice, State, Judiciary, and Related Agencies, Treasury, Postal Service, and General Government.

In the winter of 1981, after voting for President Reagan's tax cuts and budgetary package as well as helping persuade conservative-thinking Southern Democrats to vote for the legislation, Campbell urged his fellow congressmen to extend the Voting Rights Act of 1965. He became one of the first Southerners in Congress to call for amendments to strengthen so-called preclearance provisions that would require Justice Department approval of election laws. He pointed out that a straight across-the-board preclearance for the entire nation, as suggested by other Republican Southern Congressmen, "would weaken and dilute the strength of the bill, but I would like to see political jurisdictions being allowed to opt in and opt out of these provisions." In essence, he said, "I am in agreement with civil rights groups that point out that a nationalization of the act would dilute enforcement and that it would be unmanageable and probably unconstitutional." However, he asked that areas with "consistent and excellent records of compliance with the Voting Rights Act be allowed to regain control of their own election laws.

> While it is of overriding importance to protect the voting rights of all, no jurisdiction should be eternally punished for errors of the distant past.

There should be incentives to observe not just the letter, but the spirit, of the law. The possibility of relief from the preclearance requirements would provide that incentive.

You see, I learned through hard experience—way back when my friend lost that first race in 1960 because he wouldn't pay for votes—that the right to vote cannot be taken for granted, and that election laws can be unfairly applied to any minority—whether it be a people or a party. Our freedom to vote rests on both the good faith of our election officials and on the strength of our commitment to make and enforce fair and impartial election laws.

After President Reagan's director of the Office of Management and Budget, David Stockman, made sweeping proposals to reform Social Security, Campbell spoke out that many "from within their own ranks, which I may help lead," would oppose the proposed changes. Campbell said that he particularly opposed the immediacy of the impact on people who would be retiring in the near future. Campbell, who said he believed the Reagan administration had thought out other proposals thoroughly and adequately, criticized the lack of attention given "this very important step. What about the worker who, in anticipation of retirement, has given notice at the office, whose spouse has already quit, and who has sold the family home? It is unacceptable to tell that person that the rules of the game have suddenly changed and he's not going to get the money he counted on," Campbell said. While he agreed that the Social Security program was "in real trouble, deep enough trouble that its very existence is threatened," he recommended to David Stockman that he consider other options and the administration agreed.

"I am a Republican," Campbell said. "I am a Ronald Reagan Republican. But I can't condone this business of hurting the little individual out there across the country. We should be in the business of helping people while we are helping the government to get back on its feet."

In the aftermath of the Reagan tax-reduction bill's passing the Congress, Campbell joined hands with other Republicans and the Southern "Boll Weevils"—Democrats who supported the president's program—calling it "a bipartisan measure . . .designed to open up America, rejuvenate our inventive economic system, and revitalize our thinking about ourselves and our visions of the future."

The debate over the form and the extent of the bill actually began more than a year ago when President Reagan first made it an issue in his campaign. Unlike some promises made by some candidates, the president took his pledges seriously, and one of his first acts after inauguration was to propose a detailed four-point economic recovery plan. Multiyear, across-the-board tax cuts were an essential and inseparable element of that plan, and those features were the key differences in the Democratic plan and the Reagan bipartisan plan that made them worlds apart philosophically.

He failed to explain that what made it bipartisan was the crossover voting of the Boll Weevils, whom the Reagan supporters had rallied to the president's side. The loyalist Democrats continued to criticize the Reagan plan as being for the rich and not for the average American citizen. Campbell told a reporter from his home state that he believed the Reagan plan was the "best for all Americans."[6]

"Let me explain," Campbell said.

> If Congress did nothing, taxes for individuals would go up twenty-two percent in three years. Under the Democrats' bill, which provided only fifteen percent of express tax cuts, the government would have been taking more dollars from every working American by 1984. Their tax "cut" would translate into a seven percent increase over three years. Under the bipartisan [Reagan] bill, with its guaranteed twenty-five–percent tax cut, every worker in America will keep more of what he earns so he can do more for himself. Moreover, the bill contains an "indexing" feature, which I have supported since I served in the South Carolina Legislature, to ensure against the "bracket creep" that has driven working Americans into ever higher tax brackets.[7]

A Democratic supporter who held his ground behind Speaker of the House Tip O'Neill said, "Campbell is like all of the other Republicans on this issue. They explain away the inherent evils of their plan. It cuts away at the little man while lining the pocket of the big rich. In a year or two, when the personal wealth of the average taxpayers is nothing but debt, debt, debt, they'll be trying to explain it away more and more."[8]

But Campbell insisted that he had "long and publicly advocated" most of the provisions in the tax-cut plan: twenty-five–percent tax cuts over three years, automatic tax cuts afterward through indexing, a reduction in marriage penalties for couples who both work, new charitable deductions for people who do not itemize, tax-exempt savings certificates for savings and loan institutions, strong cuts in estate taxes, cuts in the maximum taxes charged on interest, dividends, and capital gains, and cuts in business taxes "to speed up depreciation to encourage expansion to create new jobs."[9]

Again, critics of the Republican administration remarked that Campbell and others were "overly enthusiastic" about their program. "What are they going to do when a year or two from putting their plan into action middle-class people are still paying high interest rates, inflation is still skyrocketing, and there's astronomically high unemployment?" asked Democratic Senator Robert C. Byrd of West Virginia. "They're moving too fast without thinking their plan through, and they're promising too much too soon. I'm afraid, deeply afraid, that the plan will backfire—and then the Republicans and the Boll Weevils will find themselves out on a very shaky limb."[10]

But Campbell was not perturbed. He cosponsored a workfare program through which recipients of federal welfare would work for the assistance they received.

What is workfare? Very simply, it's the concept that able-bodied adults should work for the value of their welfare benefits. The legislation I have endorsed would require most adults in the aid to families with dependent children (AFDC), public housing, and food stamp programs to work in public service jobs for the benefits they receive. Instead of receiving a salary or wages for their work, they would be paid with food stamps or rent subsidies or welfare payments their households would normally receive. Those responsible for the care of infant children, the disabled, and retired persons would be exempted, and special provision would be made for part-time workfare for students. The programs would be run by the states, and the states and localities—and their residents—would receive the benefits of the work performed by welfare recipients.

Campbell pointed to his home county, where a pilot program designed to test the effectiveness had been under way. Admitting that it had had mixed reviews in the first months, he stated that "workfare is a good place to start" a "self-help program" rather than simple handouts. He added that he did not believe that the program was racist "in any way" but that it "gave people incentives rather than tearing down individual initiatives."

In answer to another criticism Campbell agreed that he was ambitious.

I have grown with a party that had a long way to grow in the South, and it has come a long way. But we're still in a transition stage in the South. We have developed greatly in South Carolina, and Republicans are growing steadily elsewhere. We have quite a few young politicians in the House right now who have a wonderful opportunity to succeed—possibly in national politics in the future. One is Trent Lott from Mississippi. He has been mentioned for the U.S. Senate. Then there's Paul Trible [thirty-five-year-old House member from Virginia's Tidewater region], and I think he has a great deal of long-range potential.

The greatest problem that most of our good young people—and I'll put us all in the same category—is that we've been caught up in the federal intervention. For all of us some sort of issue seems to tarnish us on the federal and national scene. For instance, I don't know very many of them who haven't been caught since 1964 on something about the Voting Rights Act. They come out against it or its extension, trying to protect their counties or districts by taking positions that are contradictory to federal feelings. Or I don't know anybody in the group of Southern Republicans in the House or Senate who rushed out and supported school busing. All over the South they stood against it. They didn't stand against integration. They weren't George Wallaces. In fact, as I see them, they were truly very moderate people. But, as such, those things tend to work against you from time to time in a national race. If I were ever in a national race, I wouldn't apologize for anything I have supported. Hell, I'm one of those people who will go out and tell you that I'm for the Fair Housing Act and the Voting Rights Act, and I'm dead set against school busing. I don't apologize for anything. That's what I believe in. If you want me, that's what you're going to get. But to a degree all of this could hurt some of the talent coming from the South. But having said that, there's some very good people that we have down there.

I think that if a Northeasterner like a Jack Kemp got the Republican nomination for the presidency, a young Republican congressman from the South may be very attractive as a running mate. Also, a Midwesterner may go South. Probably a Westerner would go northeast, because the West tends to identify with the South. But if you reach the point where most of the West is voting Republican and the South is the swing, the way it is now, then it makes a lot of sense to go South for a Republican candidate. It's not the kind of thing I could say with a lot of probability, but it's possible.

I think we are a positive region. There's still a lot of prejudice against the South and Southerners. But the rest of the nation is overcoming that. Maybe in the next few years the nation's prejudice against Southerners will vanish altogether.

He refused to rule out the possibility of Carroll Campbell running for the U.S. Senate or some other office when the time happened to be right.

Jesse the Juggernaut

Balancing himself between being official court jester and serious political juggernaut, Jesse Helms juggled the likes of George Wallace and Ronald Reagan in his palms for a number of years. Jesse Helms had been a force in Southern politics in North Carolina long before he rode up the pike to Washington and took his seat in the Senate. He wielded an influence that was awesome to conservatives and laughable to liberals until he became king of the heap.

Back in his heyday as a homespun editorialist and outspoken local politico in North Carolina, Jesse Helms had begun to make deals with the leading conservatives on the scene—and not always with the Republican leadership. "As long as Republicans stay conservative, I'll stay in the party. When the left begins to creep into the camp meeting, I'll fight. If I lose, I'll leave. It's as simple as one, two, three," he explained with lifted eyebrows.[1]

"What most people don't understand about Jesse Helms is: he's a *good* man from a *good* family in a *good* community, and he'll fight like hell to keep it good," stated the politician's old neighbor, Lawrence "Lefty" Morrison from Monroe, North Carolina, the little town twenty miles south of Charlotte where Helms' great-great-grandfather and great-great-great-uncle settled in 1742.[2] From tough-as-nails Scotch-

Irish stock the Helms brothers farmed the ridge where the town was founded, where the Union County courthouse was built, and where the main street came alive in the twentieth century with five churches, four Republicans, a pool parlor, and one whorehouse. "It was your typical one-horse Piedmont town, sitting stale and idle and liking its staleness and idleness," described Preacher Landry Wilkins, who was born there the same year, 1912, that Jesse Alexander Helms, a towering six-foot-five-inch police and fire chief, married his distant cousin, Ethel Helms. Living three houses away from the police station when their second child, Jesse Alexander Helms, Jr., was born on October 18, 1921, Wilkins remembered, "He grew up slow and easy like the rest of us. If there was anything fast about anybody in Monroe, the boy or girl left in a hurry. We didn't have room for fast people. His older brother Wriston managed the Woolworth's that still stands up yonder. They were good, everyday kind of folks, went to church, prayed, worked, and went to church. There wasn't a whole lot to do in Monroe in the 1920s and 1930s but to go to church and work. We didn't even have fast cars back then."[3]

Like the great majority of children who grew up in Monroe, Jesse Helms went to church at least three times a week. With his older brother, father, mother, and finally younger sister Mary Elizabeth, he went to the First Baptist Church Sunday morning services, Sunday evening youth group, and Wednesday night covered-dish suppers that ended with the women cleaning up, the men sitting around and talking politics, and the children either listening to the menfolks or romping around the tree-covered yard. He grew up believing in the family, sitting on his father's knee or on the floor next to the fireplace, looking up at the giant of a man, and he carried that belief all the way to the Congress of the United States where, as the senior senator from North Carolina, he would speak out constantly for "the old ways, the family ways, the real religious ways of life in this country" and against "the promiscuous ways of the new breed of pseudo-sophisticates."[4] His father talked to him about the old-fashioned style of life that some day might disappear if evil continued to spread through the hills and hollows. And Jesse believed the fundamentalist Baptist preacher who spoke out with hellfire and brimstone against the creeping power of the devil that had already gotten as far as the big city of Charlotte and would be moving on down to Monroe it they weren't careful.

"The boy wasn't what you'd call full of mischief," recalled old friend Evans Barkley, a Monroe-raised friend who later moved to South Carolina and started an insurance agency. "He was a quiet young man. He liked to play games, have fun, swim in Richardson's Creek, and act out cowboy-and-Indian movies we saw at the Strand on Saturday mornings for a nickel. We went to school separate from the Negro children, and we didn't know any other way; it was how we grew up. The black children went to a school down past the ridge, and we went to the main school closer to downtown."[5]

Jesse Helms grew up like hundreds of thousands of other youngsters in the rural South of that period. They knew black people, had respect for some and disliked others; but they did not fraternize with black people.

He was a good boy who became a natural leader. In high school he was remembered as a good example for other students to follow. He awakened early, worked at the local newspaper sweeping floors, practiced for hours on end playing the fiddle, and enjoyed playing the tuba in the Monroe High School marching band.

When he recollected those days to audiences, his voice still trembled slightly. An onlooker could tell when his eyes watered that the days of his youth were very meaningful to him.

He was particularly fond of listening to Will Rogers on the radio, and he recalled the afternoon when he learned of Rogers' death in an airplane crash in Alaska with pilot Wiley Post. "I remember the sadness I felt. I was thirteen and a carrier for the Charlotte *News* in my little home town. It was a dreary afternoon as I delivered the sad news about," he said. All of his life he continued to peer back and remember Will Rogers' humor, looking at Congress with good-natured ridicule, and Helms said he only wished the comedian could have lived to see the Congress of the 1960s, '70s, and '80s, "when he would really have had something to talk about."[6]

Working as a soda jerk at the local drugstore, sweeping out the weekly *Monroe Enquirer*, writing up the high school baseball, football, and basketball games in his junior and senior years, and finally attending Wingate Baptist College only seven miles from Monroe during the summer after his graduation, he was a kind of all-American small-town youth. In September 1939 he traveled several hundred miles to Raleigh, where he attended Wake Forest College and proofread copy for the *News & Observer*. A year later he went to work full time as a sports reporter for the newspaper. He quit college and not long afterward fell in love with the editor of the society section, Dorothy Coble, a local girl who was pretty but not flashy and exactly what he had been looking for. He joined the navy, and his bride joined him in Elizabeth City, North Carolina, where as a specialist first class he spent World War II writing press releases. Years later, when he made speeches in favor of raising the nation's defense spending, one might have thought he had been a warrior in a foxhole when he verbalized the necessity of the U.S. "whipping to the knees the sorry communist rascals who will beat us if we don't stay fully alert."[7]

After the war he went to work as a reporter for the *Raleigh Times*, and he soon became city editor. No longer the small-town kid, he was now an experienced newshawk, and he was beginning to form the strong opinions that would be the foundation of his conservatism for the rest of his life.

Helms, who had never been fast-moving, continued his slow-motion progress in his upward climb. He quit the *Times* after an argument with printers. For a short while he worked as a radio reporter in Roanoke Rapids, then returned to Raleigh, where he took over the news department of radio station WRAL. The owner, right-wing businessman A. J. Fletcher, more or less took young Helms as his protege. Through Fletcher, and under his influence, Helms got involved in the world of politics in the late 1940s and early 1950s. As a sideline participant Helms was thrust onto the team backing a right-wing racist rebel-rouser named Willis Smith, Fletcher's chosen candidate for U.S. Senate. It was a race for the Democratic nomination, which meant winning the seat in those days in most Southern states. Smith ran a fist-shaking, name-calling race against a decent moderate, Frank Porter Graham, who had been president of the University of North Carolina. As a reporter for WRAL Helms was in on the strategy meetings primarily because Fletcher was one of Smith's leading supporters. The young reporter was not experienced enough, astute enough, or mean enough in those days to write material for the Willis Smith campaign, but he was always around the boys who put out stuff that stated emphatically that Frank Graham was soft on communism—he let any commie who came down the road speak on the campus at Chapel Hill—and even promoted big-time labor-union bosses to congregate at the school's hallowed halls. In reality Frank Graham had promoted good-quality education, built a school that was known for its high academic standards, and allowed a certain amount of scholastic freedom in the classrooms.

While he didn't write them, Jesse Helms surely read the words others wrote. He was their voice over Radio WRAL, and he spoke out with strength, lending his tonsils to a campaign of hatred. The Ku Klux Klan spread handbills reading WHITE PEOPLE WAKE UP, with slogans like *Do You Want Your Mother, Wife, and Daughter Riding Buses with Negroes?* And finally the Smith people, using the Ku Klux Klan, spread a handbill with a pasteup picture of Frank Graham's wife dancing with a black man. She was smiling, and all the viewer could see was the back of his head and his profile.

Out in the coastal boondocks KKK nightriders discovered a black man with a Frank Graham poster on his unpainted front porch. The hooded men pulled the man out of his house, stripped him, and beat him in his grassless front yard. And while other radio stations, television stations, and newspapers ran this story, Jesse Helms was broadcasting about Willis Smith signs being torn down outside Greensboro.

In one of the most knock-down-drag-out dirty campaigns in the history of Southern politics Jesse Helms was right there listening, taking mental notes, and watching every move as an intern politician.

After the first primary votes were counted, Smith trailed Graham by only a few thousand votes. Others in the race were far behind, leaving the front-runners in a runoff. But everyone, especially Smith, was dog-tired, and even a little sick of the shenanigans of the campaign. Smith retired to his house, closed the door behind him, and made utterances of quitting before he got to the final wire. Although Jesse Helms looked back from his seat in the U.S. Senate thirty years later and flatly denied anything to do with writing any of the racial slurs, he did go on the radio and urged Smith people "to go out to his house and encourage him."[8] In response to Helms' plea several hundred banded together, rode to Smith's suburban Raleigh home, stood in the front yard, and chanted for him to come out and win. Standing in their midst, with his oversized recording machine strapped around his squared shoulders was Jesse Helms, holding the microphone up to allow the crowd to speak for itself. Later, not only capturing the crowd's chants for the radio audience but introducing candidate Smith, Jesse's broadcast became the first of many during the runoff campaign. Smith came from behind, defeated Graham, and less than a year later Jesse Helms left the station with Mr. Fletcher's blessings to become an administrative assistant to Senator Smith.

As an aide on Capitol Hill Jesse Helms more or less blended into the background like the best of the professionals. His fellow administrators barely remembered him. He met his hero, Senator Joseph McCarthy, and from a distance studied his techniques. But Helms was never outgoing, always lurking in the wings, always within an earshot of Senator Smith, who died a year later, leaving Helms jobless and with a decision to make: stay in Washington and remain with the herd on the Hill who did their daily turns for the cause of national politics, or go home and develop a lifestyle of his own. With his wife Dot and their two daughters, Jane and Nancy, dutifully by his side he took the well-paying and not-too-taxing job of executive director of the North Carolina Bankers Association of Raleigh, and for seven years he wheeled and dealed for the money men of a very rich state with the lawmakers in its capital city.

A fellow lobbyist said that Jesse Helms was no song-and-dance man, the term used for the wine-'em-and-dine-'em credit card overusers, but that he was effective at working long hours and always knowing his issues as well as his people. "Nobody got the best of Jesse when it came to doing his homework," he recalled.

> He was a stickler for thoroughness, and even the most liberal Piedmont legislator would be able to rely on his facts as well as his word. If Jesse said he'd go out on a limb for somebody, they might as well look out there for him—he'd be dangling. You always knew where Jesse stood. He didn't play games with people. He was right-wing even in his youth. He was wide-eyed, listened intently, learned quickly, and put his lessons to use in the practical sense. North Carolina became a very wealthy banking state with his help. Some of the largest banks in the South grew to mammoth size because he was able to get laws passed liberalizing banking practices. Of course, if you ask any of the bankers, they will say that he made the rules more conservative by lifting restrictions; it's all a matter of interpretation. All in all Jesse Helms was a highly successful lobbyist. Most people liked him even if they didn't see eye to eye with his positions.[9]

And the bankers for whom he worked praised him, saying he did an admirable job for their association "by allowing free enterprise to work in the North Carolina banking community better than it had ever worked before."[10] And later the banking officals stepped forward and became some of his strongest and most lucrative contributors.

After he had built his name substantially as a representative of the bankers, had a comfortable brick two-story traditional home constructed on a large, oak-shaded lot, next door to his father-in-law's house, became president of the Raleigh Rotary Club, was named deacon in the Hayes Barton Baptist Church, and achieved the rank of thirty-second-degree Mason, he ran for his first political office in the spring of 1957. He won a seat on the Raleigh City Council. And with his first political victory safely in his grasp the budding thirty-six-year-old politican was no longer quietly ambitious. At the usually quiet meetings of the city fathers Helms harangued against what he considered misspending of municipal funds, occasionally dressing down the mayor and other council members with whom he disagreed. He was a slow-rolling bulldozer sweeping up the countryside of Raleigh, and when he looked out from that hillside, he saw the rest of the eastern coastal plain that held a hell-bent fury against any outside forces they considered liberal, such as desegregation of schools, laws against prayers in schools, busing to achieve integration, and any other Supreme Court-backed edict. From his view Jesse Helms saw highway signs that called for the impeachment of Chief Justice Earl Warren, and he knew most of those good people out there were ripe for hellfire-and-damnation sermons that took to task such evil outside forces. Before he finished a year on the City Council, Mr. A. J. Fletcher had talked with him again, and Jesse Helms set up a regular program that he could syndicate through the state on the Tobacco Radio Network. The old man bestowed on Helms a piece of the action, several highfalutin titles, and editorial control of a five-minute daily "Viewpoint" one-man television commentary to be run over Capitol Broadcasting Company's television station in Raleigh. His first proclamation in favor of the good life versus new-world evils was aired during the six-o'clock news in 1960, and it was followed by more than 2,700 in the following twelve years.

Over the tobacco valleys of eastern North Carolina Jesse Helms was well known for his one-sided opinions just as Ronald Reagan became known nationally for his radio diatribes in the 1970s. Jesse wasn't remembered for having the best delivery in the world. He was somewhat amateurish, but that was part of his appeal. He came off as rather studied in his effort to appear off the cuff. Looking down at his script, his eyes wide behind black-rimmed, owl-like glasses, he lingered on the words. Then he'd look up and into the camera with his heavy dark eyelashes aflutter, like he'd just been shocked at what he'd read. Then he'd haul off into something startling to those people watching and listening down there on the farms and out there in the little towns like Monroe. He'd tell them about black people demonstrating over in Greensboro or the Freedom Riders showing they could integrate interstate transportation. His voice would quaver with personal indignation.

He knew his audience well, knew how to shock them. As they sat out there in their frame two-bedroom, one-bath homes or on their cozy little farms, they'd nod and say, "Damn right, Jesse! You tell 'em!" And they would write to him in droves. There was no doubt that the 100,000 or more people who watched and listened to him nightly believed in him as their spokesman. He talked the way they wanted to talk. He spoke out against the things that were bothering them. Of course now and then somebody would disagree, but they were few and far between. Like his radio show, which had reached out to more than seventy small country stations, his television commentary was a winner. He berated the giveaway programs of President Lyndon Johnson, saying Washington was throwing away every ounce of decency left in life. He shook his finger at the Congress for passing too many social-reform laws. He gave the universities the devil for being too liberal in their teaching. He said the civil rights movement had communists in its leadership. And once he proclaimed that it would have been a better world if Senator Joseph McCarthy had been allowed to clean out all the communists from the federal government. And when he made all these statements, he held up a piece of paper like it was proven gospel by the evidence he held in his hand when the paper was actually his script or preproduction notes. And during these years he became without a doubt the best-known name in northern and coastal North Carolina.

He won reelection several times to the Raleigh City Council. If an issue came before the council and other members disagreed with Helms, they could be assured he would comment on the controversy on his television show, "Viewpoint." The others were given their chance at rebuttal, but their untrained answers usually came across as bumbling and befuddled.

When George C. Wallace came into North Carolina with his third-party campaign for the presidency in 1968, Helms arranged for the candidate "to receive all the free air time we needed to get our message over to the people," the three-time Alabama governor recalled. "He was a gracious man who had views similar to my own. When we talked, it was obvious that he hated the disruption of American life that the federal government was causing," Wallace said.[11] Like Wallace, who had stood in the door of the University of Alabama to keep black students from entering, Helms had expressed prosegregation views on many of his early Tobacco Radio Network commentaries, stating on television in 1965 that "the civil rights movement, as Dr. [Martin Luther] King called it, has had an uncommon number of moral degenerates leading the parade. The Negroes of America have a Congress that would tomorrow enact *Webster's Dictionary* into law with a civil rights label on it."[12] Also like Wallace, Helms later denied strongly that he had ever been a racist. Both insisted that they had merely fought encroachment of federal authority onto local laws.

In 1970 Helms' twenty-one-year-old daughter Nancy sat down with her father and talked about two things: her upcoming marriage and his switching from Democrat to Republican. Several days later, when he accompanied her to the county courthouse to obtain a marriage license, he also changed his voter registration. Looking back at his conversion he stated, "As it says in The Good Book, 'A little child shall lead you,' "[13] and not even the hint of a smile played on his thin-lipped, constantly puckered mouth. "There was a to-do about my changing over to the Republicans. I was a celebrity, a television personality, and a leader in my community," he said.[14] And shortly afterward his old friend and fellow conservative, attorney Thomas Ellis, spoke to him about the possibility of his running for the U.S. Senate seat held by incumbent Democrat Everett Jordan. Before Helms would agree to throw his hat into the ring, Ellis had to put all of the ducks in a row: secure Helms' position with WRAL and the Tobacco Network even if he lost the race, make sure the fund-raising tools were in better-than-working condition, and line up a strong group of Republican face-card speakers to support Helms' candidacy, including President Richard Nixon, whom he had chastised severely for kowtowing to the communists by breaking bread with them in Moscow and Peking.

Although he had been converted to Republicanism by his daughter, it took the 1972 modern political campaign to bring about his born-again experience, he later told evangelist Jim Bakker on the televised PTL Club. During a plane trip from Raleigh to a speech in Ashville, "I started looking at the lights below. I realized in each one of those houses there is a human being about to develop. All of a sudden I said, 'Jesse, what in the world are you doing in this plane?' I didn't even want to be a candidate. And for the first time, I asked the Lord to help me, to help me conduct myself properly. All of a sudden I realized the sun was coming in the window of the plane. I felt a sense of serenity I'd never felt before."[15]

William I. Berryhill, his administrative assistant in Raleigh, joined the organization in 1972 at Tom Ellis' insistence. "I went to the same Sunday school with Mr. Tom, and he approached me one Sunday after preaching and said Mr. Helms was thinking about running," said the affable administrator. "It didn't look too good at the time. I thought perhaps we could win the Republican nomination and then make a good try for the Senate seat, but winning was almost out." The bookkeeper-accountant became treasurer of the campaign against Democratic nominee Nick Galifianakis, a young moderate congressman. "It was uphill all the way," remembered Berryhill. Jesse "was a household figure throughout the eastern part of North Carolina, where

WRAL-TV beamed its signal. That was our base. But that wasn't where the votes were. Traditionally, the east was almost solid Democrat. They still remembered the Reconstruction out there on the coastal plain. They do have a strong conservative philosophy." He smiled. "On the other hand, what Republican strength there was in North Carolina came from the Piedmont and mountain counties. But we weren't known west of Greensboro. We used our conservative base to win the Republican primary, then we faced Representative Galifianakis from Durham's Fourth Congressional District [located in the heavily populated Piedmont] in the general election."[16]

While Berryhill and other Helms workers saw it as a clean, well-fought match, newspeople of the state pointed out that the Helms campaign worked subtle racism with the slogan *Jesse Helms: He's one of us* to interject the matter of Galifianakis' father being an immigrant from Greece. In November Helms won fifty-four to forty-six percent.

In Washington he discovered that being a freshman senator with superconservative ideas was not the most popular stance on Capitol Hill in 1973. He was the first Republican senator from North Carolina in nearly eighty years, and he was doggedly determined to make his mark on that austere body. When he found himself staring at the awesome interior of the great building, feeling left out when other senators played squash or tennis or met over drinks in the early evenings, he did what he had always done. He looked around for an older, more experienced gentleman who believed the way he believed. Earlier in his life, he had had the men back home, his daddy, Ray House, the deacons in the church, Mr. A. J. Fletcher at the radio network and television station, and Senator Smith. Then there had been Tom Ellis, who was only two years older but infinitely better educated and absolutely country smart. Now he looked out there on the empty floor of the Senate and saw a man who was even taller than his own six feet and one inch. Leaning awkwardly against the mahogany desk, shoulders slumped, head bowed and twisted to one side, high-pitched Southern voice drawling into a microphone, delivering well-turned phrases against the liberal doctrine of the present Congress, was Senator James Allen of Alabama. Jesse Helms sat back and listened. He liked what he heard. Senator Allen was no foreigner to him. He had read about the man's conservative philosophy, but he knew nothing of Allen's quiet, cunning ability as a parliamentarian.

Within a short while, as Allen began teaching the first-year senator the rules of the game, Helms witnessed his mentor in action. In his droning monologue, sometimes talking in whispers barely audible to the rest of the members, Allen maneuvered a piece of legislation that had been introduced by Senator Edward Kennedy of Massachusetts. Tacking one amendment after another onto the bill, deleting this word, adding another, Allen outlasted his opponents, who outnumbered him greatly. By the end of a long and grueling afternoon Kennedy ran his hand through his thick, shaggy hair and said, "Is it my understanding, Senator," speaking to Allen, "that at this point in time I will vote against my bill whether I answer 'Yea' or 'Nay' ?"[17] From his stand on the far side of the room Allen raised his large head and grinned knowingly.

Jesse Helms already knew that he had found himself an ally. Now he knew that the only way he would succeed in this intimidating hall of the legislative branch of government was to wake up earlier, work longer, learn how to wheel and deal better, and stick to his philosophical guns all the way. But, what the heck, he'd been doing that all of his adult life.

Helms became Allen's shadow, and he learned well from the old master. And after Allen died of a heart attack in his native Alabama he was missed greatly by his younger friend. "Jim Allen was a great patriot, a man who knew his business like nobody else, and a believer in the basic goodness of the people of the United States," Helms said.[18]

During the years of his first term in the U.S. Senate Helms not only polished his techniques in parliamentary procedure, he honed to a smooth sharp edge his ability as an expert negative politican. He was always against something, whether it was food stamps for the needy, sex education for the ignorant, or government-paid abortions for women who could not otherwise afford such drastic measures of birth control. And later he opposed abortions generally, disguising the negativism under the title of Pro-Life or Right-to-Life Bill, which in essence would declare that life starts at the point of conception when the fetus begins to form. This bill, which would usurp the Supreme Court's ruling against antiabortion laws as unconstitutional without going through the amendment-passing process, was pushed by most of the New Right lawmakers.

Former U.S. Solicitor General and Harvard Law School professor Archibald Cox wrote that Helms' abortion bill was

intended to overrule a 1973 Supreme Court decision holding existing antiabortion laws to be unconstitutional. By declaring that life begins at the moment of conception, the Helms bill seeks to redefine the words "person" and "life" for the purpose of the Fourteenth Amendment, thus protecting the "life" of the fetus as the "life" of a "person." The vice of this approach is its underlying premise. The Helms bill attempts to substitute legislative definitions of the meaning of the words used in the Constitution in place of the Supreme Court definitions. Even if the pro-abortion decisions are wrong, it would be worse to accept the principle that bare majorities in the Senate and House of Representatives, with the approval of the President, can change the Constitution by simple legislative definitions.[19]

With his eyelashes aflutter and his voice a smooth, strong baritone, Helms, dramatic television commentator that he was, quietly withdrew into his biblical explanation. "I believe it is time that unborn children have the right of equal protection under the law," he said.

My efforts in this behalf have brought me in touch with every possible spectrum of opinion on this immensely divisive issue. Well-meaning friends have pointed out to me the political liabilities of the stand I have taken. I have been castigated by women's liberationists, editorialists, physicians, lawyers, and every kind of ad hoc group that can afford the price of postage. I have a thick file of letters and articles containing every rationalization of abortion that the human mind can devise. Some of them are truly tragic situations, and no one could be unmoved after reading these accounts. If I had any indication toward condoning situation ethics, this correspondence, in its volume and in its intensity, could probably confirm me in it. But I oppose abortion because it is something God has forbidden to us. God's law condemns the taking of innocent life, and as a lawmaker myself, I must in conscience accept and observe the prior laws of God.[20]

In another instance Archibald Cox wrote that the Helms bill on school prayers

illustrates the other form of attack upon the Court used by foes of the Court's decisions. In order to nullify the Supreme Court ruling that bans prayer in public schools, this bill would strip the Supreme Court and federal courts of jurisdiction to hear "any case arising out of any state statute . . . which relates to voluntary prayers in public schools and public buildings." If Congress may deprive the federal courts of jurisdiction to rule upon claims that public-school officials are violating the constitutional right to be free from an official establishment of religion, Congress may just as easily withdraw federal jurisdiction to hear claims relating to freedom of speech or political association or the taking of property without just compensation.[21]

But Helms, in typical conservative interpretation, maintained that his prayer bill would not do away with the constitutional rights but would return the power of jurisdiction to the state courts, "where our religious freedoms were always safeguarded for 175 years until they were nationalized by the Supreme Court. The limited and specific objective of this bill is to restore to the American people the fundamental right of voluntary prayer in the public schools. I stress the word voluntary. No individual should be forced to participate in a religious exercise that is contrary to his religious convictions, and the bill recognizes this important freedom."[22] However, at the same time the bill promoted the exercise of having students recite prayers aloud andopenly in the classroom before all students. Helms did not recognize that this might be forcing one person's religion upon another.

Earning the title of Senator No, as he was referred to in some of the Northern and Eastern press, Helms stiffened his back against President Reagan's first Supreme Court appointment, former Arizona State Senator Sandra Day O'Connor. On the same day that her name was announced, Helms said he had talked to the president, and "he assured me that she was right on the issues that interest me and my people—especially the Right-to-Life Bill. The president said that he was satisfied that Mrs. O'Connor was opposed to abortion, and I accept his opinion," Helms stated. Later, after meeting with Mrs. O'Connor in his office, the senator said, "I'll be watching this lady's career with interest."[23]

However, try as he might, his political life in Washington was a paradox. On the one hand he was ultraconservative. He voted time and again to cut government spending and require a balanced budget, but he stood fast on his votes to beef up defense capability and add rather than cut spending. He worked and voted against the food stamp program for the poor, but he worked just as hard and voted for federal protection of the North Carolina textile industry. "If the food stamps were just for the poor and those who needed them, I might go along with it," said Helms, who was chairman of the Senate Agriculture Committee. "But right now the food stamp program money goes into the hands of the crooked administrators of the program at a local level, and, as far as I've seen, it can't be controlled."[24] But federal support for tobacco farmers was a necessity, as he viewed it. Besides, his wife had a tobacco allotment, which amounted to permission from the government to grow a certain percentage of given acreage in tobacco while receiving federal price supports. Early in 1981 Helms told Elizabeth Drew, reporter for *The New Yorker*, that he had talked with President Reagan about federal subsidies for North Carolina industries and crops. He felt confident that the president would go along with continued programs to favor tobacco farmers.

Helms continued to be ranked as one of the most easygoing,

politest, most gentlemanly and courteous congressmen on Capitol Hill. A former aide to Democratic Senator Frank E. Moss of Utah said, "Jesse Helms was known to always keep his word. If he told you he'd fight you, you better not let him out of sight; and it would take a smart, smart person to watch his every move and be able to interpret it correctly. But if he told you he was with you on an issue, you could count on his support. I would say that yes, he was a gentleman in the old sense of the word."[25]

Following him along a wide hallway in the Senate office building, his long legs reaching out in a country boy lope, he constantly grinned from ear to ear while once again denying that he was a racist. But as late as the end of 1981 he had no black employees on his staff. "I have a group of dedicated conservatives who work harder than I do, who believe in what I believe, and who are all grand people. It takes a long time to find really good people,"[26] he added. Nevertheless, he continued to oppose food stamps or any type of federally sponsored welfare program short of workfare, and when the government sent planes to bring home the bodies of people—mostly black people—killed in the mass suicide at Jonestown in Guyana, Helms said he was appalled at the waste of the taxpayers' money.

Winning no prizes from the liberal side of the fence, Helms piled up the accolades for his conservatism. He taught Sunday school, making analogies between biblical times and today's world, pointing out how the two periods correspond and how, if we don't watch our step, the United States will be dragged into pure damnation. He accepted the praises of popular preachers such as Billy Graham, Jerry Falwell of the Moral Majority, James Robinson of the Evangelistic Association, and others. In September 1978, on the eve of his reelection, conservative columnist James J. Kilpatrick praised him to high heaven, writing that Helms was indeed a noteworthy Southern senator. "In the past, these legendary figures have all been Democrats. There's a Republican in there now. Put him with Tom Connally of Texas, Walter George and Dick Russell of Georgia, Sam Ervin of North Carolina, Harry Byrd and Carter Glass of Virginia, the late Jim Allen and the Bankheads of Alabama.

"Helms shares with these predecessors one distinguishing characteristic. Like them, he is above all else a senator," Kilpatrick wrote, adding that Helms had been identified as a "redneck extremist" but "is in fact a gentle person, courteous, reserved, unfailingly polite in debate. He is a deeply religious man who lives his Baptist faith every day. And he is a prodigious worker and a tireless fighter."[27]

Jesse accepted the praise with a simple thanks. He was that kind of a person, the way fellow-Southerner Kilpatrick wrote. He was a grand old good old boy, the master of a benevolent plantation, and an opinionated congressman. He needed neither the floor of the Senate nor a soapbox to give him a forum for speech.

If this country is going to maintain a healthy and expanding economy, we must expand our overall supply of energy. Conservation alone will not provide the vital industrial growth that future generations will depend upon for jobs, security, and a better life.

Congress has already laid to rest the proposal to increase gasoline taxes. I cannot support such a tax because it will hit hardest at the people who can least afford it. I will continue to support the use of tax incentives to encourage development of solar and other new energy sources.

Taxes are too high. There is one group that is particularly hit by our tax system, and that is the American worker. It is the productive sector of our economy who should benefit from tax reductions—not the rich and wealthy [although he supported and voted for President Reagan's tax-cut program which favored the wealthy more than medium-income earners].

I came out against federal taxation of private schools, in favor of prayer in schools, and against troop withdrawal in South Korea. If we don't keep out troops in South Korea, hordes of barbarians will come down and slaughter those poor people.[28]

He talked on and on and on. Toss him a subject, and he would run with the ball. Without giving an inch, Jesse Helms continued to work against the evils he perceived in the nation's government. He believed Ronald Reagan and the Republican party were also working toward the same goals. "Southerners are good basic people. They believe in the Bible. They follow the teachings of God. Most of them strive to be like Jesus. And as long as the Republican party attempts to work within the scope of his teachings, it will win. I have never prayed I would win an election or a vote in the Senate. I believe that's up to man to decide. But we all need to have faith."[29]

The Way to the Top

Jesse Helms loved to play poker every Thursday night for nickels, dimes, and quarters at the home of his good friend Superior Court Judge James H. "Pou" Bailey in Raleigh. And it was after one of these poker festivals, where the men ate some of the best down-home cooking to be found in that part of North Carolina, that Helms' poker buddy, good friend, and political conversationalist approached him and leaned against the front fender of his car.

The friend, Tom Ellis, was a good old boy par excellence, a superior eater of good food, a senior partner in one of Raleigh's most prestigious law firms, Maupin, Taylor, and Ellis, and a thinker with a steel-trap mind. Jesse Helms looked up to Ellis, thought the world of him, and when Ellis suggested that he should run for the U.S. Senate Helms somehow knew it was only a matter of time. Ambitious young Southerners usually had somebody a few years older in whom they could put their trust, and for Jesse that was Tom Ellis.

Since his childhood days in California, Ellis had been interested in politics. After a stint in the navy he attended law school at the University of Virginia and settled in Raleigh in 1948. Within several years he jumped directly into political waters. But not without testing them first. Tom Ellis was not the kind of young man to leap before looking; he was a careful person who wanted to win. He had read about the Constitution, about the officers of that first convention in Philadelphia, and he knew without a doubt that the United States needed stronger men in its capital to do the worthy job those fathers of our country did back in the early days of independence. He had met Willis Smith and liked what he saw and heard. It would take tough conservatism, he knew, to do the job he had in mind. He moved with Smith, met a young radio reporter named Jesse Helms, and fed the reporter material that was later aired. With an iron-jawed strength he said later, "The bad thing about that race was that everybody against Frank Graham was branded a racist, but I don't think of myself as a racist, and I know Jesse Helms is not a racist."[1]

They went about their business, getting to know each other better when Helms returned to Raleigh after serving in Washington with Senator Smith. In the late 1960s Ellis bolted the Democratic party. "They got too uppity," he snapped. "They were too full of their liberal ways, and they just ran away from Tom Ellis," he said in his half-joking Tom Ellis style. "I became a Republican because I saw that within the party there could be some good conservative people, people like our founding fathers who had the best interest of this country in their hearts, elected and put in office. And when they accuse me of playing hardball, they're right. I play hardball because it's a hardball game," he stated.[2]

That was the kind of friend who approached Jesse Helms under the midnight moon and told him he had to run for the U.S. Senate in 1972. Later he paved the way for Helms by making sure he would have a job if he lost, putting a staff to work, and overseeing the operation of the entire campaign. He was the kind of friend who held his hand and told him everything was going to be okay when the votes started coming in. And he was the kind of friend who one year after Helms was elected thought up the idea of a fund-raising vehicle into which conservatives like himself could funnel their money to make sure it would be spent by true conservatives. He came up with the North Carolina Congressional Club, with former campaign treasurer Bill Berryhill as its executive director, and the kickoff was a $25-a-plate dinner for Ronald Reagan. Both Helms and Ellis were anxious about the dinner before the tickets were bought, and even they were not sure of the success of Ellis' brainchild. They were not sure until that night, when more than 1,000 supporters flooded through the front door with hands outstretched.

A few months later, on December 5, 1974, political analyst Howard Covington wrote in the Charlotte *Observer* that the club "has a healthy bank account, potential one-hundred-county political organization and, some say, the nucleus of a new conservative movement. . . Building on its cadre of those wealthy enough and committed enough to plunk down one hundred dollars a year for the honor of a couple of newsletters and sit-down dinners with folks like California Governor Ronald Reagan, the club plans to expand. Ellis wants to go after the small farmers, textile workers, and wage earners and the disgusted suburbanites who cheered George Wallace in 1972 and gave Terry Sanford the walloping of his life in the presidental primary. It's a natural coalition philosophically." [3]

Under the guidance of Ellis and Berryhill the Congressional Club prospered. Dollar after dollar flowed in. At a 1977 function 2,000 paid five dollars each for barbecue-chicken dinners to support Helms, who stood before them and promised faithfully to block the approval of the Panama Canal treaty, stop unnecessary welfare, build a stronger national defense, and halt forced busing, and the people rewarded him with a standing ovation and the promise of more money for his campaign kitty. Afterward, still grinning, he said, "My heavens, boys, I've been preaching to the choir. All these people believe in Jesse. Where I need to go is out yonder where they haven't heard of me."[4]

When Jesse and his New Right cohorts cosponsored a bill to outlaw abortions, the money poured into the coffers of the Congressional Club more than ever. Tom Ellis described the club as "an effort to counterbalance the political activities of the union bosses, the ERA crowd, and other far-left political campaigns."[5]

Berryhill left the club in 1976 to join Helms' Raleigh staff, and young Carter Wrenn became its executive director. Building from twelve to more than fifty staffers, Ellis said, "We've always been blessed with people who put the cause first. We've got to have good people. If we didn't, we wouldn't put up with them."[6] That was part of Ellis' personality all employees of the Congressional Club quickly recognized. While he had a jovial demeanor, he always meant business when it came to politics. He never dilly-dallied around. He made quick decisions that were usually right in the vote-getting process. "We're after the vote," he told his people. "We are not in this game to lose."[7] And Jesse Helms referred to him as "one of the nicest people and probably one of the most misunderstood human beings I've ever known. If people who say that Tom is a crass manipulator could know him, they would change their minds right quick."[8]

Carter Wrenn called Ellis "a very warm, personable and very considerate individual. Politically, he's very dedicated to America. He's a patriot in the old sense of the word."[9] Fellow Republican James Godfrey of Southern Pines, North Carolina, disagreed. A friend of former Governor Jim Holshouser who had got the boot from the state Republican convention in 1976 because Ellis and Helms were opposed to him, Godfrey told Raleigh reporter Sharon Bond, "I don't think Tom Ellis gives a toot and a hoot for the Republican party. If you don't agreed with Tom Ellis, you'd better get the hell out of the way. He's run a lot of good Republicans out of the party, and some of them have been in the party two or three times longer than he has."[10]

The split with Holshouser, the first Republican governor of North Carolina since Reconstruction, came when Ellis and Helms ran roughshod over party moderates at the convention. The two conservatives wanted every vote they could count for Ronald Reagan in the Californian's attempt to snatch the presidential nomination from incumbent Gerald Ford in 1976. Ellis and Helms knew they couldn't count on Holshouser and his crowd, so they shoved them out the front door on their bottoms. "Since that time there are Republicans who would say that Tom Ellis is bad for the party or the Congressional Club is bad for the party," said Ellis. "There's nothing I can do about that. I have no problem defending the Congressional Club, what it has tried to do, and what it has tried to do within the framework of the Republican party within this state."[11]

While millions of dollars were sent to the Congressional Club office, Jesse Helms worried about reelection in 1978. Jimmy Carter had won impressively in North Carolina two years earlier, after Helms and Ellis had failed to win the presidential nomination for Ronald Reagan at the national convention. Also, Democrat James B. Hunt, Jr., won the governor's race with sixty-five percent of the vote that year.

In the meantime Helms managed to have his name tagged to every piece of conservative legislation that came out of the Senate and spoke out for much that failed on the floor. And when he spoke out against liberalism in the Congress, the Congressional Club capitalized on it. New Right direct-mail expert Richard A. Viguerie put the finishing touches to the appeals and later said, "When we send out an appeal for funds over Senator Helms' signature we get three to five times the response that we get if it is a simple request from the Congressional Club."[12]

Still, Jesse worried. He had never lost a political race, and he did not wish to lose one now. He was the godfather to the New Right by now. He had worked hard on that image, and he continued to develop it. He called Tom Ellis almost daily, and he always asked about how much funds were being delivered across the threshold. Ellis reported "one," "two," then "three," then more; it looked as though their campaign chest might reach $4 or even $5 million. That sounded better to Helms, who by then was running back and forth from Washington to North Carolina by private jet every weekend, making speeches, appearing in church, actually eating the mounds of barbecue that was cooked in the pits by the good solid citizens who wanted to see their candidate chomp down on the smoked meat, and appearing at church again on Sunday evenings before flying back to the capital.

Howard Covington wrote that when Helms was in Washington he walked, talked, and acted like a Republican, but when he was in North Carolina "he seldom mentions the party. He says he is not running away from the Republican party but in ways not running with it." In the state where Republicans were still outnumbered three to one, Helms' people spent nearly $100,000 for Jessecrats—Democrats for Helms—and the Congressional Club was termed "all but a third party in this state," while Ellis "tried to persuade people that Jesse is a bipartisan candidate." At the same time, according to Covington, Democratic opponent John Ingram accused, "Jesse is ashamed of the Republican party. He won't associate with any Republican candidates. He's so ashamed of where he is on the ticket, nobody's going to be able to find him."[13] But State Republican Chairman Jack Lee of Fayetteville appeared on television to endorse Helms, then he was followed by every Republican conservative Helms could find inside or outside North Carolina.

Jesse spent $7,460,966, during the campaign. Most of the money went toward accumulating more and more addresses for his Congressional Club mailing lists. On election day he received 619,151 votes at a cost of more than $10 per vote in campaigning expenses. Ingram, the former insurance commissioner with little more than $250,000 and a campaign personality almost as flat, pulled 516,663 votes. But to have heard the rhetoric that screamed from the national conservative press after the victory, an onlooker would have thought Jesse Helms had an edict from heaven instead of a fairly close win.

With the Helms' money machine hardly depleted even after the big spending of the campaign, the computer banks were freshly filled with new names of solid contributors. Raising $1.2 million during the first nine months of the off-election year 1979, the Congressional Club gave $1,100 to Organized Christian Churches, a Winston-Salem-based fundamentalist group; $3,040.40 to the North Carolina Right-to-Life organization in Cary to fight abortion legislation; $2,600 to the Stop Equal Rights Amendment Political Action Committee; $1,000 to Kentuckians for Louie Nunn, the unsuccessful GOP candidate for governor; $33,000 to pay off debts to direct mail expert Richard Viguerie; and $4,576 as a loan to the state Republican party. The club showed a million-dollar budget for the year with twenty-six salaried employees. The staff was almost doubled the following year, when the club began raising more funds to gear up to support Ronald Reagan and other conservative candidates around the United States.

Democratic Governor Jim Hunt, who had beaten Republican David Flaherty by more than 500,000 votes in 1976 and was seen as the strongest potential candidate to take on Jesse Helms in 1984, became the most frequent target of attacks by the Congressional Club in 1979. The club spent $25,000 on a September advertising campaign showing that the Hunt administration had awarded more than $1 million in job-training contracts to the AFL-CIO and two companies headed by Wilbur Hobby, president of the North Carolina AFL-CIO, through the federal Comprehensive Employment and Training Act (CETA). Sixty thirty-second ads showed stacks of $100 bills with hands reaching out and grabbing the money and giving it to another, while the question was asked: "What does the state do with your money?" At least thirteen television stations refused to run the ad, but it was estimated that much damage was done by its appearance elsewhere.

In 1980, after easily defeating two democratic opponents by more than two to one, Hunt faced Republican I. Beverly Lake, Jr., a state representative, in the general election. In this race more ads were run against Hunt. Also, a Southern Pines conservative minister who had been close to Helms, the Reverend Kent Kelly of the Churches for Life and Liberty, claimed that Governor Hunt had lied about his stand on abortion, death penalty, liberalization of divorce, drug, and liquor laws. Part of what the Charlotte *Observer* showed as the Congressional Club's "Big Lie" was a promotion that proclaimed Hunt rated only ten percent with conservatives to Lake's ninety percent. In November Hunt counted 1,143,145 votes to his opponent's 691,449.

However, the *Observer* reported that the biggest of the "Big Lies" was promoted in East Carolina University Professor John P. East's campaign against Democratic incumbent U.S. Senator Robert Morgan. The Jesse Helms–Tom Ellis machine reached down and hand-picked East, an Eisenhower look-alike with a bald head and forceful jaws who had assisted Helms in writing the Reagan-conservative-oriented platform of the 1976 Republican national convention. The man, who was confined to a wheelchair, had never run for political office and had no record, but he showed strength in his strong conservative outlook, and the Republican nomination was his for the asking. And while Morgan was jousting for the Democratic nomination, the Congressional Club paid for high-priced television spots showing all of the positive traits of Mr. East's character. An alert attorney who had practiced in Greenville from 1960 to 1964, an ex-Marine, a Republican national committeeman, the forty-nine-year-old East held his law degree from the University of Illinois and doctorate from the University of Florida. The advertisements were strong, dynamic, and positively conservative. Then, as soon as Morgan won the Democratic nomination and the two were in face-to-face combat, the Congressional Club pulled out all of the stops. Its advertisements borrowed heavily from old campaigns throughout the South: Morgan was painted as the Washington-oriented, liberal-minded incumbent Democrat. "What has he done for you today?" the ads read. As an extra added attraction, Helms twisted the arm of his fellow Republican Howard Baker of Tennessee with whom he had argued over the Panama Canal treaty but at whose insistence Helms had turned off an all-out conservative attack on the treaty. Baker made several stops throughout the Piedmont, speaking for East, saying that while they "disagree upon a few issues," they "will agree on infinitely more," and added, "There's no requirement that we agree on everything."[14] More than $600,000 was spent on television ads in the last six weeks, stating that incumbent Morgan had supported "the giveaway of the Panama Canal," had voted "to send hard-earned American dollars to help communists in Nicaragua," had opposed efforts "to strengthen our defense by voting against the B-1 bomber," and finally had voted in favor "of giving away our tax dollars to aid New York City." When the final vote was counted, East edged past Morgan with 898,064 votes to 887,653. In the aftermath Morgan told the press that he blamed Tom Ellis and Jesse Helms for his defeat, calling them "masters of deceit."[15]

After the race Helms and Ellis posed proudly next to the senator-elect in his wheelchair. Defending his position with John East, Ellis said:

> We felt we had some ideas on how to run a winning campaign, and John agreed to put himself on the line to represent the conservative cause. But I'll tell you, we didn't win the victory; the victory belongs to the folks who cared enough about the country to contribute their money and time to the East campaign and the Congressional Club. They made the difference. I think we know how to get conservatives elected, how to put the nuts and bolts together to go over the heads of the liberal editors and TV commentators and get the conservative message out there to the people on TV. When John East started running for the Senate, less than five percent of the people in the state knew who he was. We turned that around and gave the people a chance to know John, the type of man he is. That's why he was able to win and that's what it's going to take to elect more people like him to government. The Congressional Club can be the most effective organization in the country when it comes down to doing the hard work it takes to win an election.[16]

By working successfully with both the East and the Reagan campaigns at the same time, the Congressional Club's organization proved it was capable of spreading itself around to multiple conservative causes. Also, in 1980 it helped out several statewide campaigns other than East's, making sure that those politicians who were opposed to Jesse Helms and his conservatism were defeated or badly damaged at the polls. And the club contributed to other congressional campaigns in the South, West, and Midwest. In addition it raised more than $5 million under the label Americans for Reagan, spending it primarily on the presidential campaign in North Carolina to build on the Republican foundation there.

Despite the overwhelming success of the club, Ellis was determined not to sit still. He pressed the fifty-plus staff to continue its hard work, and into the off-election year of 1981 the offices in the suburban park outside Raleigh buzzed with activity. The club sent out propaganda opposing the Equal Rights Amendment, renewal of the Legal Services Corporation, and welfare for the needy.

People around the United States continued to send their money to the club, usually with letters proclaiming their admiration for the work being done by Senator Helms. A cattle rancher in Russell, Kansas, who sent $250 in 1978 and $250 again the next year, said, "I sent the money to Jesse Helms. It's for him and his cause. When I first heard him talk at a convention in New Orleans, he reminded me of the kind of people who used to be in charge of this country. He represents to me America when it was at its best. We've tried the liberal thing. The crime is up, the divorce rate is up, illegitimacy is up. It looks to me like the whole damn thing is falling apart." An eighty-five-year-old widow of a construction engineer from Port Arthur, Texas, said she sent $150 in 1979"because I just like what he stands for. I know he will spend it the way it should be spent." An independent oil producer from Dallas who gave three $100 gifts said, "To me Jesse is probably the most articulate conservative spokesman in the Senate—even more so than John Tower. He represents a body of thought I don't want to see defeated in the Senate." And a New Jersey bookkeeper who sent the club $75 six times in two years said, "It's simple. He's the greatest American living today."[17]

And while the money flowed into the offices of the Congressional Club, Jesse Helms spoke to overflowing crowds in California, Washington, Illinois, and London, England, and was invited to appear on popular television shows in the United States and abroad—as though he was looking beyond North Carolina at future political horizons.

Southern Sex Czar

Jeremiah Denton was a man of action. He was ready to move. He had been confined to a solitary cell in North Vietnam for more than seven years. By the grace of God he made it back home. He stepped off the airplane onto the runway at Clark Field in the Philippines with his fellow officers and hundreds of enlisted men. While millions of Americans watched on television, he dropped to his knees, kissed the ground, and uttered with trembling lips, "God bless America."

He knew that it was time to act even before Paul Weyrich of the Committee for the Survival of a Free Congress flew down to Mobile, Alabama, and sat with him and talked about how the federal government needed a genuine American like Jeremiah Denton in Washington. It was nice that a good conservative patriot like Ronald Reagan was running for the presidency in 1980, he thought, but Admiral Denton knew that he didn't need anybody's coattails to run on; he would do very well with his service record and his devotion to his country and his Lord and his belief that the United States had been running wild with free sex and an absolute lack of morals. While he had been imprisoned by the Viet Cong the country had become a virtual Sodom and Gomorrah, and now it needed a crusader to wash it clean. A true believer in old-fashioned conservatism was one thing, being white from Alabama was another, and holding to the true Catholic faith was even more reason for Denton to believe in himself as a candidate, or so he told a group of backers in the ballroom of a luxurious resort, the Grand Hotel in Point Clear on the eastern shore of Mobile Bay.

Jeremiah Denton disregarded a historical fact: nobody from Mobile, the state's oldest and most predominantly Catholic city, had ever been elected to the U.S. Senate. People in the northern hill country and Birmingham's steelmill valleys and in the rich Tennessee River crescent had always voted for Protestants, with the exception of John F. Kennedy, who had projected above their Bible Belt mentality. Mostly they had preferred Church of Christ Campbellites. But here he was, not altogether ignorant of the political facts, lowering his head ever so slightly and looking out into that audience. His stance was not unlike that of their hero, Ronald Reagan, though he was short and Reagan was tall. Nevertheless, he was a real live hero, not one who had to be projected onto a silver screen. Jeremiah Denton spoke out in his Southern-tinged voice that sounded more like sandpaper rubbing over rough glass. His words were audible when he said, "It's time someone started speaking out for morality in this country. Good old-fashioned morality!"[1] And his audience stared up into his line-mapped face capped with gray-sprinkled wavy hair, his lips a thin moving curve as he spoke, and they nodded their heads. "It is time that someone spoke out for the American family, family life, and against the immoralities that have crept up on us and have taken control of *so* many lives," he was saying, speaking out, nodding his own head, his gray-splotched brows furrowing over his deep-set eyes, and creases paralleling up the center of his forehead. "When I came back from Vietnam, what I saw . . . "[2]

It was mid-July of 1965 when he was flying a mission over North Vietnam. After his controls failed, he attempted with all of his might to keep a hold on the jet. When he slammed his left foot hard against the rudder, he snapped a tendon in his thigh. The engines didn't respond. The plane went into a roll. His heart pounded. And Jeremiah Denton knew fright. He and his bombardier-navigator ejected. "Like Alice in Wonderland, we were falling from one world into another," he wrote in his autobiography, *When Hell Was in Session*.[3]

He wrote later that the North Vietnamese, when they captured him, acquired an average product of Middle America. And he believed staunchly in the values of that product. "My heritage, training, and background made me the very antithesis of everything my communist captors stood for," he stated. For his heart and soul belonged to God, country, and family, although that family had been split asunder when his father left his mother when Jeremiah Denton was fourteen. Still, his mother instilled a deep religious belief in her son. "My religious upbringing and my mother's strong influence shaped my character, although my father worried that my life was too sheltered," he explained.[4]

Before his father left, the Denton family had moved from one town to another, one hotel to another. His father became embarrassed that he had not gained the wealth he thought he should have, and finally he left the family in Mobile. An old acquaintance from the port city remembered, "I think Jerry always remembered that time in his life with bitterness. He went to private Catholic schools: St. Mary's elementary and McGill Institute, where he was a tough athlete, a quarterback on the football team and shortstop in baseball, leader of his drill squad, always adequate but never superior. But he seemed to glory in the strict regimentation of the Catholic church, military academy, and organized sports."[5] And after he saw a Robert Young, James Stewart, and Lionel Barrymore movie, *Navy Blue and Gold*, he decided the Naval Academy was the school he would like to attend. He accomplished that goal and graduated with honors from Annapolis in 1946.

Nearly twenty years later, while he was languishing in a North Vietnamese prison camp, his childhood in Mobile stood him in good stead. He never had any doubts about his country. Not once, he remembered, did he question the goodness of the motivation of the United States' involvement in Southeast Asia. Lying in solitary confinement, he remembered carrying an American flag in a parade in downtown Mobile when he was seventeen, and even then he knew that it was a great honor. And in the painful silent hours of darkness he remembered the band playing the national anthem. And he wrote that "even now, tears come to my eyes when I hear those pure, sweet strains. I wish every American could share the feeling of love and gratitude that I have for this country and her people, and the sense of urgent necessity to protect her."[6]

There was no doubt about his heroism. In many of those black moments, crouched in a filthy hole, he remembered in detail the U.S. Code of Conduct, particularly Article I: "I am an American fighting man. I serve in the forces which guard my country and our way of life. I am prepared to give my life in their defense." And Article II: "I will never surrender of my own free will. If in command I will never surrender my men while they still have the means to resist."

He wondered about the last phrase, but he knew that he was continuing to fight under Article III: "If I am captured I will continue to resist by all means available."[7]

Jerry Denton had always felt a strong love for his country, for honor and duty, and he talked frequently with his few close friends about his belief in these abstract emotions while he was growing up. He had felt left out, different, and perhaps alone after his father moved on and left behind a broken home. But his mother was strong, and she transferred her strength to him.

Near the end of his first year of captivity he refused to write a biographical account for the Viet Cong to use as propaganda. When he refused, the interrogator jerked back his arm and slapped it forward, catching Denton on the side of his face. When the man's fist hit his face, Denton fell back. He looked up in a daze while the poker-faced Vietnamese reached down, picked him up, and hit him again and again. Each time the interrogator was careful not to strike the prisoner in the eyes or mouth. And at each blow Denton reeled backward. He felt sick at his stomach with the beating: his first taste of real brutality as a prisoner. And when Denton refused again to write anything, the Cong interrogator "took me by the cuffs, dragged me into one corner and threw me down. He turned off the light and left. I heard the key turn in the lock and I was alone in total darkness."[8]

He was moved from camp to camp, each worse than the one left behind, and he was tortured over and over, and finally he was brought before a camera and questioned. The reporter asked routine questions about his background before he began making a speech about the bombing of North Vietnam. Although Denton did not listen to the words, he looked around the bamboo room. In a daze he glared into the blinding floodlights aimed into his face—and he blinked. At that moment he knew that they were playing into his hands. Looking into the lights again, he blinked again. He was frightened, but he knew what he had to do. Then he stared straight into the camera's lens. He blinked once slowly, remembering the Morse code that he had learned so many years before. Then he blinked three more times—each time slowly. "A dash, and three more dashes. A quick blink, slow blink, quick blink.

"T . . . O . . . R . . .

"A slow blink . . . pause; two quick ones and a slow one; quick, slow, quick; quick.

"T . . . O . . . R . . . T . . . U . . . R . . . E . . ."[9]

Over and over he blinked out his message, and Naval Intelligence picked it up; for the first time U.S. officials knew that American POWs in North Vietnam were being tortured.

While in solitary confinement Denton thought not only about carrying a flag in a parade; he thought a great deal about his country and what made it strong. For him strength was the key to survival. His battle was a moral one, and he found that when he prayed, his strength was renewed. It didn't cross his mind that he might be released, return to the U.S., and run for political office. He didn't pray for such a happening. He prayed only for freedom, for his country to survive, and for the safety of his family back home. In the solace of prayer and in his own minute ways of communicating with fellow prisoners Denton remained a leader. He was the highest ranking officer, and he knew he must do everything in his power to make sure that morale was kept as positive as possible. He prayed with his men and for his men, he told them the best way he could that everything would be all right and that their families would be waiting for them when they returned, and he gave them the comfort of knowing that he was praying daily. He told them that he believed that the United States would prevail because it lived by faith and that the primary philosophy of ardent faith was Love Thy Neighbor.

Finally he was liberated, the highest ranking officer in the first wave of freed POWs. After he came home to Alabama and was reunited with his wife, Jane, and five sons and two daughters and several daughters-in-law he had never seen, he began to take notice of some strange occurrences. At least they were strange to him—and uncalled for. In what he called "some dark corners of America"[10] he saw a new permissiveness: advertisements for group sex; pornographic magazines right on the stand where children could look up and see naked women and naked men in full color in front of their eyes; flashing lights beckoning men into massage parlors he knew were only cheap camouflage for sidewalk houses of prostitution; lurid and lustful signs marking X-rated pornographic movies; and long-haired hippielike young people who obviously were the population of a drug culture. He saw it and at first couldn't believe it, then was completely revulsed by a nation gone wrong.

During the next year he saw his heroic president, Richard M. Nixon, who had greeted him at the White House and who had become his friend, resigning and leaving the highest office in the U.S. under the pressure of accusations of wrongdoing. Such happenings—seeing the unraveling of the Watergate scandals on television, hearing from his military and political friends in Washington, recognizing the damage to America's very foundations that was taking place before his eyes—Jeremiah Denton was sickened. He knew he had to act.

Seeing these changes in his world made him begin thinking that he had to do something about the deterioration of the old-fashioned moral values. First he became the director of an organization called Coalition for Decency, accepting a salary and contributions from persons who were also interested in washing clean the smut that was so ever-present on the streets and particularly on television, where any child could see without really trying. He watched the television shows and lambasted the ones that permitted too much of what the producers referred to as T-and-A, or tits and ass. In his letters to his members, a coalition put together through his growing friendship with New Right conservative Paul Weyrich, he called for boycotting products sold by companies that advertised on, and paid for, shows he found too promiscuous or tended to promote promiscuity or to idealize homosexuality.

Denton had been quoted once as stating he would like to pass a federal law making adultery punishable by death, but he denied ever making such a statement. He explained to Myra MacPherson of the *Washington Post*:

> I have said, on several occasions, that historians will tell you there are two requirements for societal well-being. One is agriculture. People have to eat, and need hides for protection against the elements and so forth. The second requirement is the need for procreation to sustain the tribes and family life. In my speeches I give examples of societies which are extremely primitive. What you might call sustenance-level civilizations such as some of the tribes of Tibet or Afghanistan way out in the hills. They are so aware of the truth about the necessity for agriculture and family life that if you steal it's almost invariable that the penalty is cutting off your hand because what you're doing is taking away a necessity. And adultery is a capital crime without exception, because it upsets the society so much and deprives it of one of the basic necessities for survival. Now when we get to our development of society we don't have to do that. If I'm unfaithful to my wife, they don't have to kill me because it's not going to disturb the national welfare that much. But were we a tribe of twelve families, it would. And zap!

While he told one Alabama reporter, "I don't want to be known as the Southern Sex Czar. But something *has* to be done before we are completely overrun by promiscuity," he said to Ms. MacPherson,

"I'm not a nut on the subject but I do believe there is a problem. No nation can survive long unless it can encourage its young to withhold indulgence in their sexual appetite until marriage!"[11]

With the knowledge that he had to act to clean up the filth that had layered the society he knew before he went off to fight in Vietnam, he clasped hands with Paul Weyrich, who walked with him and talked with him and prayed with him. "I knew that he would make a great statesman," the head of the Committee for the Survival of a Free Congress remarked. "He had the kind of drive and total belief in himself and in the cause of conservatism that we had been searching for," he added.[12]

First, however, Denton faced opposition from a Republican in the primary, which was unusual in the Deep South state. The opposition was a traditional Black Belt country club Republican, Armstead Selden, who had served in the U.S. Congress back in the sixties as a Democrat. He had always carried water for the national Republican party, had kept close ties to the national machine, and had as his campaign manager fashionable Don Collins, who had converted to Republicanism on the floor of the State Senate in the sixties. Selden's people came out of the courthouses, while Denton's stepped straight out the front doors of the churches, and there were considerably more churches than courthouses. In the meantime young, tall, handsome Jim Folsom, Jr., scion of the famous old political dynasty started by James Elisha "Kissin' Jim" Folsom, who had served two terms as governor in the forties and fifties, defeated Democratic incumbent Donald Stewart. While many political observers thought Folsom would be a shoo-in against a Republican Catholic from Mobile, these commentators didn't reckon with the military hero factor or the new strength of the Moral Majority in the South. In spite of Denton's out-in-the-open enjoyment of a glass of Jack Daniel's or a cold beer now and then, which had been taboo in Alabama politics for the twenty years George Wallace had been in power, the leaders of the Moral Majority listened to Denton's talk against teenage sex and adultery, and they were sold on his beliefs. Besides, he had been courted by the most conservative of them all, Paul Weyrich, and that put him right with the New Religious Right. And former President Nixon had broken his political silence and had sent Denton a $1,000 contribution.

Before the two candidates met in a statewide televised debate, Denton arranged to sit down and talk with media and issues consultant Joe Azbell, the gregarious behind-the-scenes adviser to three George Wallace campaigns for the presidency. "When we talked for nearly three hours at the Governor's House Motel, he sipped beer and obviously enjoyed himself and took in the issues. He was a very likeable but somehow strange individual. I liked him, but I didn't know until the day of the debate whether he would use my advice or not," Azbell, who had handled dozens of political campaigns in the southeast and southwest, recalled.[13] Others indicated that Denton was not the typical Southern Republican candidate, would not follow national party leadership, and did not own the local rank-and-file Republicans.

But Denton did it. He stepped out strongly on the issues in the debate, while young Folsom hemmed and hawed about his stands. And two days before the general election the chairman of the state Democratic party, George Lewis Bailes, in a speech in Huntsville questioned Denton's competency, saying, "If he was smart, why did he get captured by the North Vietnamese?"[14] And Denton's people knew that with this comment spread from one end of the state to the other his election was all but sealed. On Tuesday, after Denton had spent $855,346 to his opponent's $356,647, he squeaked by with 650,362 votes to 617,175 for Folsom.

Before he was sworn into office, Denton spoke out against the very people who had supported him the heaviest—Jerry Falwell and the Moral Majority. He told *Wall Street Journal* reporter James M. Perry that he had some serious questions for the organization and its leadership. "I don't see black people on the board of the Moral Majority. I don't see the Moral Majority supporting the commandment, 'Love Thy Neighbor.' " Denton continued that he spoke directly to the leader of the Moral Majority, the Reverend Jerry Falwell, at a meeting of fundamentalist groups, and Falwell agreed that there were too few black people in his organization. Denton was adamant. "That's what I have to say to them: Put up or shut up! Prove you are Christians! What's the essence of Christianity? It's love the Lord thy God, love thy neighbor. So I say, 'Prove it! Prove it! Get some blacks in this group because they are more interested in saving the family structure in this country than anyone else.' "[15] Several months later the Reverend Falwell told a group in Montgomery that he thought Denton was "doing a great job, keeping the faith, and working hard for all of his followers."[16]

A tough individualist, Denton went his own way on Capitol Hill but always under the leadership of Paul Weyrich. He was erratic, telling one reporter one story and then denying it to the next, playing quotation ping-pong so often that many journalists tired of his accusations and denials. One thing for sure, he was almost impossible to categorize.

While on one hand he preached for a stronger and wider-ranged defense, he stated early on that he was not opposed to the Jimmy Carter-backed Panama Canal treaty to allow Panama to operate the canal because it was no longer efficient for U.S. vessels, and "you could sabotage that canal with a Boy Scout troop."[17] While he stated that he was against welfare giveaway programs, he spoke out loudly in favor of continuing the peanut subsidies, without which many farmers in Alabama would suffer. He was given more power probably than any other freshman who ever entered the Senate. He was certainly given more than any other in the Ninety-seventh Congress, being appointed to four committees (Armed Services, Judiciary, Labor and Human Resources, and Veterans' Affairs), and being named chairman of two subcommittees, while serving on seven other subcommittees. Under the Labor and Human Resources Committee, he was named chairman of the Aging, Family, and Human Services Subcommittee, where he believed he could streamline government's welfare system, making it a Republican-backed workfare, as well as building the government's responsibility to promote the family in society. But with all of his power he expressed anger when he was not appointed to the Foreign Relations Committee, where he felt that he could do more good than any other.

In his role as chairman of the subcommittee on Security and Terrorism Denton underwent what *The Conservative Digest* termed an attack and a propaganda blitz from U.S.S.R. newspapers *Pravda* and *Izvestia*. Saying that Denton was a "vulture" who as "the chief fighter against international terrorism" was threatening to upset detente, *Pravda* initiated the articles that continued with *Izvestia* publishing an account entitled "The Admiral Eradicates Subversion," in which it was stated that he was treated "humanely" by the North Vietnamese because "they let him live." But while *The Conservative Digest* found the articles disgusting, they failed to point out that such an attack could not be better publicity for a New Right senator.

In an article in *The Digest* Denton outlined the basic goals of his subcommittee's work:

> While terrorism was once largely confined to single national states or political units, international terrorism often involves the citizens and authorities of several nations. In Chicago, for example, in 1978, Croatian nationalists held the German consulate hostage. The purpose: to force the release of Croatian terrorists in Germany awaiting extradition to Yugoslavia.
>
> International treaties and conventions, diplomatic accords and foreign policy concerns often severely hamper the efforts of law enforcement agencies

to deal with terrorists in their own jurisdictions. Thus France, in the course of improving its relations with hard-line Arab states such as Syria, Iran, Iraq, and Libya, has become a favored haunt—and battlefield—for international terrorist organizations sponsored by those states.

International terrorism is as much a foreign policy problem as it is a domestic law enforcement dilemma.[18]

Denton continued that most experts on the subject of terrorism agreed that the infrastructure of the international organization of the criminal groups could not function without "tremendous support and direction that the Soviets and their clients provide. The Iranian hostage crisis, the killing of Americans by Puerto Rican separatists, the attempted assassination of President Reagan, and a bloody shootout between Ku Klux Klan and Communist Workers' Party terrorists—these and other similar incidents raise serious questions for Americans. Are we adequately protected against terrorist acts both abroad and in our own land? If so, how?

"Because of the great freedom of movement possible in the United States, international terrorists enter, leave and move about this country almost at will," he added, stating that communication between all types of extremist groups "can take place virtually without the knowledge of American law enforcement agencies."

Because any American inside his or her own country could be the victim of a terrorist attack like those that citizens read about taking place in Paris, Rome, Belfast, Tel Aviv, Madrid, Johannesburg, Manila, or Beirut, the senator stated, his subcommittee on Security and Terrorism planned to discover means by which the United States could become secure again. Denton said that it was time someone spoke out against the threat of terrorism, quoting German theologian and Nazi holocaust survivor Martin Niemoeller, who said, "In Germany, they came first for the communists, and I didn't speak up because I wasn't a communist. Then they came for the Jews, and I didn't speak up because I wasn't a Jew. Then they came for the Catholics, and I didn't speak up because I was a Protestant. And then they came for me, and, by that time, no one was left to speak up."[19]

While those around him spoke promisingly of the future of Republicans and the Republican party in Alabama, Denton refused to be interviewed about his party. "He's too busy with other things to talk about politics," said his press secretary, Steve Allen, a former weekly news editor and graduate of Birmingham's Cumberland Law School. Young Allen did not wince when asked about the future of Republicanism in Alabama. He pulled out statistics, figures, charts, and graphs, and for a moment appeared to speak like an echo of Kevin Phillips from Nixon's early days in the presidency. "In Alabama in the 1980 general election, you could not be sure who was running on whose coattails: Jeremiah Denton on Ronald Reagan's or Ronald Reagan on Jeremiah Denton's. From the very beginning in Admiral Denton's race, it was a high-risk Machiavellian campaign strategy; everything was against him except his high visibility and his unequivocal honor as a prisoner-of-war in Vietnam. He was very clear on the issues and where he stood on the issues, and the people liked that and voted for it," he added.[20]

Allen, who said that he might return to Alabama and run as a Republican candidate some day, estimated:

Republicans might win one of every ten races in the South in order to build a strong two-party system. But why not? Why not continue the high-risk strategy? That's what it will take, I believe, to break the old-time prejudice against Republicans in the South that was perpetrated by the Democrats through the years. The good thing about a Ronald Reagan vote for president—and an awful lot of so-called Democrats all over the South voted for him for president—is that once they have voted for one Republican it will be easier for them to vote for others. That is why, also, we need to have someone running for every place on the ballot in every election. And we need good competition in our own party in the South to build our party.

Today there is not one district in Alabama that isn't winnable by the Republicans. There are three or four key counties in the state, that if they went Republican, a Republican governor could be elected. One time not long ago it was hopeless; or, at least, it looked hopeless. South Carolina is very much like Alabama politically. While South Carolina is smaller, it is similar geographically, from the ocean to the hills, and today it has some very strong Republican areas. The Republicans will be working hard in Alabama as they will be in all Southern states. And if the Democrats nominate Walter Mondale in 1984, they'll throw away Alabama and most of the South. And Republicans will be waiting for that kind of move, and we will continue to have strength in fine senators like Senator Denton who will build on that strength.[21]

The Damning of Dixie

The Birmingham, Alabama, chapter of the Ku Klux Klan of America did not put out a position paper on the Jeremiah Denton-Jim Folsom race for the U.S. Senate. But they put out typewriter-paper-sized sheets with large headlines: JEREMIAH DENTON ALMOST DIED FOR THE WHITE RACE. In smaller letters were the words: *Jim Folsom's Father Invited Niggers to the Governor's Mansion*. Under the smaller letters was a paragraph explaining that Governor James E. "Big Jim" Folsom had met and drunk whiskey with black New York Congressman Adam Clayton Powell in the governor's mansion back in the 1950s. Even though Denton denied the Klan, the organization nevertheless put out more than 25,000 sheets against his opponent. And after he was elected and listed the KKK among terrorist organizations such as the Italian Red Brigades and the Japanese Red Army, Klan leaders at a rally in Decatur stated, "Jeremiah Denton is a better man for the white people of America than another Democratic politician who would give away another chunk of our country to the Negro race and the Communist Party." And another said, "Senator Denton is a friend of the Ku Klux Klan. He is in favor of the family unit and against abortion, just the same way we are. We want to continue to fight the evils that are destroying this country, and that's the same thing he says every time he stands in front of a microphone."[1]

Randall Williams, journalist and director of Southern Poverty Law Center's *Klanwatch Project*, pointed out that Klan leadership throughout the United States "put out political rhetoric that could easily be interpreted as pro-Ronald Reagan in nature and content."[2]

In the general election of 1980 President Jimmy Carter chose the Labor Day political rally at Tuscumbia, Alabama, to make his first speech. Speaking elsewhere, Reagan accused Carter of talking "in the city that gave birth to and is the parent body of the Ku Klux Klan." And while shock waves of such an accusation swept the South, and Carter somewhat sanctimoniously apologized to the city and the area for Reagan's "mistake," and Reagan's headquarters asked him also to apologize, the Reagan people kept their candidate quiet. They knew exactly what they were doing: they were trying to keep the onus of the KKK off their candidate, while the Southern strategists like Lee Atwater knew good and well that the Ku Kluxers could do nothing but support Ronald Reagan. After all, white-gowned members of the Klan had demonstrated against Carter at a north Alabama airport and a block away from the rally where he spoke. And not two weeks earlier Louisianan Bill Wilkinson, wizard of the Invisible Empire of the Ku Klux Klan, had spoken out strongly against Carter and his "giving the whole system of government over to the Negro people." [3] When Wilkinson, who led white-caped demonstrations in Montgomery, Decatur, Knoxville, Atlanta, Jackson, Baton Rouge, and Little Rock, said in the summer of 1979, "It is good to see that out there in front all these good white people have gathered to tell Washington that they are sick of the government niggertickerton and trying to get the nigger and the liberal vote," the white folks who cheered knew that he meant: *Vote Against Carter*! When he added, "We are sick of supporting the blacks while they multiply like rats," the white people who applauded and catcalled his remarks knew he was in favor of doing away with giveaway welfare programs just like the Republican conservative Ronald Reagan. And when he said, "Go out there and vote for the best white man's candidate, Ronald Wilson Reagan, for President of the United States, because he will do away with keeping niggers in the rich-house and white people in the poorhouse,"[4] there was no doubt about what he meant.

In Nashville, Tennessee, two of Wilkinson's members, Dennis Mangrum and Ann Reeves, told an interviewer from NBC-TV's "Today" show in October 1980 that they were a part of the local Ronald-

Reagan-for-President campaign. Working out of a red trailer parked on a city street corner, the two campaign workers were described by local Reagan officials as being good workers for the organization. Jere Griggs, chairman of the Tennessee Reagan campaign, said in a statement that he assumed all volunteers shared Reagan's goals and interests but that he had "neither the means nor the inclinations to make background checks" on everybody."[5]

In the meantime Carter, speaking in the Reverend Martin Luther King, Sr.'s, Ebenezer Baptist Church in Atlanta, expressed his sorrow that he was running against "a racist." His accusation, obviously not as orchestrated as Reagan's earlier remark, spread quickly across the nation. Middle-of-the-roaders appeared shocked that the president would call a good man like Reagan such a name, and avowed racists were glad that the question was out in the open.

In North Carolina the White Knights of the Ku Klux Klan as well as several other factions worked against Democratic candidate Robert Morgan. "We put out more than fifty thousand pieces of literature in country stores from one end of the state to the other," said Larry Grant at a Raleigh rally. "We didn't come out in support of John East, but we let it be known that we were against Morgan's liberalism. People got the point,"[6] he added. The same sort of smut sheets had been distributed against Senator Jesse Helms' opponent, John Ingram, in 1978. But nobody put their finger on East or Helms as supporting the Klan, but in more than eight years in the Senate Helms never hired a black staffer. The senator told journalists that it was always difficult to find qualified people.

No longer the basic brogans-and-overall stereotype of the Kluxer, some younger leaders of the Klan were more in the gray-pinstriped-suit crowd. The most visible of them was David Duke of Louisiana. Born July 1, 1950, he became active in far-right politics in the sixties when he was still in high school. The son of an engineer, Duke was born in Tulsa, traveled with his family to The Hague when he was in kindergarten, and attended private military school in Georgia. Duke told prize-winning journalist Patsy Sims, who wrote the definitive book *The Klan*, about his metamorphosis from youthful liberal to confirmed racist by the time he was seventeen. When he was twelve, he said, "I imagine I'd already read as much as people twenty-five, and I was becoming a liberal. I really was. I had read some of these books that were very much pro-black and trying to instill a guilt complex in the white people for being white. You might say I was committed reasonably and emotionally to liberal ideas."[7] However, he told Ms. Sims that one book, *Race and Reason: A Yankee View*, started him off, and in the next four years he changed, until as a high-grade-average student at Louisiana State University in Baton Rouge he became known as "the Nazi of LSU." He was the outspoken anti-communist leader of a small but fervent group of like-thinking students. In the fall of 1980, leaving his position as grand wizard of the Knights of the Ku Klux Klan in Metairie, Duke ran for the state senate, speaking out against Jimmy Carter's candidacy under the auspices of his new organization, the National Association for the Advancement of White People. "It is time we cast aside the cloaks of the Ku Klux Klan," he said in the aftermath of quitting the KKK for the NAAWP.[8] And one of his local chapter presidents, William B. Dunston, reiterated his sentiments: "No sheets or pillowcases flopping in the wind will be able to turn us around. Mr. Duke has fired a shot to begin a battle in this area, but he is not aware the people here are united in a way he will not be able to overcome."[9]

In his shaggy-sandy-haired, mustachioed, silver-voiced movie-star manner, the former LSU ROTC cadet who had once scored 173 on an IQ test personified the youthful right wing. Breaking down the issues, he sounded like a rough-hewn echo of the national Republican advertisements.

However, in the final analysis, Duke's politics were too wishy-washy for the Klan and too way-out for the Republican leadership. Still, as far as the Deep South was concerned, he was very much a part of modern-day Republicanism in his view of the issues.

He said,

> White people are facing massive discrimination in employment, promotion, scholarships, and union admittance. White people must be entitled to civil rights too. I favor enacting legislation specifically making it illegal to enact so-called affirmative action programs that discriminate against white people. Welfare has gone far beyond the level of charity and reason. A workfare program must be instituted for able-bodied welfare recipients; that is, they must work in menial jobs for the state in order to receive their welfare money. No workfare, no welfare! Because welfare has become practically a hereditary institution, welfare mothers should be given financial incentives to have fewer children. That is the only real solution to the welfare problem.

Again, echoing Reagan's national plan, he advocated a reduction of taxes:

> I pldge to vote against all attempts to raise taxes on the middle class. State spending should be cut and all surpluses should be returned to the

taxpayers. State taxes on oil at the well-head should be increased and taxes at gasoline pumps should be abolished. Tax breaks should be established for gasohol manufacturing concerns producing gasohol for Louisiana consumption. Black political pressure groups have prevented judges from dealing harshly with the greater portion of violent criminals. We must have mandatory penalties for convictions of violent crimes, and an iron-clad law guaranteeing that repeat offenders are jailed. Criminals should be forced by law to pay restitution to victims. Public officials should have stiff penalties for misuse of public funds.[10]

Although he attempted to whitewash his image, Duke had a history as a firebrand for the American Nazi party in Louisiana and later with the Ku Klux Klan. He worked his way up to grand dragon of the state and national information director of the organization. He became the hooded empire's best-known spokesman, appearing on "Today," "Tomorrow," and "A.M. America" national television shows.

In 1980, after Duke announced that he had left the Klan for his NAAWP to run for political office, a Klan publication was spread through southern Louisiana disavowing any KKK connection with the candidate. Duke received some of the Klan's antipolitical dirty work. "The Truth about David Duke," stated, "Duke claims to have 'inherited' his klan from a mysterious New Orleans man using several aliases, but whose real name is Jim Lindsay. The fact is that Lindsay was never in the klan. Duke alleges that his klan can trace its roots to 1956. The fact remains that he founded his 'klan' in 1973 and incorporated it in 1975. It has never been sanctioned by a legitimate Klan organization."

The one-page legal-sized sheet continued that Duke was the "darling of the talk show circuit" because "he is the judas goat leading the klan movement to slaughter. He has neutralized more good men than the communists could ever expect to accomplish by any other means. No one before has ever had the exposure via the news media than has Duke."

The sheet stated that Duke had exposed woman jockey Mary Bacon as a Klan member "in violation of his Klan secrecy oath. Duke placed ads on radio prior to the Walker, Louisiana, rally announcing that Mary Bacon would make an appearance in support of the Klan. Mary Bacon was astonished and shocked that Duke had exposed her without her knowledge. When she arrived at the rally reporters besieged her and taunted her to make a speech. Duke pulled her onstage and off of America's best-known thoroughbreds. Dutch Masters cigars and Revlon cosmetics cancelled their advertising contracts with Mary Bacon. Today, Mary Bacon is reduced to riding quarter horses."[11]

Duke, as soon as he tried to become respectable and shed the Klan, received the same kind of treatment that he and the Klan had always dished out in political races. Of course, Duke was defeated—but all across the South these same kinds of sheets about other candidates—mostly Democratic candidates—were being put out wherever the vote was predominantly white.

In the fall of 1980 more than a thousand persons gathered near the birthplace of the Klan at Pulaski, Tennessee, where one of the hooded figures standing behind a podium in the flickering light of the gigantic burning cross told of the six young Confederate veterans who met late Christmas eve in 1865 in a law office to discuss the formation of their new order. "The Ku Klux Klan of America formed around the Den, our smallest enclave, to protect the citizens of our families from the onslaught of the outside world," the speaker said. And another speaker told about the changing politics of the time, that it was time "white people stopped kowtowing to the likes of nigger-loving politicians who stand in our midst and tell us one thing then go off to Washington and do something else. If we cannot find people to seek political office in our own folds, we should find the best white person for the job and vote for him."[12] And there was little doubt at that time who the KKKer meant.

During the same time, in Atlanta, an old holdover from the 1950s and 1960s, J. B. Stoner, who had been convicted by an Alabama jury of the 1958 bombing of a black church in Birmingham, ran for the U.S. Senate under the National States' Rights banner in Georgia. Stoner shook his fist before the crowds that gathered to see all of the candidates and screamed that "niggers are causing ninety-nine percent of the problems in the cities of the United States. You can take the African out of the jungle, but you can't take the jungle out of the African," while other candidates on the dais squirmed and looked away, flushed with embarrassment. "All civil rights laws should be repealed, then all of the niggers in America should be rounded up, put on ships, and sent back to Africa where they can build their own society. If they're able!" he shouted so loud his throat almost closed. "We could send them some food stamps and some welfare for a short length of time—until they're able to take care of themselves." He went on and on about how the blacks were "merely tools in the hands of the Jews, who want to control the world" and destroy all white

Christians. And he added that it should be against the law to practice "the Jewish religion" in the United States. "I favor confiscation of all ill-gotten Jewish wealth and resettling the Jews in this country on an island off the coast of Africa, probably Madagascar," Stoner advocated.[13]

An onlooker who stood and nodded occasionally and shook his head in disagreement to some statements, but who stayed and heard all of Stoner's words said:

> I'm not a member of the Klan, and I'm not a member of the National States' Rights party, but some of the things that Mr. Stoner says I know are right. For one, he says the black people are getting more rights than the white people in the South, and that's right; they get more welfare, food stamps, and the law's on their side; you see 'em riding down the road in a Cadillac full of children and you know they're going to pick up their welfare check, and you know it isn't right. It just isn't right. The Democratic government of Lyndon Johnson and Jimmy Carter turned everything over to the blacks. It doesn't seem to matter whether they cheat, whether they spend my tax money for welfare and food stamps, as long as we feed the black people. Well, I'm sick of all that. Back in the sixties and early seventies I voted for George Wallace for president whenever I had a chance, because I thought he said the right thing; he understood what was happening up there in Washington, and he wanted to do something about it. I don't consider myself a racist; I'm for black people having their rights; I don't want them sent back to Africa; but I'm also for white people having a few rights too. I think it's time this government was turned around. I'll vote for Ronald Reagan for president because I think he wants to turn it around and give some of the government back to the white people. I guess it's just about that simple.[14]

Not unlike other right-wing groups that supported Reagan throughout Dixieland in 1980, the Ku Klux Klan came out in opposition to some of his programs after he entered office in 1981. The Klan's official publication, *Thunderbolt*, criticized him for being too easy on welfare programs, not acting fast enough in favor of workfare as an alternative, supporting the Zionist causes of Israel rather than the more militant sides of the Arab nations, and failing to back U.S. Senator Jesse Helms' antiabortion bills. When Reagan named Sandra Day O'Connor to the U.S. Supreme Court, the KKK joined hands with the Moral Majority in speaking out against the new justice's "liberal stance on abortion, school prayer, and other pertinent issues," according to an anonymous writer in *Thunderbolt*. "The time has come for all conservatives to unite and be heard as one voice throughout the land. That is why we voted for a conservative to sit in the White House, that is why he has always had our support, and that is why now we must protest his backhanded kind of treatment of the people who have been his bedrock support in the South."[15]

The New Religious Right

More than 5,000 believers in the New Religious Right hitchhiked, drove, flew, and bicycled to a meeting in sunny Dallas, Texas, in August 1980 to hear their favorite political candidate, Ronald Reagan.

In the so-called National Affairs Briefing, sponsored by the non-denominational Religious Roundtable, a group of ministers founded and headed by Edward McAteer for the purpose of coordinating conservative causes in political activities among Christian leaders, Reagan spoke out like an old-time evangelical preacher. "When I hear the First Amendment used as a reason to keep traditional moral values away from policymaking, I am shocked. The First Amendment was written not to protect the people and their laws from religious values, but to protect those values from government tyranny. But over the last two or three decades the federal government seems to have forgotten both 'that old-time religion' and that old-time Constitution," Reagan said.

Shouts of "Amen!" filled the auditorium.

"Because of your hard work, your basic belief in Christian principles, your organized efforts on behalf of Christians in government is the real reason for the new vitality in American politics. Religious America is awakening—perhaps just in time for our country's sake,"[1] Reagan continued. And his message was spread across the Bible Belt through such groups as McAteer's Roundtable, Robert Billings' National Christian Action Coalition, Billy Melvin's National Association of Evangelists, the Moral Majority, John Beckett's Intercessors for America, the Reverend Billy James Hargis' Christian Crusade, the Reverend Pat Robertson's Christian Broadcasting Network, Bill Bright's Campus Crusade for Christ International, and other old-timers such as Major Edgar C. Bundy's Church League of America and Robert Welch's John Birch Society. With a combined membership of more than ten million the organizations joined in the effort to broadcast, telephone, visit neighbors, and fill the air with the word that Ronald Reagan was the man for the presidency. They said he fulfilled the promise that all good Southern Christians—not to mention those from the Midwest, West, East, and places in between—had been waiting for, to put the right man into the White House.

And less than six weeks later Reagan dipped down into Virginia and reconfirmed his belief in the Reverend Jerry Falwell's Thomas Road Baptist Church in Lynchburg. Condemning the "expulsion of God from the classroom," Reagan also told the meeting of the National Religious Broadcasters Association, "Because you are professionals, I know how much you respect and strongly support, as I do, the separation of church and state." In an auditorium at Liberty Baptist College, a religious institution built on a red-clay hillside near Lynchburg with funds collected by Falwell, Reagan remarked that the basis of his campaign was religious strength. He added that Christian conservatives were "absolutely right on key moral issues like prayer in the public schools. But I would be absolutely opposed to a state-mandated prayer. On the other hand," he said, "I have always believed that a voluntary, nonsectarian prayer in our schools was perfectly proper and I don't think we should ever have expelled God from the classroom."[2]

Promising to use the "bully pulpit" of the presidency to exercise what he called "moral suasion," he added, "I believe that the halls of government are well nigh as sacred as the churches, temples, and synagogues of our religions."

According to Howell Raines, a reporter covering the event for the *New York Times*, Reagan took questions only from representatives of "the religious media," who "greeted Mr. Reagan's answers with applause and amens." Raines wrote that Reagan was "unusually talkative as he arrived at the campus. First he asserted that Mr. Falwell, founder of the church-based political movement called Moral Majority, had not questioned the ability of Jews to reach God with their prayers. 'Dr. Falwell never made the statement attributed in that question,' said the candidate. 'He never said that. It was someone else who said that.' Later, Mr. Falwell confirmed he had said that only those redeemed by Jesus Christ could have prayers answered, but he blamed unscrupulous journalists for labeling this view as anti-Semitic."[3]

About this same time, primarily because of the National Affairs Briefing in Dallas, which had been such an out-and-out political forum for Reagan, Marion G. Robertson, known as Pat, resigned from the Roundtable. He told his people of the "700 Club," a daily television talk show with religious guests, that God wanted him out of politics and more concerned with religion. He canceled his scheduled appearance at the National Religious Broadcasters meeting. A graduate of Yale Law School and a powerful teacher of the ways of Christ through the medium of television, Robertson told his audiences the best thing people can do for the country was to pray and to write their congressmen about the laws they did not think follow the Christian perspective.

In the meantime Falwell became more and more active in the political arena. He and the Moral Majority had targeted liberal senators Birch Bayh, Frank Church, John Culver, George McGovern, Warren Magnuson, Gaylord Nelson, and Donald Stewart, and millions of dollars were raised, primarily through the direct-mail operations of Richard A. Viguerie, who had become known as the money man of the New Right. He had started by raising funds for Alabama Governor George C. Wallace, about whom he had doubts because Wallace was a Democrat and "not one-hundred percent conservative. He had a lot of populist, non-conservative ideas. But he and I agreed on about eighty percent of the important issues, social issues like busing and law and order, and the need for a strong national defense." Although he received criticism from old-line conservatives, Viguerie later wrote, "My working for Wallace—although I don't think I realized it at the time—was the beginning of my thinking in terms of coalition politics. I was encouraged by the fact that other conservatives like Paul Weyrich and Jeffrey St. John, the author and TV commentator, were meeting and talking with Wallace."[4] Since Wallace, Viguerie had assisted in electing conservatives like Jesse Helms, Strom Thurmond, Jim McClure, Orrin Hatch, Phil Crane, Mickey Edwards, Larry McDonald, Bob Livingston, Phil Gramm, and Bob Dornan. McClure of Idaho became influential as chairman of the Senate Steering Committee and repeatedly attacked opponents of nuclear power. Crane, a congressman from Illinois, chaired the American Conservative Union before he launched a dead-end campaign for the Republican presidential nomination in 1979–80. Dornan, a representative from California, had been a Los Angeles radio broadcaster when he originated the idea of the POW-MIA bracelet in 1970. Congressman Edwards of Oklahoma was a behind-the-scenes Capitol Hill backer of Ronald Reagan in the Core Group and became chairman of the American Conservative Union in 1981. McDonald, a congressman from Georgia, voted across the board against President Carter's plans in the Ninety-fifth Congress and was known as one of the most conservative Democratic Boll Weevils who supported President Reagan's administration. Livingston of Louisiana was elected to Congress to fill the First District slot vacated by F. Edward Hebert's retirement. But in 1976 Livingston was defeated by Democrat Richard Tonry, who was later accused of vote fraud. Livingston won in a special election in 1977. Since that time he gained the reputation of being a very conservative congressman. And Gramm was counted on repeatedly to support Reagan's tax cuts and budget cuts as a true-believing Democratic Boll Weevil.

When he was criticized as being a dictator of the New Right, Viguerie vehemently denied the charge.

These people do not work in that way. They work together. They believe in the work ethic. They work night and day to expand their leadership and their programs, educate each other in winning techniques and build ever larger and more influential coalitions. What they work with is a well-oiled machine: internal dynamics. Some people think we are a big conspiracy. Others think we meet and vote on everything we do. Others think I give orders to everyone. These are all false ideas. I have helped start a number of New Right groups, but I don't "control" any of them. When we get together, we never vote on anything. Usually someone leads the discussion, but he has no more authority than anyone else present. We exchange information. We brainstorm new ideas. Some people volunteer to do something or commit their organizations to do specific things. But no one gives orders like a commander-in-chief or a godfather. Some gatherings are weekly, some twice a month, some annually, and so forth. But the majority are ad hoc. We meet to work on special projects, say a piece of legislation. We meet as often as is necessary to do the best job we can for the conservative side of the issue. We often bring in different leaders for different kinds of issues. We are creative in convincing different groups that their interests are the same as ours in particular battles. That's how we got a broad spectrum of allies to fight instant voter registration, taxpayer campaign financing and other liberal election law power grabs."[5]

An energetic, bald, athletically trim man with shifting, alert eyes that flash with ideas like a pinball machine ringing up scores, Viguerie stated:

> I have an attitude regarding the New Right that it's almost like a family—and I'm in no way comparing it to an organized crime family, but there are certain code similarities. If there's any problems in the family, you keep 'em in the family. It's a great no-no to go outside the family, so to speak. And when a family member asks me for something, I don't say, "I don't think that's right." Sometimes I might think it's dumb. Sometimes I might think it's a waste of time. But, you know, if they want it, fine, because I'm going to call them tomorrow and ask them for something. And I just believe that we should have a good close working relationship."[6]

Respected not only by his conservative brethren, the Texas native of Louisiana French ancestry, who graduated from the University of Houston before he traveled to New York and got involved in Republican politics, was introduced to the George Wallace operation through a liberal contact. Morris Dees of Montgomery, who had been responsible for the supersuccessful direct-mail fund-raising for George McGovern in 1972, suggested to the Wallace people that they get one of the best in the business—Richard Viguerie.

Back when he was testing his youthful wings in New York, joining the Young Americans for Freedom as its executive secretary when it was $20,000 in debt, Viguerie breathed new life into the sagging conservative organization. He moved the main office south to Washington, D.C., wrote letters, and solicited contributions from people who had given $50 or more in the Barry Goldwater campaign. From that first successful makeshift attempt he went on to handle conservative after conservative, turning down anybody with whom he did not agree most of the time. He moved fast and unpredictably from Wallace to former Texas Governor John B. Connally in 1976 after Connally turned from Democrat to Republican. Then he attempted a takeover of the waning American Independent party, then jumped aboard Phil Crane's presidential try, then moved on to the Ronald Reagan campaign that was building steam in the late spring of 1980. "My business decisions are dictated one hundred percent by politics,"[7] he bragged, and he named the top conservative political action committees as his clients: Jesse Helms' Congressional Club, Terry Dolan's National Conservative Political Action Committee (NCPAC), Paul Weyrich's Committee for the Survival of a Free Congress, and Howard Phillip's Conservative Caucus.

By 1981 the Viguerie Company was based in Falls Church, Virginia, employed more than 300 persons, mailed more than 100 million letters a year, grossed more than $5 million dollars annually. The quick-thinking Christian fundamentalist who, according to associates, practiced what he preached, admitted that his two heroes were "two Macs": Senator Joseph McCarthy and General Douglas MacArthur, both of whom stood strongly against communism and espoused an iron-willed and unbending conservatism.

With his highly successful magazine, *Conservative Digest*, as well as his biweekly newsletter, *The New Right Report*, he informed his publics about the goings-on, the goods and the evils, and who was straying and who was working hardest for the conservative point of view. An example of the NRR's reporting from the South was shown in a 1981 issue under the headline: "Freshman's Fundraising Success Startles Skeptics." Editor James L. Martin wrote:

> The pundits called his 1980 election to Congress from South Carolina's heavily Democratic Sixth District a "fluke," nothing more than a rejection of the Abscam-tainted incumbent, John Jenrette. In 1982, it was universally predicted, a "clean" Democratic nominee would, with little effort, unseat the freshman Republican. But Representative John Napier recently startled those same experts, in South Carolina and throughout the nation, with what Representative Guy Vander Jagt (R-Mich.) called "probably the most successful freshman fund-raising event I have ever been to." Having raising forty-thousand dollars at the door and another fifteen thousand dollars in pledges, the thirty-four-year-old congressman has forced a drastic re-evaluation of his re-election chances. Such Reagan administration heavyweights as counselor Ed Meese, White House political chief Lyn Nofziger, Interior Secretary James Watt, and Secretary of Energy James Edwards came to pay tribute to Napier, who also greeted over forty of his House colleagues, including five Democrats. "The extent of Democratic support for John is impressive," said Don Wallace, agribusiness consultant and long-time Democrat.[8]

With inspirational articles like this, Viguerie helped his followers keep (and extend) the New Right faith.

From the hillsides of Lynchburg, where the Reverend Jerry Falwell's "Old-Time Gospel Hour" originated, broadcasting his message to the millions of followers throughout America, to the small churches dotting the plains of West Texas, where the individual fundamental preachers spread the word, the Religious Right got its message over during the final weeks of the 1980 presidential election. While the Southern Baptist Convention let it be known that they would stay with born-again Democrat Jimmy Carter, the fundamentalists who had split from the organization allowed that they would back born-again Governor Reagan. And, as reported in *Time*, Falwell's Religious Right was primarily Southern: "His fundamentalist following so far remains overwhelmingly white and heavy with farmers, blue-collar workers and small businessmen."[9] Unlike Ronald Reagan, on issues, he had always been conservative. But like the new conservative Reagan, they counted the same constituency in the late 1970s and early 1980s.

After statehouse rallies in Mississippi, Tennessee, and Georgia back in 1979 Falwell gave luncheons for the local fundamentalist preachers. In Alabama Governor Fob James, a Republican believer in Democratic clothing, and his charismatic wife, Bobbie, played host to Falwell, who prayed over the group and stated, "It is too bad, O Lord, that there are not more true Christian politicians in this world like your servant Fob James and his lovely wife. Too many conservative Christians out here in this world take the easy way out, hide from public office and public commitment. It is time that we stirred the souls of our brethren, shook them loose from their stay-at-home attitudes, and got them out to the polling places where their collective voice can be heard."[10] And at the height of the dinner he looked up from his roast beef and English peas and mashed potatoes, turned his head sidewise in a Ronald Reagan-style pose, grinned widely, and said, "But with the help of all of you, we will find victory at the polling places in the future. I know you will do it." And he told the preachers gathered around them, "If there is one person in this room who is not registered to vote, repent! It's a sin!" By now his smile had vanished. His face was a picture of chubby seriousness. "That is the weapon of the Christian life. It is the only way we are truly able to criticize the government. If we vote, we make ourselves heard. If enough of us vote, our government will change."[11]

The following year Fob James became the only Democratic governor who did not announce himself in support of Jimmy Carter. And a year after that James became a regular visitor to the White House, visited five state capitals in the South to sing the praises of Reagan's tax-cut program, and was appointed by Reagan to the Commission on Intergovernmental Relations. In his own state James failed to push most of his own programs through the Legislature, though when he was elected in 1978, James' high-powered political adviser, Deloss Walker of Memphis, told a celebrating crowd in James' home town of Opelika, "Today our man got more votes than any other Republican in Alabama's history." [12]

Time reported that "Falwell's habit of mixing religion with American chauvinism and military policy does not sit well with many born-again churchmen." Then the magazine pointed out that Jimmy Allen of the First Baptist Church of San Antonio, Texas, and past president of the Southern Baptist Convention warned that joining hand in hand with political organizations is dangerous for the church. But Falwell dismissed such criticism by stating, "The issue is survival. America must be turned around." And he added, "Jesus was not a pacifist. He was not a sissy."[13]

Growing up in the medium-sized Virginia town of Lynchburg, population 85,000, Jerry Falwell was a popular student at the largest high school, Brookville, made a solid A average, and played varsity baseball and basketball. Although his mother encouraged him, he seldom if ever went to church. On Sunday mornings his mother turned on the radio to Charles E. Fuller's "Old-Fashioned Revival Hour," which he would listen to from beneath the covers. Although he later professed to enjoy the program, which eventually led to his own broadcast career, during those days he had little time to think about religion. But as an eighteen-year-old sophomore at Lynchburg College he saw the light, was born again, and immediately transferred to Baptist Bible College in Springfield, Missouri. In 1956, when he finished seminary, he returned to his home town and started the Thomas Road Baptist Church with thirty-five members in an abandoned Donald Duck bottling plant, the soft drink that has become a symbol of his driving success. In his plush offices in the nation's second-largest church, which had grown to a membership of 17,000 by 1981, he displayed the bottles he found in that old plant twenty-five years earlier.

Explaining his involvement in politics, Falwell stated:

> I believe that human beings are put upon this earth with a brain with which to use. The good Lord meant for people to go out and use what they have in a constructive way, to try and stop whatever hell-on-earth that might be awaiting us. And one way He means for us to work is through the exercise of the vote. The more I study the history of America, the more I see that the Lord was the motivating force in making this a free political society. We are not combining church and state the way some people say we are; no, we are using the freedom we are granted under the Constitution of the United States to turn this country back around toward positive goals.[14]

"We are not partisan in our politics," he went on to say of the Moral Majority, which he founded "to bring back the kind of leadership we have been missing for a long, long time." And he added, "If

Jimmy Carter had been leading his country the way he should have been, the Moral Majority would have backed him with the same strength and conviction we brought to the Ronald Reagan campaign."

Falwell walked with Reagan and talked with him and he became convinced that he was the man the country needed in the presidency. The senators whom Falwell and his group decided were objectionable prior to the 1980 elections were all Democratic, and their opponents, backed by the Moral Majority, were all Republicans.

"I don't see why ninety-nine percent of all Americans don't sit back and listen and follow Jerry Falwell's preachings," said a member of the church standing in the five-acre parking lot on the hillside overlooking the rich, rolling hills of Virginia. "He's a strong, level-headed, beautifully spoken individual who believes with all of his heart in the teachings not only of the Bible but also the United States Constitution and the Declaration of Independence. He speaks out from his pulpit as a grand philosopher who has given all of this a great deal of thought. He's not a ranter and a raver, he's quiet in his words and devout in his message; you always have the feeling that he has spent a lot of time with the Lord before he comes before you with his words."[15]

Although Falwell made himself known as a believer in the positive, he was totally against the wrong kind of politics for America, against abortion, pornography, sex education in schools, the Equal Rights Amendment, the giveaway programs of a welfare state, communism, and liberalism. "Every time a country begins to lean and give way to the left, allowing itself to be duped by people who think government can solve all problems, it is in trouble. When government grows too big, becomes all powerful, religion begins to deteriorate. And then society begins to be infiltrated with immoral false idols," he warned.[16]

Yet he also recognized that the New Right could possibly go too far, but added:

> I don't think the people that I know, who are on the conservative side of the spectrum, are radical or foolish. I think we all know that to do what our opponents did—and that's go so far to the right that it's ridiculous—will cause the same reaction a few years from now as has happened to them. I think what we have to do is come back to some reasonable middle-of-the-road position on the issues. There had to be some reactionary movement to slow down the liberal steamroller, because during the sixties and by the mid-seventies, the liberal perspective on moral and social issues was literally bowling its way through, and people on our side had to do what those people did twenty-five years ago. We had to become revolutionary. Once a line

of thought is invited to the table, radical action is over and then one can express his views; so can all the rest, and the end result is that somewhere in the middle of the road there's an acceptable and reasonable compromise.[17]

But, try as he might, his smooth sophistication gave way to a slightly raised voice when asked about homosexuality, which he regarded as "moral perversion." He believes that acts between two people of the same sex should be "crimes carrying prison punishment."

He ended most of his well-spoken sermons with pleas for money. One resident of Lynchburg who had quit the Thomas Road Church several years back said,

I don't question Jerry Falwell's goodness. I think he really does mean everything he preaches. But he is forever and ever asking for money. He'll stand up there and tell you he needs this many million for that and that many million for that and dig a little deeper for the Lord. He's not a squanderer, he builds his schools and his churches, and he lives in a very comfortable house and drives a nice car. But when you see him out at the airport getting into his private jet and see his picture in this magazine and on all these television programs from California and South America and England I get a little perturbed that my money is being spent on his and other church people's luxuries. I got tired of sitting there and listening to him beg and plead, and I just never did go back.[18]

Falwell also did his begging and pleading on his "Old-Time Gospel Hour," selling people Bibles, sending them a newsletter and a "hotline report" and a "special news periodical" if they would only send $12 a month and then $15 a month. As a member of his Fifteen Thousand Club a person would receive a box full of cassette tapes of Dr. Jerry Falwell's talks, a copy of his book *Armageddon and the Coming War with Russia*, and a personalized certificate, all for only $100, which would be renewable the following year.

What he lacked in loudness Falwell made up in persistency and audacity. His asking for more and more money seemed to be a never-ending merry-go-round. Selling "Jesus First" lapel pins for $25 each, parchment Christian bills of rights for $50, and easy-to-put-together, do-it-yourself patriotic flag kits for more appeared time and again in his brochures, church bulletin boards, and in his TV sales pitches.

Working side by side with Falwell, Viguerie, et al., were Paul Weyrich and his Committee for the Survival of a Free Congress and Coalitions for America as well as Terry Dolan and his National Conservative Political Action Committee, known as NCPAC. Weyrich, a Roman Catholic, prayed with his fellow Roman Catholic Jeremiah

Denton and talked the retired admiral into running for the U.S. Senate. He later commented, "Bringing Denton into the political folds of a foundering nation was the best contribution I could make to the cause of a free society and a free Congress."[19] And it was Weyrich who joined with the Moral Majority in the sponsorship of such bills as Senator Paul Laxalt's Family Protection Act, designed "to bring the family back into the legal system of American life and strike down legally so-called gay rights, ERA philosophies, and other immoral stands that should be out-and-out illegal,"[20] according to the overseer of Christian rights, as Weyrich fancied himself.

As an under-forty pusher of conservatism, Weyrich put his finger on the pulse of the Southern electorate when he tapped Denton for the Senate. The son of a German immigrant to Wisconsin, Weyrich was taught early in life to admire the life and philosophy of Robert Taft, his conservatism and his isolationism. Along with Terry Dolan, Weyrich was one of the first after the 1964 presidential debacle to turn against Goldwater and his brand of conservatism in favor of the more radical right. He told free-lance writer Peter Ross Range, "We are radicals who want to change the existing power structure," and the team struck out on its own path. Ronald Reagan, he said, "has made a good beginning (as president) in a number of areas. His rhetoric has been good, he has a positive upbeat style, but it's still early. His administration is moving toward some bad policies. I'm told he will be pushing for so-called 'soft loans' in foreign aid, and that's unacceptable."[21] And he and Dolan and Falwell and others of the New Religious Right heaped criticism on the president when he appointed Sandra Day O'Connor to the U.S. Supreme Court. Weyrich fed his friend Jeremiah Denton a hundred questions to ask Mrs. O'Connor in the public hearings before the Judiciary Committee. Denton asked most of them in repetitious fashion, not seeming to know what he was asking her about, and she answered the questions fully and appropriately, and Committee Chairman Strom Thurmond gave Denton thirty minutes extra. At the end of that time Denton still didn't have what he wanted. It became obvious during that hearing: Weyrich was putting words into Denton's mouth, and the Senator from Alabama was going along with the script.

While Weyrich bragged of Denton's election that "more than any other victory this is a CSFC win," and Denton wrote that the Committee for the Survival of a Free Congress was "the main force," Weyrich was also responsible for other Southern Republican wins. Senator Paula Hawkins of Florida received CSFC backing in the primary, runoff, and general elections, and she too openly thanked Weyrich and his people for their assistance. And when the Republican nominee to the Senate from Georgia, Mack Mattingly, faced four-term veteran Herman Talmadge, Weyrich traveled south to lend a helping hand. In Atlanta during the summer Weyrich trained 200 ministers on the importance of getting voting-record information to their congregations. Weyrich brought along a training film produced by CSFC, which was shown in more than 400 rural churches, encouraging Christian participation in the political process. And, as in the other races, CSFC contributed funds to Mattingly's campaign coffers.

John T. "Terry" Dolan was not unlike Weyrich in his headstrong seeking of Republican conservative victories. The son of a Boston stockbroker, the young attorney became involved in 1977 with a group of youthful Republicans campaigning independently to defeat Henry Howell, a Democrat seeking the Virginia governorship. According to Alan Crawford in his book *Thunder on the Right*, the campaign was "so tawdry that the Republican opponent, John Dalton, disavowed it." Dolan had formed the Independent Virginians for Responsible Government, acknowledging "that the effort was to defeat the Democrat."

"We don't care about Dalton," Dolan said. Virginia Congressman J. Kenneth Robinson signed a letter, written by Dolan and an associate, that called the opponent a "radical" and distorted his position on busing; this letter was mailed throughout Virginia. Dalton called on Dolan's group to cease its activities, calling it "unnecessary and counterproductive." At least two television stations in Roanoke had refused to air the commericals, Crawford reported. He also said that Dolan described the pitch of his organization as, "Let's get rid of the bastards," in his fund-raising appeals, "to make 'em angry . . . stir up hostilities. We are trying to be divisive . . . The shriller you are, the better it is to raise money." And his National Conservative Political Action Committee raised more than $5 million dollars in 1980, but reportedly contributed only $182,000 to candidates while it called itself "the group that spend more than $5 million to elect conservative candidates." Nevertheless, it continued to raise more and more money, which insiders said would be spent "heavier and heavier on conservative Republican candidates throughout the South. We believe that the South is the place where most of our potential voters are located, and we plan to blitz the area during the next six years. It is our number-one target."[22]

Together with the New Republican Victory Fund, created by

political consultant and Reagan campaign aide Charles Black, the National Republican Candidates Committee, and one-issue groups like the National Pro-Life Political Action Committee, it was expected that more than $5 million in campaign contributions would flow south to conservative Republican candidates during 1982 alone. By 1984 conservative PAC group leaders hoped that contributions to candidates in the South would triple. At an organizational meeting of Southern Republicans in early 1982 in Florida it was estimated that more than $30 million would be spent on midterm elections during the year in the South. The general mood of the meeting was: we will spend money, we will train our people, we will organize, and we will win.

The New Old Republican Order

The year was 1964.

It had been a long, hot summer of campaigning across the foothills into western Tennessee, down in the lush valleys of the Civil War battlefield at Shiloh, and back home again to the mountains of Appalachia.

The thirty-nine-year-old man, who looked even younger with his brown hair cropped close above large ears, slipped off his horn-rimmed glasses and wiped the sweat-created fog from the lens.

When he looked up and squinted his eyes down the main street of the town of less than a thousand, looking with nearsighted vision across the gold and brown leaves of late autumn, he thought about his aching right hand and arm and elbow and shoulder. He enjoyed campaigning, but it was rigorous. He had shaken hands with several thousand people since a three-o'clock-in-the-morning shift change at a plant outside Knoxville. He had talked with people along the streets of a half-dozen towns not unlike the one he was now covering. He was bone-weary but ready for the 100-mile trek across the winding roads back home to Huntsville, a little hamlet of less than 500 where he had been born and raised. He was glad he had a driver. Perhaps he could sleep for an hour or so before arriving at the farm where his wife, Joy, who been out campaigning herself, would be waiting with the children.

Just as he turned toward the open back door of the car, a voice interrupted the twilight silence. The young man pivoted and looked through the slanted sunbeams toward the grizzly chinned old man who stood ten or twelve feet away. To the politician, who was also a better-than-average photographer, the man looked like a perfect portrait of these hill folks. He was framed in a halo of glimmering, autumn leaves. His face was strongly mapped with heavy lines. His eyes were piercing in the day's last glowing moments. In fact, Howard Henry Baker, Jr., wished he had his thirty-five-millimeter camera with him. The man would have made a magnificent character study. "Yes, sir," Baker said, squinting his eyes and looking at the man.

"What you going to do if you get to Washington?" the man said flat-out, a stream of brown tobacco juice following his words from the edge of his mouth.

"Well, sir," Baker started. He was amazed that there was one person in the town who didn't know his stand on the issues. It was a stand he had drawn so well and talked about so animatedly that he had been sure everybody in Tennessee would know it by election day.

The men who sat on the bench next to the courthouse watched in amazement. Years later they remembered that the young man began making his speech with fire in his eyes and purpose on his tongue.

For more than ten years Baker had been an attorney. And for the past five or six he had become well known throughout these hills as one of the finest criminal lawyers a person could hire. He had a grand reputation for presenting cases with persuasive arguments to the jury panels in the small county seats, winning freedom for his clients and pocketing big fees along the way. Now he was arguing to a jury of one, though not unaware of the others who were sitting and listening nearby.

Halfway through his speech, his voice raised higher than usual, his words cracked slightly as he made a point. "Do you know what is happening to this country? Do you know?" he asked.

The old man, watching intently from a few feet away, spat a long stream of tobacco juice onto the sidewalk.

"Our country is being led straight to the damnation of socialism!" Baker answered himself.

> If we do not stop the free-spending programs being put into operation by the liberal Democrats in Washington, we're going to lose this country!

And we've got to stop throwing all of our hard-earned money away by sending it to foreigners in Africa, Asia, South America! What do we get back from doing that? I'll tell you! Nothing! Absolutely nothing! Those people take our money and turn their backs on us! If we needed them, they'd leave us in the lurch! And look what we're doing to the Negro people in our society! I believe in every man having a chance! An equal chance! But there's no reason to give people everything just because their skin is a different color! Right this minute, President Lyndon Johnson has got his Voting Rights Act passed through Congress to make sure every Negro person in the South votes. That's what it does! Pure and simple! But I tell you, I wouldn't vote for a bill like that that puts shackles on just one section of the country and pays no attention to the North or the East. They can be prejudiced all they want, according to that law, and nothing will be done about it. Well, I don't like that! I'd do all I could to stop that kind of lawmaking!

When Baker finished his harangue, standing there flush-faced and breathing deeply, the old man stared at him and stated, "Well, you better go get you some sleep right now, 'cause you look too tuckered out to do much lawmaking." And the man turned and spat again and walked away.

When Baker looked over at the others on the bench, they chuckled.

Baker said nothing for a moment. Then he said, "See y'all later," and waved good-bye. "I'd appreciate your vote," he called.[1]

Watching the little town, which looked like so many other Appalachian villages that dotted the mountains, disappear out the window, Baker leaned back and closed his eyes. But he had a hard time sleeping. He thought about the old man who had listened but apparently had not been moved. He thought about the others who had laughed. He wondered whether they would vote for him his first time out. People said he was a bit presumptuous, going out all over the state of Tennessee looking for votes for the U.S. Senate when he could have had his father's old congressional seat with ease. He had decided to hell with it; he wanted to be a senator. That was where the power was.

He had grown up with Republican politics in his blood, raised in a part of the state where Parson Brownlow had been the ruling force through Civil War days, a section that had never really and truly seceded from the Union. The Bakers had settled there back in the eighteenth century, and most of young Baker's ancestors had been politically involved. His grandfather had been a judge. His grandmother, who lived past her hundredth year, had been the first woman sheriff in Tennessee. And his father, Howard Henry Baker, Sr., had represented the Second District, which stretched the width of the state and took in Knoxville, in the U.S. House of Representatives from 1951 until his death earlier in 1964, when the governor appointed young Baker's mother, Irene Bailey Baker, to succeed her husband.

Howard Baker grew up in the woods around Huntsville, playing cowboys and Indians like the other little boys. He was sent off to Chattanooga to McCallie School when he was fourteen because the local public schools were just not quite good enough for the kind of education his family thought he needed. When World War II broke out, he was not old enough to go directly into the army, as he wanted; he had to finish high school first. But as soon as he left, he entered the navy's V-12 program in engineering at Tulane University in New Orleans. And before the war ended, he served on a PT boat in the South Pacific.

Without experiencing combat, which was most young Southern boys' dream—after all, he had read Sir Walter Scott and knew Ivanhoe, and he too had Scotch blood flowing through his masculine body; and he had ridden in his youthful imagination with Jeb Stuart and Stonewall Jackson through mountains and valleys just like the ones of East Tennessee—he returned to his homeland and enrolled in the University of the South at Sewanee. Several years later he moved on to the University of Tennessee, where he graduated with a law degree in 1949.

He gave politics several thoughts. He was a good campus politician, having been elected president of the student body in his senior year, and he was sure his friends from school would help if he asked.

However, he had seen the disappointment on his beloved father's face when he had run for governor in 1938 and lost. And he remembered the same look, the hard work and the screaming silence of defeat two years later, when his father ran for the U.S. Senate and lost. It was not yet time for Republicans statewide, even in Tennessee.

Deciding on the law, Baker entered the firm that his grandfather Baker had founded in 1885. His first years were not filled with the hardships of many young lawyers directly out of school. For the first year or so he felt his way around the practice like most beginners. But he was earnest, hard-working, and eager, and every established attorney in Knoxville and most of the small towns through the Cumberland Mountains all the way to the Kentucky line knew that it wouldn't hurt to help young Baker. And they knew it even better in 1950 when Howard Sr. finally succeeded in politics and was elected to the U.S. House of Representatives.

The next year, after the elder Bakers moved to Washington, the young man met the daughter of one of his father's best friends. The young woman, Danice Joy Dirksen, the daughter of Senator Everett McKinley Dirksen, was a bright and beautiful companion, and late in the summer of 1951, after the flamboyant senator had decided that he would campaign hard for his friend Robert A. Taft for president, the young woman brought her suitor to the Dirksens' rented cottage on Chesapeake Bay in Maryland.

Baker and Dirksen went on a walk together along the beach, where the young lawyer told the older man he wished to marry his daughter. Dirksen, whom Baker considered to be the most formidable character he had ever met, stopped immediately and turned to Baker, squinted his eyes thoughtfully, and twisted his head sidewise in his wise-old-man gesture he was fond of posing on the Senate floor or before large Republican audiences in his home state. He stopped, but he continued to listen. And when Baker was finished, the older man guided him back to the cottage, where he asked his daughter if she had considered a time for the pending wedding. "Yes," she said. "January twenty-second."

Her father threw back his massive head and laughed joyously. "Well, you've figured out all the details without me, haven't you?"[2] When he turned to his wife, he discovered that while he had been busy with politics, the two women of his family had already made all of the arrangements. His daughter told him she had absolute confidence in Howard's persuasive ability. Dirksen turned and shook Baker's hand and said that of course they would have his blessings.

During those first months and years, getting to know Dirksen and already having respect for him, Baker learned much about the sophisticated and complicated work of an extremely powerful U.S. senator. As chairman of the Republican Senatorial Campaign Committee, Dirksen moved about the country, made speeches, met with local committees, and worked arduously in an attempt to gain the presidential nomination for Ohioan Taft. Baker was kept busy with his law practice in Tennessee, where his legal interest in banking, coal-mining, and real estate development earned him the reputation of being an excellent business attorney as well as a trial lawyer, but he also listened to his father-in-law talk about what he was doing in Republican politics. Dirksen lost his fight for Taft but became a strong supporter of Dwight Eisenhower. And other than his father, Dirksen and his politics had the most profound influence on the brilliant young lawyer.

A few years after they were married, Howard and Joy Baker produced a son, Darek, who later became a banker, and a daughter,

Cynthia, whom they called Cissy, who worked in Washington as a television news producer before she returned to Tennessee to run for a congressional seat. Through the years of the children's growing up Baker piled up one success after another, accumulating well over a million dollars in assets including real estate and other holdings. Baker obviously enjoyed the law. He gloried in building up his own personal wealth apart from his father's, which would some day be his. He liked the people of his state and particularly of the mountains. But it was only a matter of time, he felt, before he too would enter politics. He had a strong sense of belonging within the Republican party and wished to enhance it, as he realized it had given so much to his and Joy's families. And, although Joy later told writer Myra MacPherson that politics had "nullified my personality" and "I always felt I was sort of an appendage,"[3] Baker spent much time talking about his possibilities in the future. His friends in Knoxville saw his moving into the political arena as an inevitability, and when his father died in 1964, they expected him to announce for the House. But he chose the more difficult Senate seat left vacant by the death of Estes Kefauver.

Following many other trips into the hills and across the valleys, Baker listened intently on that cold November night when the votes were counted. His had been an emotional campaign. Many times, on many street corners, he had been as enthusiastic as he was in talking to the old man in the little town yet it was not atypical for the people to stare at him coldly, perhaps not understanding. By that night in November, when he talked with supporters in all parts of the state until late in the evening, Baker was—as the old man had said—"tuckered out." And by midnight he knew he was a loser.

But he didn't quit. He continued his lawyering, and he kept on campaigning. He spoke to audiences in civic clubs and political gatherings, and he modified his stand to one not quite so vehement or so radical as he had taken in the previous campaign. He had thought about it long and hard. He had always enjoyed his moments of solitude in the mountains, and he took walks and shot pictures with his camera, and he worked by himself in the darkroom, and he read. He came to the conclusion that the country was not exactly going to hell under the Democrats. When Barry Goldwater, his conservative hero, had been defeated, the world had not ended. And his own defeat certainly did not stop life. He felt deep in his bones that he would be senator one day, and when that day arrived, he wanted to be the best senator he could possibly be, and that would take study and work and a wide knowledge of the issues he would face. In that respect he would need to know the Democratic point of view as well as the Republican. He knew that the old man in the little town had been right in his own way. He had been saying, Go home and sleep and rest and think.

Two years later, after his initial entry into politics, Howard Baker had found a style of his own. He was no longer young Baker. He was a sort of Southern Ivy Leaguer, an educated mountain man who had been to Washington a few times, had a good Republican background, had read some books and put them to use, and had mixed and mingled with educators not only at Sewanee but Tulane. He was married to a good woman and had two fine children, he talked sensibly and straight out, and a majority of those people who listened to him in 1966 thought he was the person they wanted representing them in Washington. By election day he had put together several traditional Democratic groups, including thirty-five percent of the black vote of Tennessee, which was a very high percentage for a Republican in the South in the twentieth century.

After his win Baker became outspoken on the need to attract more blacks into the Republican party. He spoke across the South on the subject and encouraged local organizations to go out and find black voters to support the Republican ticket. He took a stand against his father-in-law on a federal open housing law in 1968, when Dirksen described him as "not kin to me but he does have a legal relation to the family." Baker voted with him on one version of the legislation, however, and it was Baker who, with his newfound maturity in negotiation, discovered a way to write the law so that Dirksen could support it. Given his son-in-law's version of the bill, Dirksen decided to vote with him and the younger Republican senators who wanted to give their party a more progressive appearance. Dirksen explained his shift in typical rhetoric: "One would be a strange creature indeed in this world of mutation if in the face of reality he did not change his mind."[4]

Such mannerisms and ways with which to turn the tide of favoritism did not go unnoticed by the freshman senator. While he was a fast learner from Dirksen and other older, more experienced lawmakers, he also made friends with other young Republicans like Mark Hatfield of Oregon and Charles Percy of Illinois. He sat with Senator Dirksen, whom he called Mr. D, on many private occasions and listened to his pointed analogies about some bit of drama that was presently happening on Capitol Hill and how it might compare with some historical happening. Just as he felt a strong sense of history, he saw the same thing in his father-in-law, who had attempted several times to win the Republican nomination for the presidency but had never succeeded. Baker respected what he saw and heard in his father-in-law, and they never asked each other for votes to further a particular cause. When they disagreed, they decided to do so quietly without causing each other unnecessary personal embarrassment.

As a freshman Baker knew that he had to disagree with Dirksen on his proposed reapportionment bill, which would allow variations in constituencies of congressional districts up to thirty-five percent. Taking a stand diametrically opposite to that of his ultraconservative 1964 campaign, Baker went to his father-in-law's office and said, "Senator, I'm going to be against you on this thing. I owe you the courtesy of telling you. I feel deeply on this." Dirksen eyed Baker for a moment before saying, "Howard, my only advice to you is this: if you are going to fight, try to win."[5] Baker went directly and allied himself with Senator Edward Kennedy of Massachusetts, who was also serving in his first term, although he had about four years of experience at the time. Together Baker and Kennedy wrote an amendment to reduce the allowable variation of any district to ten percent, which would mean the state legislatures would have to work harder to give blacks and other minorities an equal opportunity at representation. Baker and Kennedy used every political tool they could manage, while Dirksen worked against them. The two young senators did not stop until the Senate approved their amendment forty-four to thirty-nine. The elder statesman-minority leader had been defeated by the two freshmen.

Until Dirksen died in September 1969 Baker continued to learn from him. He was the grand old man of Republican politics, and Howard Baker was the attentive student. While Baker generally followed in Dirksen's conservative footsteps—one of his first steps as a new senator was to allow state governors to veto federal grants-in-aid during the Nixon administration—he backed all major civil rights legislation. When he looked back at his own political childhood, he saw the conservatives had done very little for him. Baker realized that back in 1964, when he was running for the Senate and Barry Goldwater was running for president on the Republican ticket, Goldwater's proposal to sell the Tennessee Valley Authority to private enterprise was not exactly popular in his state and did nothing but cost both candidates votes. Baker stayed with the Republican administration, voting for and supporting Nixon's ultra conservative Southern appointments, G. Harrold Carswell and Clement F. Haynsworth, to the U.S. Supreme Court. He also voted for the District of Columbia crime bill's no-knock and preventive-detention clauses. He spoke out strongly against forced busing to promote racial integration, and he backed amendments to the Education Act of 1972 that limited the use of federal funds for busing. However, just as ardently he backed the extension of the Voting Rights Act in 1970 and 1972, and he endorsed the nomination of Judge Benjamin Hooks to be the first black member of the Federal Communications Commission. In all of his stands having to do with racially oriented issues he was not unlike the old populist Republicans of the hill country in the late nineteenth and early twentieth centuries: he was for allowing the blacks an equal opportunity, but believed—as most of his white constituency believed—that the government could go too far, and thus he attempted to balance his votes accordingly. In the same manner, becoming more and more the arbiter between conservative and liberal factions of his party, he opposed gun control with vigor and was proud of his stand when he met with mountain folks who disregarded his civil rights votes because of his pro-gun and pro-strong defense moves when he spoke out and voted for antiballistic missiles and supersonic transports.

During his first term in the Senate he went home to Huntsville frequently. He enjoyed the quietness of the ten-acre estate, where he built the county's first tennis court. And he loved walks through the Cumberlands and talks with the local people. They kept him in touch with what was happening back home. In 1972 he was reelected with relative ease, defeating flamboyant Democrat Ray Blanton sixty-two to thirty-eight percent while spending $830,769 to Blanton's $224,653 in the general election.

In 1973, after he was named by minority leader Hugh Scott as the ranking Republican on the Select Committee on Presidential Campaign Activities, otherwise known as the Watergate Committee, he emerged as the shining light in President Nixon's own party. While Democratic Senator Sam Ervin of North Carolina stood out as chairman, Baker was a stern juxtaposition to the country wit of the older gentleman. Baker's personal prestige and honor shone through brightly over the nationwide television coverage. Although he was criticized for behind-the-scenes maneuvering to protect Nixon, a former deputy counsel to the committee, Terry Lenzner, told a reporter that he "never saw any attempt to undermine our investigation because it was a Republican president."[6]

Baker's weighty, philosophical-sounding statements and his lawyer-oriented questions of witnesses gave him a statesmanlike pose he carried well. In retrospect, he recalled, "Nobody on that committee was more diligent in doing what I announced that I was going to do: that was, to follow the facts wherever they led. Remember, I started those hearings convinced Nixon was innocent. And it wasn't many days [of hearing testimony] until I realized that we had quite a different situation on our hands, and I made that statement: that it was going to be painful, it was going to be difficult, but Republicans were going to follow the inquiry wherever it led us and let the chips fall where they may. And I think we did that with a vengeance."[7]

With his public image more or less solidified as a strong politician who would not allow party allegiance to stand in the way of his fight to better the nation, Baker had shown the American public he was ready for more responsibility. Stating in a speech within the next few years, "Vietnam and Watergate are behind us, and America's greatness is ahead of us,"[8] he believed sincerely that his time had come.

When Spiro Agnew stepped aside as vice president, Baker was mentioned as a choice to replace him. But after his stand to go after the truth in Watergate, he knew better than any that he would not be Nixon's pick—and he more or less silently backed Gerald Ford, with whom he had worked for a number of years in Senate-House-related measures. After speaking out with force for a "new and better United States of America in which all people can work side-by-side"[9] in the keynote address at the Republican national convention in 1976, he became Ford's statewide campaign manager in Tennessee. Although Baker worked actively for him, Ford lost to Carter fifty-six to forty-three percent.

In the following year Baker labored to become senate Minority Leader, the post once held by his father-in-law, but he lost a close vote, sixty-nine to seventy-one. A year later, however, he won the position and became the new voice of opposition during the Carter administration. When Baker called for the establishment of a special prosecutor to investigate the peanut business back in Plains, Georgia, and how it might have contributed to Carter's presidential campaign, the White House withdrew the use of an air force plane in which the senator planned to travel to China the following week. Instead of calling a press conference and lambasting the administration, Baker characteristically quietly canceled the trip in order not to make a public squabble.

During the late 1970s he continued to believe that he would be a good candidate for president. He believed that it was in the nation's best interest to ratify the Panama Canal treaty, and he worked with the Carter administration to accomplish the ratification, although he knew by doing so he would be losing a certain amount of his ultra conservative constituency. It was as though he was pulling himself out of an eventual race for the presidency. "I gave the logical arguments, showed how the treaty needed to be passed by Congress and how the canal was no longer a strategical necessity for our country and how it was by no means a giveaway to Panama or any other country," Baker said later with certain resignation.[10] When he attempted to explain this to his Republican brethren, the right-wing faction of the party came down on him with both feet.

He should have known the superconservatives of his own party would be after him. They had criticized him before when he had supported forceful environmental-protection laws. In the early seventies he had played an important role as a member of the Public Works Committee in the development of clean-air and clean-water bills. The conservatives had shouted and pointed toward him and called him names, although he voted in favor of the supersonic transport program and the construction of the Alaskan pipeline.

On the first of November 1979 Baker stood in front of colleagues, press, and curiosity seekers on Capitol Hill and announced, "I am a candidate for President of the United States. Throughout our history, days of trouble have turned into years of pride through a renaissance of the American spirit. We will recover in pride, but only if we are honest enough to admit our peril." He took several swings at Reagan, placing him with Carter as another with Washington inexperience and saying that a candidate that was too far to the right "will not bring the unity we need."[11]

He was off and running, but he faltered almost immediately out of the chute when the Maine primary, which he was supposed to win, saw him defeated by John Connally. He lost his footing and thought about resigning from the Senate in order to spend all of his time running—but quitting was not and had never been his style. He had come a long way since that late afternoon in the small town in the Cumberland Mountains when the old man had put him down with a curt comment. Yet, time and again he found himself having to choose between making a tough decision as minority leader or pushing it aside and going out on the campaign trail full time.

As this tug-of-war was taking place, political consultant John Deardourff, who with Douglas Bailey ran the Baker race, told writer Richard Reeves: "I don't know if it can be done. We can't make him [Baker] understand that no one understands him. People out there can't make sense of what he's saying. He has a legislative mind; he doesn't understand the process of winning a presidential nomination. He sees the world as a dish, and his job is to divide up the food on it. He can't take his eyes off the plate; he can't look up and offer any vision. We have to get him to understand that this isn't the same as mediating between liberal and conservative Republican senators, say, Jesse Helms of North Carolina on the right and Jacob Javits of New York on the left.[12]

Baker's presidential campaign never again got back on track—if it ever had been running smoothly in the first place. He won fewer and fewer votes in the primaries, and finally, after New Hampshire, he was not a power to be reckoned with.

But he pulled himself together politically, and after Ronald Reagan won the nomination, he worked for his election in Tennessee, where Reagan beat Carter by little more than 4,000 votes out of more than 1.5 million cast. As soon as Reagan won the general election and the Republicans won control of the Senate, Baker called Reagan's closest political friend, Senator Paul Laxalt of Nevada, and asked for his support in the upcoming in-house elections as Senate majority leader. Baker knew that if Laxalt wanted the position, he would have Reagan's support and be difficult to beat. Laxalt agreed to back Baker, who became a staunch supporter and in-the-trenches worker for Reagan's budget-cutting and tax-cutting program. Even as the conservatives continued to attack him for putting the so-called economic recovery program ahead of the social issues of right-to-life, antibusing, capital punishment, and family protection, Baker continued to lead the legislative pack.

The Long-Distance Runner

The man with the high, sloping forehead that had been tanned by afternoons in the cool Atlantic breeze looked down the powerful ridge of his prominent nose at the crowd that stood mesmerized in the waning South Carolina sunlight. He spoke about foreign problems, synthesizing a complex text into language that could easily be grasped by these hill-country people, but not talking down to them because they knew and respected him as being a part of the very soil on which they stood. He had been with them since they were little children, and they had been with him ever since they were old enough to vote—and perhaps even before then. Once, years ago, he had spoken louder and faster and with more zest; now he weighed his words with absolute surety, and they understood. When he told them this country needed to arm itself with mightier weapons, they knew he was correct; they nodded their heads in unison. As far as these people—mostly white with a smattering of blacks—were concerned, Strom Thurmond was their leader just as he had been for the past half-century, since the day he was elected to the state senate in 1933.

Now he was speaking at his fourth stop of a long day, which included meeting with a group of ladies at midmorning in a town 100 miles from where he now spoke, having lunch with Civitan club members in another hill town, and now talking to townspeople who had always agreed with his populist-conservative style of politics which he had learned from the old-timers in his hometown of Edgefield way back when.

On this afternoon in 1978, running for his fourth term in the U.S. Senate, he finished speaking and stepped back to listen to the enthusiastic applause. Moments later, while the sun was going down and the hills were turning cool, Thurmond's athletically lean body bent without effort to pick up children and nuzzle their faces close to his and kiss their cheeks and hold on to a curvaceous coed from a nearby college and press the palm of a businessman. He answered their questions quickly but personally, giving each a second of his time while his piercing eyes narrowed and focused on them—just them—and his ears perked like the finest-tuned professional. When he heard appeals from the people, he needed only to flick his head in the direction of an aide who stepped forward at once to register the request in his handy notebook.

"I've been watching old Strom come into these hills for twenty or more years, and he's gotten better at his politics than he was back in the fifties," said James G. Ethridge, a native of Anderson and a resident of Columbia. He had driven out into the hills to hear his senator talk. "He's more natural with his politicking now than he was back then. He used to step out on a stage and holler some words, and it was kind of like 'We've got to stop the niggers!' And now he knows what he wants to say without getting everybody upset about a problem they can't solve anyway. He's more natural and more mature. Maybe it's because he's married to a young woman and has got four little children of his own with the oldest one no bigger than that,"[1] and he held his hand waist-high and smiled.

In the meantime the old-time race-baiter Strom Thurmond moved into a cluster of black people. He grabbed the big hand of a black man in a gray three-piece suit and pushed his ear down to the man's mouth and closed his eyes momentarily. When the man finished saying his words, Senator Thurmond straightened, took a firm hold on the black man's shoulders, and stared directly into the man's eyes from no more than six inches away. Thurmond nodded and mumbled a word or two, and the black man grinned and nodded with him. They shook hands again, and Thurmond eased into the backseat of a waiting automobile that would take him home to Aiken, a town of about 13,500 in the Piedmont.

Less than two months later, after beating his opponent fifty-six to forty-four percent, James Strom Thurmond celebrated his seventy-sixth birthday on December 2, 1978.

Three years later, after Ronald Reagan had stomped through the South and won the presidency and the Republican party had won a majority in the Senate, he was elevated to president pro tem of that body—the third in line to ascend to the presidency if something happened to President Reagan and Vice President George Bush. As chairman of the Judiciary Committee he wielded ironclad strength and made sure the new president's first choice for the Supreme Court, Mrs. Sandra Day O'Connor, was approved by an overwhelming majority. As second-ranking member of the Armed Services Committee and chairman of the Subcommittee on Military Construction, he carried on the stranglehold South Carolina had had on military bases since the late Representative Mendel Rivers had dominated the similar committee on the House side years earlier. Thurmond made sure the South continued to control most of the power in military bases. As second-ranking member of the Committee on Veterans' Affairs the retired army reserve major general remained the top candidate among the hundreds of thousands of American Legionnaires throughout his state.

In the textile mill town where Thurmond was raised politics was a way of life. His granddaddy had returned to the state capital of Columbia after riding with General Robert E. Lee in the Confederate Army and found that town destroyed by General William Tecumseh Sherman's Union Army. Corporal George Washington Thurmond stepped through the rubble of more than eighty blocks and 1,400 buildings that had been burned to the ground. He moved south into the country and eked out a living from the rocky soil for his family and talked constantly about the way the North never let them forget, putting poor uneducated blacks into the state legislature, which was controlled by carpetbaggers who were parasites in the tortured land. As his son John grew up, he heard story after story from his father, and the young man experienced the Ku Klux Klan, the desperate nightriding of the white Southerners who were frustrated by the power the Republican Yankees held over their laws as well as their businesses. John Thurmond read the law and made friends with the man who was to become the most powerful populist politician of them all—"Pitchfork Ben" Tillman, who articulated the troubles of the times in the late nineteenth and early twentieth centuries and who gathered in more votes than anyone who faced him as he became governor twice and later senator four times and ruled South Carolina politics. Tillman ranted about the "nigger problem"[2] and swore that he would solve all the ills that were squeezing out the poor farmers of his state. John Thurmond was hired as Governor Tillman's lawyer and was anointed political boss of Edgefield County, already known as the home of governors. On a day just before the turn of the century John Thurmond was sitting in the barbershop in Edgefield one afternoon, passing the time of day talking politics while a stranger from out of town was getting a shave and haircut. When the barber finished with the man, who was a drummer for a drug company, the man sat up in the chair, looked straight at Thurmond, cursed several times, and said he would be ashamed to have one thing to do with a no-good sorry scoundrel like Ben Tillman. John warned the man, who challenged him to go outside. On the street the salesman pulled a knife from his pocket. John Thurmond drew a gun from the inside of his coat and shot the man dead on the main street. Within two weeks an Edgefield County jury found John innocent of the charge of murder.

John's wife, the former Eleanor Gertrude Strom, was a leader in the local temperance union and in the First Baptist Church. In a strict household she raised three sons and three daughters, using the Christian ethic as the guiding rule. The next-to-oldest son, James Strom, worked at his chores on the farm, then trotted to town daily and spent his time sitting around the county courthouse and listening to the tales about his father's friend, "Pitchfork Ben." He itched to get his hands and heart and body and soul into the political merry-go-round.

Before most of the new Republican leadership of the 1980s were born—even while Jesse Helms was still in grammar school about 150 miles away in Monroe, North Carolina—Strom Thurmond finished Wingate Junior College and Clemson College, where he ran on the cross-country track team. He read the law at night while teaching agriculture and coaching football and basketball in his hometown. In 1928, at the age of twenty-five, he was elected superintendent of education in Edgefield County. Two years later, when Jesse Helms was only eight years old and four-year-old Howard Baker was still in knee-pants, Thurmond was admitted to the South Carolina bar, and three years afterward he won a seat in the state senate.

When he got to Columbia in 1933, he learned the workings of the senate, continued to listen, and took on the beliefs of his political ancestor, "Pitchfork Ben." In those days he was a Democrat because that's what he had to be to get elected in South Carolina. He not only worked his way into the leadership of the state's upper chamber, on one Saturday during a regular session he entered a mule race with other politicians. "I knew mules, so I picked a long-legged one whose ears laid back," he said later. And he rode the mule to victory at the racetrack near the capital, leading a writer of the time to state that such was "invaluable training for a man who has to deal with a legislature." [3]

After five years of experience in the senate he was elected circuit judge at the age of thirty-five, and during the next four years he pronounced death sentences on four persons after juries had found them guilty, and all four died in the electric chair. One was a white youth from the hills who nearly decapitated with a dull knife the sweetheart who jilted him. Another was a black man who killed his wife and a white woman who tried to help her. The third was a seventeen-year-old black sharecropper who murdered a wealthy white landowner with whom he had argued over work. The last was a black man found guilty of raping a young white woman. Thurmond was applauded by the people of his circuit as a hero after he single-handedly persuaded an armed killer to give herself up. She was Mrs. Sue S. Logue, whom he had hired during the Depression as a teacher despite a school board rule that no married women could teach. Thurmond insisted that she be hired because there was a shortage of teachers at the low salary the county was paying. Another board member, however, questioned the woman's morals. Several days later the woman's husband approached the board member, named Timmerman, and pulled out a pistol. But Timmerman was quicker on the draw and killed Mr. Logue. A jury found him innocent on the grounds that he shot in self-defense. Within a few days Timmerman was mysteriously murdered by gunfire.

Almost ten years later it was discovered by the Edgefield County sheriff that police elsewhere had caught Timmerman's assassin, who confessed to having been hired by Mrs. Logue and two of her brothers-in-law. The sheriff and a deputy traveled to Mrs. Logue's house. When he walked through the front door, he was shot dead. The deputy opened fire. He killed two of the Logue brothers before he too was cut down. As the bloody scene unfolded, an angry armed mob gathered. Judge Thurmond arrived, walked toward the house, shouted that he was unarmed, and flipped aside his coat to prove his statement. Continuing to talk, Thurmond walked to the doorway. Within minutes Sue Logue stepped forward and handed him her gun. Before another judge she was tried and later electrocuted. And the people of the area hailed Thurmond as a hero.

On the day after the Japanese attacked Pearl Harbor Thurmond joined the army, and during his tour he did not sit behind a desk in Washington or make movies in Hollywood. Serving in the Eighty-second Airborne division, Thurmond landed by glider on Normandy Beach in France on D-Day, and by the end of the war he held seventeen decorations including the Purple Heart, Legion of Merit, and the Bronze Star for valor.

There was no doubt in his mind what he was going to do when he had put the war and the army behind him. Back home he returned to the bench, then resigned his judgeship in May 1946 and started running for the office of governor. He had heard the call of higher politics, and he wasn't about to let it escape his grasp. He was a hero, and while the taste of heroism lasted, he would make the most of it. He traveled from American Legion Post to AmVet Club to Civitans to Kiwanis. He spoke to the Ku Klux Klan open meeting in Orangeburg and the Ladies' Auxiliary Club in Greenville. He told them basically what they wanted to hear: he was back from the war to clean up South Carolina, and he wanted to do it with their vote in the gubernatorial election, and they clapped and hollered, "Hallelujah!" Their boy had come home to lead them.

It reminded him of his granddaddy returning to a war-destroyed Columbia. The people had been beaten down pretty badly, first by the Depression, which took their money and food and clothing, and then by the war, which took their sons and left their daughters husbandless. The people were ready for somebody they could look up to, believe in, and respect. And that was what he gave them.

Never married, he was known as a rounder with the women, always picking the best-looking and the one with a hint of mischief in her eye. He danced well, and he held his ladies close, and they said he never took no for an answer. "Strom Thurmond was bald-headed when he was forty years old," recalled an acquaintance, John Jeffers Langhorn, "and he never drank or smoked, but he was strong with the ladies, if you know what I mean. He had an eye for the best-turned ankle in the crowd, and apparently he kept up that reputation years later."[4]

When he ran for governor at age forty-four, he met attractive brownette Jean Crouch, the twenty-one-year-old daughter of an old family friend. After he won the office, he moved her into the governor's mansion and named her his personal secretary. When the pristine matrons of historic Charleston told the new governor that only a Miss South Carolina could preside over the Azalea Festival in that city,

Thurmond appointed Miss Crouch Miss South Carolina and accompanied her to the port city where the first shots of the Civil War had been fired. Not long afterward he dictated several letters before saying, "Now, take this down: My darling Jean . . . Loving you as much as I do . . . I want you to be my wife without too much delay."[5] She nodded and moved to another room, where she typed out her acceptance.

While he was feeling his way into his first year in the governor's chair, where he was the tenth native of Edgefield County to sit, and while he was courting his lovely fiancée, a civil rights storm was brewing over the Southland. He described it as a New Reconstruction in which the democratic leadership was imposing Force Bills not unlike the kind the Radical Republicans pushed upon the South after the Civil War. He pointed out that the antipoll tax law being advocated by President Harry Truman "would take from you the right to regulate your own elections" and that the antilynching law "would provide the opening wedge for federal control of your police powers." He said the antisegregation laws recommended by the President's Committee on Civil Rights "were taking social engineering to the fartherest extreme. When will they learn, as the South has learned, that you cannot legislate racial harmony?" And he stated that the FEPC (Fair Employment Practices Committtee) imposed by President Franklin Roosevelt in 1941 by executive order "would force all business and business relationships into a Washington pattern guided and enforced by a federal Gestapo."[6]

Even with his FEPC President Roosevelt had been careful to keep the Southern leadership under his wing while angering them with such action. He explained that it was merely a temporary wartime effort, and he doled out favors to keep them from leaving his ranks. Nevertheless, Roosevelt did more to impose federal authority on the states than any political leader since Lincoln, and this infuriated Thurmond. But Roosevelt always mollified Southern politicians with handouts, and in Governor Strom Thurmond's office in Columbia his portrait hung in 1948 alongside the blank space where Harry Truman's portrait had once hung.

Truman did not pacify his Southern brethern. In October 1947, when Truman urged Congress to enact his Civil Rights Committee's recommendations to outlaw anti-Negro practices in the South, the brushfire spread rapidly across the old Confederacy, and the cry went up for secession from the Democratic party.

Politically, however, the white South had no place to go. Southern governors, meeting at Tallahassee, passed a resolution urging Harry

Truman to reconsider. But, as *Time* magazine in October 1948 pointed out, "Truman, son of a Confederate father, might have found some way out. But by now he was caught in a crossfire. Northern labor leaders and old New Dealers, whooping for disciplinary action against the unreconstructed South, and fishing for liberal and Negro votes, seized control of the Democratic convention at Philadelphia and rammed the President's civil-rights recommendations into the party platform. That did it. Harry Truman was stuck with his civil rights and the South was stuck with its revolt."[7]

Thurmond had led the South Carolina delegation to the convention. He was chairman and national committeeman, and he had supported the nomination of Senator Richard Russell of Georgia. He considered the support of Russell to be a protest that could help the South and keep it from revolting. He remembered "Pitchfork Ben" Tillman's advice to other populist-thinking Southerners, telling them to think populism but remain Democrats. However, after he and his delegation were seated, Thrumond saw no way out but to walk. Also, as he talked it over with his people, he saw that if he was to have a chance in 1950 against Democratic Senator Olin D. Johnston, who was preaching the national Democratic doctrine to South Carolinians, Thurmond needed to take his stand.

When he moved, he did so with authority. There was no doubt who the leader of the Dixiecratic walkout was. Strom Thurmond led the way.

Three days later the angered Southerners met in convention in Birmingham, Alabama, where they formed the States' Rights party and nominated Thurmond as their presidential candidate. He told the crowd, "We have just begun to fight," and held skyward the hand of his running mate, fifty-three-year-old Mississippi Governor Fielding L. Wright, who *Time* called "as smooth and cold as a hardboiled egg."[8]

When Thurmond, always accompanied by his bride with shoulder-length ringlets, campaigned in Baltimore, he stated, "Those who follow the banners of the States' Rights Democrats are determined that the evil forces which have seized control of the national party shall be cast out. The tides of that great party will flow like muddy water over the sands and rocks and be purified. The impurities of that party—Harry Truman and all his followers—will be deposited like sediment on the banks."[9] Pundit H. L. Mencken described the presidential race as satisfactorily scandalous, with Truman being "shabby mountebank," Dewey a "limber trimmer," and Thurmond as "the best of all the candidates" with "all the worst morons in the South for him."[10]

The forerunner of George Wallace politics—although as a member of the Alabama delegation to the Philadelphia Democratic convention Wallace did not leave with the Dixiecrats but remained behind to make friends with civil libertarian Hubert Humphrey—Strom Thurmond, like the Wallace of later years, denied being a racist. "I don't hate Negroes," he said. "I'm a realist. I know what the situation is in my community. I know what the white people think. I know what all the thinking people think."[11] And in Augusta, Georgia, after he and his wife led a long line through a tent in which a buffet of home-cooked food was served, he told a crowd of more than 3,000 that he, like most Southerners, feared "a new kind of police state with all power centered in Washington." And he added that "there are forces at work in this country today which would lead our people down the same pathway to the total state that was traveled by the people of Germany, of Italy, of Russia. Harry Truman, Tom Dewey, and Henry Wallace [the Progressive Party of America candidate] are birds of one feather. All three are kowtowing to minority blocs by advocating the so-called civil rights program. This time they cannot fool the people and especially the Democrats of the South. The Jeffersonian Democrats have spewed out of their mouths that mongrel outfit which captured our party at Philadelphia."[12]

In the meantime, *Time* questioned, "But if it was states' rights that Thurmond was battling for, what was the theoretical difference between him and a lot of northern U.S. citizens who were equally apprehensive of Big Government?" And, answering its own rhetoric, the magazine stated, "The main front of the Dixiecrats, indeed, was a Southern upper crust of mill owners, oil men, tobacco growers, bankers, lawyers who might have felt more comfortable voting Republican. Would the Dixiecrat party be a kind of political decompression chamber for conservative Southerners, on their way to the Republican party?"[13] Although the question was not answered for nearly twenty-five years, it certainly proved prophetic in Thurmond's case by the mid-1960s.

It was pointed out in numerous publications that Thurmond's appeal was not merely states versus the national government, but was racist in nature. Thurmond allowed that he would not deny black people the opportunity of gaining an education or getting a job. But neither would he encourage a black person to study and work for a better education or job, and voting was the last thing he wished the blacks to be involved in.

Speaking in Montgomery, Alabama, and Jackson, Mississippi, Thurmond shook his fist toward the North. "They want us to integrate," he cried out, "while the white people in the North continue to live separate from the Negro. What they preach is hypocrisy, pure and simple!" And across the South scholars bantered about the question of segregation versus integration. It was pointed out by newsmen that in the North hotel owners did not allow Negroes to register at some establishments and real estate salesmen would not sell them homes in some neighborhoods, and a study by the Southern Regional Council in Atlanta showed, "The South certainly has no monopoly on prejudice and discrimination." However, the report added that the hypocrisy of the North was not a good excuse for the South, adding that it was no good for the South and Thurmond to say: "You are as guilty as we are; therefore leave us alone in our guilt."[14]

Nevertheless, the Deep South felt comfortable with its spokesman, giving him 1,169,021 popular votes and thirty-nine electoral votes. He carried Alabama, Louisiana, Mississippi, and South Carolina, and held one electoral vote from Tennessee.

Even without the Solid South Truman and the Democrats beat the Republicans. And several months later, when Governor Thurmond escorted his first lady to Washington to appear in the inaugural parade, they rode in a long black limousine. When their party neared the reviewing stand and the president saw that it carried the South Carolina governor, Truman turned away and chatted with someone until the delegation had passed.

Thurmond never slowed. While on one hand he was a progressive governor, with John Gunther's popular 1948 book *Inside U.S.A.* describing him as a "liberal governor,"[15] on the other hand he remained true to old-time racism. He carried out his inauguration promise to "streamline state government,"[16] reorganizing the bureaucracy with the help of his legislature. He raised the teachers' pay scale, built dozens of new schools, and appropriated money for vocational education. He constructed hundreds of miles of farm-to-market roads, raised standards for hospitals, and improved rural health facilities. He called for the establishment of a merit system in hiring state employees, a secret ballot in state elections, and regulations to control child labor. Going before the legislature, his lean, six-foot frame ramrod straight, he asked for more funds for Negro education, including graduate schools for Negroes and an industrial school for Negro girls. In May 1947, when a black accused of killing a white man was lynched in Greenville, Thurmond ordered special prosecutors to assist in the federal investigation. Although the thirty-one men arrested were later acquitted by an all-white jury, the *New York Times* commented, "There has been a victory for the law. A precedent has been set,"[17] and a New York *World-Telegram* editorial stated, "In this case, we think it must be said that the South Carolina government made a determined effort to do its duty."[18] On the one hand Thurmond spoke out against allowing blacks to vote in state primaries. On the other hand he preached that "we must be forever aware of the 'equal' part of 'separate but equal.' We cannot give our Negro citizens second-class facilities."[19] However, he continued his attacks on the FEPC, calling it "the closest this country has yet come to communism. It would turn this nation into nothing more than a police state."[20]

In the last year of his term as governor he ran against Democrat incumbent Senator Olin D. Johnston. During the summer of 1950 they jousted like two angry knights. Johnston, a big man with a barrel chest, rounded stomach, and deep gruff voice, gave Thurmond some of his own medicine. He called the governor "a downright out-and-out nigger-lover." Before a crowd of more than 4,000 at a baseball park in Charleston the two squared off in a speaking contest. Johnston won the toss of a coin and spoke first. He turned toward Thurmond, who was seated next to his pretty young wife, pointed his finger at the bald-headed governor, and said, "Had I been Governor Thurmond I would never have appointed the nigger physician from Charleston, Dr. T. C. McFall, to displace your beloved white physician [on the State Medical Advisory Board]."

The white people cheered, and the 400 blacks booed.

Johnston rared back his head and bellowed, "Make those niggers keep quiet!"[21]

And with such rantings and ravings, saying that he hated President Harry Truman worse than Thurmond but could do more damage from within the party than Thurmond, a Dixiecrat, could do from outside, Johnston convinced the South Carolina electorate to vote for him, beating Thurmond 178,000 to 154,000.

Thurmond returned to the practice of law, and it was not long before he was making in excess of $100,000 a year. But he did not allow his politics to stagnate. He and his wife jogged together in the early mornings, and in the evenings she accompanied him to rallies all over the state, where he lambasted the federal government's encroachment. In 1952 he joined with seventy-two-year-old Governor James F. "Jimmy" Byrnes, a legendary politician in his own right, in an attempt to persuade the state's voters that Republican candidate

Dwight D. Eisenhower would be a better president than Democrat Adlai Stevenson. Thurmond's speeches became tinged with pro-Ike sentiment, saying, "I support General Eisenhower. I served under him during the war and consider him a great leader."[22] The Democratic leadership in the state was shocked by the out-in-the-open Republicanism of Thurmond and Byrnes. They were probably more shocked by Byrnes, since he had been a member of both houses of Congress and had served on the U.S. Supreme Court for a year before he resigned at President Truman's insistence to become secretary of state; later he was Truman's White House domestic chief. Nevertheless, Thurmond and Byrnes put together an organization that captured slightly more than forty-nine percent of the votes for the Republican ticket and continued to anger the Democrats.

Two years later, on September 1, 1954, the Democratic incumbent U.S. Senator, Burnet R. Maybank, died five days before the deadline for the Democratic party to certify its unopposed nominee and two months before the November 2 general election. In a hurried session two days after Maybank's death the state Democratic executive committee met in Columbia. The forty-six-member group immediately ruled that under state law there was not enough time to hold a special primary to nominate another candidate. After much clashing of ambitions, while Byrnes sent emissaries to meet with them and Thurmond's name was mentioned prominently more than several times, the committee settled upon one of their own, a singularly powerful state senator and Democratic national committeeman, Edgar A. Brown.

Within hours of the decision Thurmond visited with Byrnes in the capitol. The two tested the water with a few telephone calls and decided that their loose-knit organization to win votes for Eisenhower was still basically intact. Although they would not have the opportunity to place Thurmond's name on the ballot, they decided that he would campaign as a write-in candidate.

No other person had ever been elected to the Senate on a write-in vote. The mere fact that he would go ahead with such an attempt showed something fierce about Thurmond's persistence as an individual and his philosophy as a personal gambler. The Democratic leadership snickered at the audacity of the Thurmond-Byrnes ploy, and they said publicly that it would be impossible because not ten percent of South Carolina's voting population could spell Strom Thurmond—and if the name was not spelled correctly, the ballots would not count.

Governor Byrnes asked the attorney general for a ruling on the matter, and he ruled that the name did not have to be spelled correctly but had to be written in the proper place on each ballot. He also stated that the Thurmond people could not give out stickers with the name already printed on paper that could be stuck on the ballot—the name had to be actually written on each ballot.

Again, Thurmond and Byrnes worked together. They came up with one of the most intensive six-week educational campaigns ever devised. Their workers went out to every corner of the state, met with other Thurmond-followers, educated them, and they in turn educated people on every block of every small town. Most newspapers around the state cooperated with the effort, reprinting sample ballots on their front pages and showing how and where the name had to be written. Sample ballots were sent to every county, distributed door to door and to virtually every boxholder in post offices and rural routes. Each showed exactly where the name was to be written with arrows pointing to the bold print: STROM THURMOND.

Thurmond himself traveled and spoke in every county, outlining verbally how the Democratic executive committee "met behind closed doors to handpick a United States Senator." And he promised, "If you vote for me, I'll resign before the next regular primary and I'll allow you to make the choice. I do not believe a few selfish politicians should meet in Columbia in a smoke-filled backroom and pick a Senator for you."[23]

And on November 2 he received 143,444 write-in votes to 86,525 for Edgar Brown, who later blamed Byrnes, his personal friend of many years, for his loss. He told friends that Byrnes had never forgiven him for being the one to inform him during the Democratic national convention in 1944 that Byrnes would not be the vice-presidential nominee.

After winning his unprecedented victory, Thurmond immediately dissolved his now $200,000-a-year law partnership and resigned as president of the Aiken Federal Savings and Loan Corporation. He was appointed by Governor Byrnes on December 24, 1954, in order that he could gain at least two weeks of seniority over other entering freshman senators. He served his appointed term until January 3, 1955, when he was sworn in for his full six-year term.

Thurmond never forgot his promise to the voters. Although close friends and supporters advised him that it was unnecessary, Thurmond sent a letter of resignation to Governor George Bell Timmerman in March 1956 stating that he would step aside as senator as of April 4, when he would stand for nomination in the regular Democratic primary.

Timmerman appointed Greenville attorney Thomas A. Wofford to fill the seat, which Wofford promised to relinquish in November.

Thurmond, who campaigned hard to keep his job, won the nomination and the general election with little or no trouble.

As senator, Thurmond had already spoken out against the U.S. Supreme Court's *Brown* vs. *Board* decision to do away with the separate but equal concept of public education. "I reject the philosophy of the sociologists that the Supreme Court has any authority over local public schools supported in part by state funds. The Court's segregation decision has set a dangerous precedent. If, in the school cases, the Court can by decree add a new constitutional provision, not in the written document, it might also disregard the Constitution in other matters. Other constitutional guarantees could be destroyed by new decrees," he said in early March 1956. He also stated, "I hope all the people of this nation who believe in the Constitution—north, south, east, and west—will support every lawful effort to have the decision reversed. The Court followed textbooks instead of the Constitution in arriving at the decision. We are free, morally and legally, to fight the decision. We must oppose to the end every attempt to encroach on the rights of the people." Sounding like echoes of John C. Calhoun from the past and George C. Wallace in the future, Thurmond continued:

> Legislation by judicial decree, if permitted to go unchallenged, could destroy the rights of the Congress, the rights of the states, and the rights of the people themselves. When the Court handed down its decision in the school-desegregation cases, it attempted to wipe out constitutional or statutory provisions in seventeen states and the District of Columbia. Thus, the Court attempted to legislate in a field which even the Congress had no right to invade. A majority of the states affected would never enact such legislation through their legislatures. A vast majority of the people in these states would staunchly oppose such legislation. The people and the states must find ways and means of preserving segregation in the schools. Each attempt to break down segregation must be fought with every legal weapon at our disposal. At the same time, equal school facilities for the races must be maintained. The states are not seeking to avoid responsibility. They want to meet all due responsibility, but not under Court decrees which are not based on law.[24]

Thurmond continued the refrain that was repeated again and again throughout his lengthy tenure: "The white people of the South are the greatest minority in this nation." And he added that "they deserve consideration and understanding instead of the persecution of twisted propaganda. The people of the South love this country," he swore.

"In all the wars in which this nation has engaged, no truer American patriots have been found than the people from the South. I, for one, shall seek to present the views of my people on the floor of the Senate. I shall fight for them in whatever lawful way I can. My hope is that consideration of our views will lead to understanding and that understanding will lead to a rejection of practices contrary to the Constitution."

He didn't dillydally around when anyone asked him about his politics. He was a South Carolina Democrat, proud to be sitting in the upper house, and often described himself as "an old-fashioned Democrat of the states' rights, free-enterprise, individual-liberty school."[25] To him Roosevelt's New Deal and Truman's Fair Deal only managed to pervert the name of the party with socialism and communism.

He was always known as a fighter, and he enhanced that image by speaking for twenty-four hours and eighteen minutes—a Senate record—against civil rights legislation in 1957. Several years later, when he was more than sixty years old, he got into a shouting match with former Senator Ralph Yarborough in a hallway outside a committee room. They shoved each other playfully, then Thurmond suddenly reached out, took a hold around Yarborough's neck, and wrestled him to the floor.

During the fifties, when he was lambasting the unanimous Supreme Court *Brown* decision in speeches before conservative audiences across the Southland, he remarked, "If the two major political parties do not respect the wishes and beliefs of large segments of the people, then I can see how a third party could arise again. For myself, I hope to stay within the present framework of the Democratic party, but I shall not hesitate to do what I think best for my state and my country."[26]

While feuding not too silently with the Democratic leadership, Thurmond continued to take part in party affairs and was a delegate to national conventions in 1956 and 1960, although the latter was a halfhearted participation because his beloved Jean died in January 1960. He grieved hard, and his friends came to his side, and those closest to him encouraged his political growth, although he was fifty-eight years old.

During the early 1960s he kept his finger on the pulse of South Carolina and recognized that it was changing. State Republican Chairman J. Drake Edens, Jr., the heir to a chain foodstore fortune, put together a party organization stronger than the Democrats had ever had, and in a special election in 1962 the Republicans elected the first state legislator since Reconstruction. The candidate for the U.S. Senate, W. D. Workman, a Columbia newspaper editor, going against incumbent Olin Johnston, received a startling forty-three percent of the vote. In private conversations with friends Thurmond speculated that Republicanism in South Carolina was to become a permanent part of politics, and he wondered if it was not time to make his move. After all he had been a Republican in spirit and philosophy for most of his career. No longer could an old-time populist continue honestly to call himself a Democrat.

By 1964, after President John Kennedy had been assassinated and President Lyndon Johnson had initiated his liberal Great Society programs, Thurmond could hold back no longer. He not only identified with Barry Goldwater conservatism, he could not abide the Johnson style of government. And when Johnson teamed with Hubert Horatio Humphrey, the author of the civil rights planks of the 1948 Democratic platform that had irked Thurmond and other white Southern Dixiecrats so much, the senator from South Carolina announced that he was breaking with the Democrats for good.

In a fifteen-minute talk telecast throughout the South Thurmond's hoarse but emphatic voice stated, "The Democratic party has abandoned the people. It has repudiated the Constitution of the United States. It is leading the evolution of our nation to a socialistic dictatorship." He said that he wished to urge all Southerners to "stand up and fight to elect Senator Barry Goldwater president" and to fight for the Republican party, "which supports freedom, justice, and constitutional government."[27]

Some supporters at the time said Thurmond had been worried that Governor Donald S. Russell would challenge him for his senate seat in 1966 and that he could fight such a challenge better from the Republican side of the fence. On the night of September 17, 1964, when he made the announcement with a gold elephant pinned to his lapel, Thurmond said, "I can only follow the course which, in my heart and conscience, I believe to be in the best interest of our state, our country, and the freedom of our people."[28]

Thurmond met Goldwater the next afternoon at the Greenville-Spartanburg Airport and introduced him as "my candidate for president." To crowds at Al Lang Field in St. Petersburg, Florida, and Cramton Bowl in Montgomery, Alabama, Thurmond spoke out for his candidate and his new party. "It is time we quit hiding all the communists and the commie-lovers in our government," he spat. "It is time we had a brave and honest and decent representation of the people of this country." His was the language of the people of the area. While Goldwater was a quiet Westerner, the voice of the intellectually oriented conservative, Thurmond was a down-deep, strong-as-swamp-water hater of Supreme Court rulings and a down-and-out champion of white supremacy. It didn't take the white Southerners two seconds to figure out what Strom Thurmond was talking about, and the blacks who had recently been enfranchised by the Voting Rights Act knew they had to vote in the opposite direction. "The little people of this nation have to have a big friend in Washington—and the only friend that can be is Barry Goldwater,"[29] Thurmond told the crowds, and the white majority whooped and hollered and clapped. They also knew old Strom was up there in Washington, and he, too, would be watching out for their interests.

Goldwater swept the Deep South, including South Carolina, but he lost every state outside the five in Dixie with the single exception of Arizona. Two years later, with Thurmond leading the Republican ticket in South Carolina, the elephants made their first major inroads into state politics. They won seventeen seats in the 124-member house and six in the state senate. Thurmond himself won reelection easily. Republican candidates for governor and lieutenant governor each tallied more than forty-one percent of the vote. And Marshall Parker, Republican nominee for the U.S. Senate seat left vacant by the death of Olin Johnston, came within 11,000 votes of beating former Governor Ernest Hollings. According to Jack Bass and Walter DeVries, authors of *The Transformation of Southern Politics*, the 1966 elections "set in motion trends that continue in South Carolina politics. They established a challenging position for the Republican party and a base for two-party politics."[30] From that time until recently the black voter found Thurmond's segregationist image the same as that of the Republican party in the state. And the returns that year reflected a basic economic split among urban white voters, a division that Bass and DeVries wrote has continued.

Thurmond backed Nixon in 1968 and helped carry South Carolina with a thirty-eight-percent plurality even though fellow-conservative Southerner George Wallace was in the race. However, local Republicans did not continue to win by riding Thurmond's coattails, losing seventeen of twenty-five seats in the legislature. In the race for a full six-year term in the Senate, Hollings beat Parker by more than 150,000 votes.

Although Thurmond lost the tenure he had gained as a Democrat, he soon became a power to be reckoned with on the Republican side of the aisle in the Senate. Back in 1964, when Thurmond switched parties at the age of sixty-two, no one would have bet more than a nickel that he would ever see the day when he would be king of the hill as he had been at home. But Thurmond persisted.

No matter what the stargazing strategists surmised, Thurmond became Mr. Southern Republican. He pledged to fellow Southerners that Nixon would be more effective than Wallace in slowing forced school integration. And he promised the people of South Carolina that Nixon would provide protection for the state's ailing textile industry. Later, after the state went for his man, he cursed the Nixon people for not halting desegregation at once. "Nixon's boys are kowtowing to the northeastern establishment labor bosses and race agitators, and I'm tired of fooling around with them," he stated.[31] But he got three of his former aides posts with the new government: number-one administrative assistant Harry Dent became Nixon's Southern political adviser in the White House, J. Fred Buzhardt became general counsel of the Defense Department, and R. Alex McCullough was named director of the Export-Import Bank. Other former members of his staff were appointed to regional jobs throughout the South. And Nixon sought Thurmond's advice before making any Southern appointments, including Alabamian Winton "Red" Blount as postmaster general.

While campaigning for Nixon in 1968 Thurmond met a twenty-two-year-old beauty queen who caught his eye. Nancy Moore, a senior at the University of South Carolina, said later that the tall gentleman with the youthful twinkle in his eye and fire in his gentle voice was "the most handsome man and the most intelligent speaker I had ever had the pleasure of meeting."[32] And on December 12, 1968, a week after his sixty-sixth birthday, they were married. Winning an honest-to-goodness Miss South Carolina who was one-third his age, Thurmond told a friend, "I prefer the smell of perfume to the smell of liniment."[33] And little more than a year later their first child, Nancy, was born, and fellow senators threw a baby shower—another first for him and the Senate—in the hallowed halls, with one politician giving a pair of diapers with a Confederate flag emblazoned on the seat. Not missing a chance to make political hay out of the new addition, Thurmond had sent his pregnant wife home to Aiken in order to have their child born on South Carolina soil. He was at her bedside after the healthy baby was delivered, and within hours he posed with his new daughter. Next year he traveled around the state with "my two Nancys," letting all the people see his wife and baby.

It was during the year before the baby arrived that pint-sized

Newberry College freshman Lee Atwater first met the senator during a summer internship in Washington.

> What impressed me right off was his total lack of ego. He was a humble man. I was struck by that. I think there's two keys to his personality: humility and determination. He is more humble than anyone else I know, and he possesses absolute determination. He has never backed down from any challenge in his entire life. And after that, his philosophy is that nothing does the job like down-and-out hard work; he believes that there's no secret to success short of blood sweating out of your pores. In my years of working with him, I learned more than anything else that it takes living the right kind of life to succeed; he impresses those around him with that feeling that you must lead the life in order to get the good things out of it.[34]

In 1972 Atwater was his college coordinator in his race for reelection. While critics said he was too old to win the young vote in the state where more than 170,000 persons under twenty-one would be allowed to go to the polls for the first time, Thurmond won all fourteen mock elections on college campuses. It was not the first or the last time Thurmond would prove his resilience. "I have always worked to make sure my people back home are taken care of," he said. "I believe the way they believe, and that's what has kept me in office for so long. I am a man of independence. I have proven that I will go with any party, if that party goes with me and South Carolina. My job is to protect the interest of my people. That elected me, and when I do not accomplish my job, I will no longer be senator from South Carolina."[35] His former aides agreed without question that Thurmond was the inveterate campaigner. He never allowed a constituent to come to his Washington office and leave without seeing him. Even if they had to call him off the floor, Thurmond would see the visitor and talk and listen. "If a man waits until election year to campaign, he's waited too long," Thurmond said.[36]

In 1978, when he was up for his fifth full term, he again defeated his opponent. Thurmond was a slicker of a Capitol Hill politician. He held babies and kissed them. He hired blacks on his staff in Columbia. He attended meetings with black preachers and politicians.

> I have never been against you. You know that. I've been fighting for your rights just as much as I've been fighting for the rights of white people. Yes, I stood up and said George Wallace was a good Southerner and a good politician and a good man. He was basically for the same thing I was for: good government and less federal government. When you let the government tell you everything you can do and can't do, you'll be controlled by Washington. I don't think you want that any more than Strom Thurmond wants it.[37]

And he received a rousing round of applause.

To the outsider who thought of him as a racist who broke away from the Democratic party and led the Dixiecrat parade, Strom Thurmond's words might appear incredible. But to most of the people of South Carolina who had watched him through the years, this was another of his political coups. To I. S. Leevy Johnson, a black who served in the South Carolina legislature, "he is a master politician. He is very adroit, very astute, very sensitive to issues. He knows how to adjust to changing times. You may not like what he produces, but you have to give him credit. He gets things done."[38]

His power, which continued to grow yearly, reminded one reporter of a teacher in a kindergarten class at Greenville back in 1971. She was leading her young students through the hymn, "Jesus Loves Me," and she kept hearing something wrong in one part of the song. Finally she asked one little boy to repeat the line, "Little ones to him belong, they are weak but he is strong," and he stared up with big round innocent eyes and sang, "They are weak but he has Strom."[39]

They had Strom in South Carolina. And when he backed former Texas Governor John Connally in the Republican primary in 1980, it was assumed by most that Connally would win just as Nixon had in 1968 and 1972; even outsider Gerald Ford got forty-three percent against Georgian Jimmy Carter's fifty-six percent in 1976. But this time the young men he had taught so well—Carroll Campbell and Lee Atwater—came up with a candidate the voters could not refuse. Ronald Reagan captured the imagination of South Carolinians just as he did that of Alabamians, Mississippians, and other Southern states. And as soon as Reagan won the primary, it did not take Thurmond two shakes of a mule's tail to find his way to Reagan's tent and grasp his hand and join the team.

With the Republicans winning a majority in the Senate and Strom Thurmond taking firm control of some strong spots in that body, George Wallace commented, "Ol' Strom's got the power now, boy. They better watch out!"[40]

He did have power. More personal power came his way than had ever been his. Overnight he was chairman of the Senate Judiciary Committee and second-ranking Republican on the Senate Armed Service Committee, and his muscles held tightly to positions across the Southland, beginning with young Atwater in the White House in the same job Harry Dent once held. He said:

> When I was a Democrat, I was a good Democrat. I left the Democratic

party to show them something, to demonstrate that a part of our land did not agree with the liberal communistic approach to government that many Democrats were taking. Finally, in the early sixties, the Democratic party left me. I could not in good conscience continue to be a Democrat. Now I am a Republican. I'm proud to be a Republican. For the first time in a long, long while the Republican party is really acting the way it should act in my estimation. Today we have a clear hold on conservatism within the party. I do not think the Republicans will let go of that. It is what elected Ronald Reagan president. It is what gave the Republicans a majority in the Senate. Now the party needs to win control of the House. Then it will really be able to act as it should.[41]

As third in line to the presidency, more than any other time in his long career he was Mr. Southern Republican. He continued to run three to five miles every day, do fifty or more pushups every morning, spend time with his wife and four young children, and tend to his business in Washington and South Carolina.

Thurmond was seen by Southern Democratic colleagues as a stiff-necked old rascal just waiting to show his fox's claws and fangs. He was a wily devil who knew more about the Senate than two-thirds of the membership. He wouldn't go along with the New Right boys like Jesse Helms and Jeremiah Denton—he thought they were fools because they had no elasticity, and he had learned to bend through his many years of making laws. He knew that a politician had to bend. He had blacks on his staff, he sat and listened to women's libbers, and he had an agile brain. He was still tough. Perhaps he was the toughest and the strongest of them all.

Some Other Southern Republicans

After the 1980 elections more Republican politicians held office in the South than any other time since Reconstruction. These ranged from senators to governors to state legislators to county comissioners to mayors.

SOME SENATORS

Back in the early 1970s, just twelve or thirteen years after he moved from his native Indiana to Georgia, Mack Mattingly traveled through the Tobacco Roads of his adopted state and spoke to Republican party meetings in towns like Waycross, Cairo, Vidalia, Snapping Shoals, and Plains. Never more than several dozen and sometimes as few as a half-dozen party members showed up at the local cafe or community center. He told them about the lonely times when he ran for Congress against Bill Stuckey of Eastman, Georgia, when he was beaten soundly but not totally, and when he made up his mind that the Repulican party was here to stay in the Peach State. He found a home on St. Simons Island, sold business machines for IBM, and became Republican party chairman in 1975. "I knew all the time that one day those meeting rooms would be overflowing, that they would be calling out my name as a Republican, and that this state would be represented in Congress by a Republican senator,"[1] he recalled. And people started believing in him, those handfuls here and there, and in 1980 he went after the seat that Herman Talmadge had held for twenty-four years. Talmadge had been whipped down by a divorce, accusations from a former staffer that he used official funds for his own personal purposes, public confession of alcoholism, and a tough primary and runoff with a formidale opponent. When Talmadge faced fresh, clean-cut, well-spoken nice guy Mack Mattingly, he looked like the worn-out old mule running against a sleek young thoroughbred. With Talmadge trying to put on a new face by shelling out more than $2 million on campaign cosmetics, Mattingly spent little more than $500,000 to become the first Republican since 1871 to be elected senator from Georgia. He received fifty-one percent of the vote, approximately 25,000 more than Talmadge, with more than 1.5 million cast.

Although he was a new man in the Senate, Mattingly was a member of the prevailing party, and he was given chairmanship of the subcommittee on Legislative Branch, perhaps because he had worked with the Republican National Committee's Economic Affairs Council and was familiar with Ronald Reagan's economic-recovery program. As a member of the Appropriations Committee and Governmental Affairs Committee, Mattingly spoke out frequently in support of Reagan's tax cuts and budget cuts, even while back home in Atlanta a columnist for the *Journal-Constitution* wrote that Mattingly's victory was a "fluke" because of the time and the opposition. The writer added that Georgia was far from Republican simply because it had elected one to the U.S. Senate.

Similar attitudes were voiced in Mississippi after handsome, forty-year-old Jackson attorney Thad Cochran, who had served in the U.S. House of Representatives for five years, became junior senator on a plurality vote. Outspending both of his opponents, Cochran won with forty-five percent over Democrat Maurice Danton with thirty-two and black Mayor Charles Evers, brother of slain civil rights worker Medgar Evers, with twenty-three percent. Cochran won his heaviest votes from the more heavily populated municipalities, carrying only his hometown of Jackson, while Danton got most of the rural white voters and Evers carried the blacks. Serving on the Agriculture, Nutrition, and Forestry Committee and Appropriations Committee, he was shortchanged by the Repulican leadership in 1981 by receiving chairmanship of only one subcommittee, Agricultural Production,

Marketing, and Stabilization of Prices, but the graduate of the University of Mississippi did not let it stall his work. "He listens to more people than either one of our Democratic senators, John Stennis and Jim Eastland, did. He is more open to suggestion, doesn't turn his back on the liberals or the blacks, and he may very well be in the Senate for a long time to come,"[2] said Mississippi Native Winifred Green. A conservative, Cochran was never denounced by the New Right, but the leaders of the religious-political groups did not count him as one of their flock.

Another senator not listed among the membership of the New Right is John Tower of Texas, who ran against Lyndon Johnson in 1960 when LBJ ran for both the vice presidency and the Senate. In that race Tower received forty-one percent. But after Johnson won with Kennedy, Tower got the majority of the vote against an extraordinarily conservative Democratic candidate in the special election in 1961. Since then he has become a stronger and stronger vote-getter in his home state, although every six years the Democrats pull a different type of candidate out of the hat to try and unseat him. A man with a deceptively soft smile and a biting wit, he served as chairman of the Armed Services Committee.

Paula Hawkins became the queen of the Southern Republican senators when she captured the conservative central and panhandle counties of Florida, but she knew she had to work hard and listen to the moderates to keep the crown for more than one term. Winning in 1980 in a hard-fought primary and in a general election during which her Democratic opposition spent more than three times her campaign budget, Ms. Hawkins joined the Senate after a ride on Ronald Reagan's coattails. In a state that has reelected a senator only once since 1964—Democratic Senator Lawton Chiles in 1976—Paula Hawkins left little doubt about her conservative stance. She accepted help from the New Religious Right, embraced Paul Weyrich and his Committtee for the Survival of a Free Congress, and steadfastly voted for President Reagan's program during her first year in the Senate. Pensacola journalist Virginia Gibson, who covered the Senate race, said, "Paula Hawkins is one of the new right-wing people who is against everything and for Ronald Reagan. When she served on the Florida Public Service Commission she got the reputation of speaking out against any positive move toward the twenty-first century. If Reagan's popularity holds, she might keep her job down the line. If it doesn't, she'll be gone."[3]

In Virginia wealthy landowner-attorney John W. Warner had a

woman by his side who didn't hurt in his squeak by his Democratic opposition in 1978. Warner's wife, actress Elizabeth Taylor, was an asset to his campaigning, and he was the first to admit it in every planned tent barbecue stop across the triangular state. Ms. Taylor spoke out for her husband at many of these occasions, and she shook hands, smiled, and spoke with thousands, and her autograph became the most popular from the Tidewater to the mountains. The owner of a cattle farm in Middleburg with lush, rolling, emerald hills and a plush country mansion, former Secretary of Navy under Presidents Nixon and Ford, Warner won his election over Democrat Andrew P. Miller by less than 5,000 votes with little more than 1.2 million cast, although he outspent Miller more than three to one. In the Senate the tall, aristocratic Warner built a moderate-to-conservative record. Within two years he became the fourth-ranking Republican on the Armed Services Committee, chairman of the Energy and Mineral Resources subcommittee, and generally commanded respect among the new majority.

FOUR GOVERNORS

After some forty years of control by Tory Democrats in the statehouse, Texas elected Bill Clements—"Don't call me William!"[4]—an individualistic, big-business-oriented Republican who told his advertising and behind-the-scenes people to "spend everything you need to spend in order for Bill Clements to win." And in 1978 they spent a record-breaking $7 million to eke out a 16,000-vote victory over former Attorney General John Hill, with 2.3 million-plus votes cast. The brash governor, who made no excuses for pushing free enterprise and big business to the hilt, told *Texas Monthly* writer Stephen Harrigan, "I'm a nuts-and-bolts guy. I'm a fire-by-friction man. I'm not long on self-indulgence. I'm a why and wherefore guy. You know, when you're raised during the Depression, there is indelibly imprinted upon your being your impressions of that period. I don't know of anybody that went through that so-called quote-unquote Great Depression that was not tattooed in the process. But irrespective of the circumstances of the times, you have to maintain a sense of humor and perspective." Then he leaned forward and added, "Nothing is ever so bad that it can't be worse. Or better. Think about that." And with such a complete statement of his philosophy and personality, the father of the Clements offshore oil-drilling platform, which earned him millions, showed part of the reason Republicanism had made gains in the Lone

Star State. With the help of a Demo-turned-Republican, John Connally, Clements and the Republicans considered that they had taken over in the beginning of the eighties. "We have gotten the first inch," he said. "It won't be long before we get the first mile."[5]

In Louisiana, with the wildest, craziest, most unusual politics in the United States, it upset few that the first Republican governor since Reconstruction was elected. Dave Treen was almost opposite from Huey P. Long's Share-the-Wealth populism. A nice, gray-haired, middle-aged totally ultraconservative Tulane University political science and law graduate, a persistent politician who lost mostly because he was a Republican when he ran twice against the more moderate Hale Boggs in the sixties, he finally won in the Third District for Congress in 1973. The year before that he ran against Edwin Edwards for governor and fared pretty well with about forty-three percent of the vote. He was chairman of the Louisiana Republican party, member of the State Central Committee, chairman of the Louisiana Young Republican Federation, and had been delegate to Republican national conventions every time back to 1964 when he was a Goldwater supporter. He got his training, and he persisted. His Congressional District was out of Metairie, across the Mississippi River to the west of New Orleans, going from the high-rent district of suburbia to the sugarcane fields and rice patties of New Iberia Cajun country.

Also, Treen was blessed with a tough seven-man Democratic fight that got so down-in-the-gutter dirty that Lieutenant Governor James E. Fitzmorris, who lost to Louis Lambert by less than 3,000 votes, joined most of the other Democratic candidates in supporting Treen the Republican in the general election. Not only did they endorse Treen, most campaigned openly against Lambert. After taking office Treen became an ideal toward which Southern Republicans strived. In Mississippi and Alabama the party looked toward Treen, said he was running the state like a good businessman, and claimed that they would soon field candidates who would do the same. He not only embraced one of his former Democratic opponents and made him his liaison between the governor's office and the legislature, he pushed enthusiastically "to provide the opportunity for each and every person in our state to realize maximum economic opportunity."[6] Though he did not promise "a chicken in every pot," as Huey Long had promised in the 1930s, Treen made education "the bedrock of our hopes for a brighter and better future. Our resources must be focused on the critical needs of education: improving the pay for our public school teachers who, for the most part, have done an outstanding job under trying and difficult circumstances; a system of merit pay to encourage greater proficiency by those who are entrusted with the instruction of our children."[7] He went on from there with detailed improvements he attempted to implement.

While Treen set the trend, Frank White of Arkansas fit the Southern Republican mold. Another highly successful businessman, he was an outspoken conservative running in 1980 against a thirty-four-year-old one-term Democrat, Bill Clinton, who had been beseiged with problems arising from the Cuban refugees sent to Fort Chaffee during the Carter administration. While Clinton had to deal with the problems of crime, an overflow of foreigners in the area near the Oklahoma border, as well as rising state taxes, Frank White spoke out against these "Democratic issues."[8] A native of Texarkana who moved to Little Rock and became a banker, White made an impressive stumping speechmaker. He won fifty-two percent of the vote and continued to speak out against liberal fiscal policies.

In Tennessee Lamar Alexander had been beaten by Democrat Ray Blanton by more than 100,000 votes in 1974, but in 1978 the ex-reporter walked the length of the state speaking out against Blanton's gubernatorial record. The tall, gaunt, Lincolnesque Alexander spoke in a quiet drawl and apologized to the people from Memphis to Gatlinburg, telling them he was downright sorry he had slipped up four years earlier and let Blanton beat him. Not saying much about his present opponent, Knoxville banker Jake Butcher, Alexander concentrated on the earlier race and Blanton's mistakes. And this time Alexander won over Butcher by almost the exact number of votes that had turned in the opposite direction earlier. The graduate of Vanderbilt and New York University Law School, former aide to Senator Howard Baker, Jr., and spokesman for the Tennessee Republican party then watched from the sidelines as Governor Blanton took advantage of his last days in office to pardon a number of state prisoners. After Alexander was inaugurated, U.S. Justice Department people moved into Nashville and indicted the former governor. Afterward, Alexander held the reins of government tightly and became a more-or-less political saint, compared to Blanton's tainted image.

A BUNCH OF CONGRESSMEN

One of the most respected of the young Republican Southern congressmen was Paul S. Trible, Jr., of Virginia's First District. Before he was thirty years old, Trible scurried around the Tidewater lowlands of the Hampton Roads area, knocking on doors, speaking to people personally, and showing off his fresh, blond-haired, blue-eyed charm on a one-on-one basis. While the Democrats battled among themselves, Trible did what was necessary to win in the general election. A hard worker on behalf of President Reagan, Trible served on the Armed Services and Budget committees.

The senior member of Virginia's overwhelming Republican majority of congressmen was William C. Wampler, who was first elected at the age of twenty-six in 1952. However, after one term he was defeated, but managed to win again in 1966. His Ninth District's Republican tradition was almost as old as the party itself. The ranking Republican member of the Agriculture Committee, Wampler, the brother-in-law of Senator Howard Baker, was also the second-ranking member of the Select Committee on Aging.

A newcomer on the scene in North Carolina in 1980 was thirty-five-year-old William M. Hendon of the mountainous Eleventh District, with Asheville as its cornerstone. Not depending on the Jesse Helms machine to pull out a victory over one-time Democratic incumbent Lamar Gudger, Hendon bore down hard on Jimmy Carter's liberal presidency, concentrated on building up himself and Ronald Reagan and the Republican party, and he drove a mule in front of a wagon throughout his district. People liked the young businessman's down-home approach and his youthful enthusiasm.

The veteran Republican congressman from North Carolina, James T. Broyhill, who entered Congress at the age of thirty-five in 1962, would become the chairman of the Energy and Commerce Committee if the Republicans win a majority in the House. A member of the family that owns Broyhill Furniture Factories in the Tenth District, he has constantly spoken out for less government regulations in business and energy concerns. When the Department of Energy was created, Broyhill worked quietly but effectively to attach a sunset amendment whereby it would be dismantled by the end of 1982 unless Congress authorizes its continuence.

In 1972 James G. Martin began representing Charlotte, North Carolina, in the U.S. Congress. A former chemistry professor at Davidson College and a member of the Mecklenburg County Board of Commissioners, he worked with quiet effectiveness on Capitol Hill as sixth-ranking Republican on the Budget Committee and seventh on Ways and Means. Charlotte political observers believed that as long as he continued to protect the textile and garment industry in Washington, he would continue to be elected.

Thomas F. Hartnett was one of Lee Atwater's congressional candidates in 1980. He won the low-country First District around Charleston, South Carolina, by defeating Charles D. "Pug" Ravenel, against whom Atwater had campaigned when Ravenel took on Strom Thurmond for the Senate. The voting public was reminded of Ravenel's "New York position," and Hartnett won fifty-two to forty-eight percent. Serving as a new member of the Armed Services Committee, Hartnett was seen by some other Republican leaders as having good potential for the future, although he kept a relatively low profile.

Floyd Spence of Columbia, South Carolina, had served in the State House ten years when Lee Atwater's Baker & Associates helped him defeat Democrat Tom Turnipseed in 1980. Two years earlier he had beaten Jack Bass, a well-known and respected newspaperman from Columbia who was coauthor of *The Transformation of Southern Politics* and several other books. As ranking Republican on the Standards of Official Conduct (Ethics) Committee, Spence was characterized by the authors of *The Almanac of American Politics* in 1981 as "the kind of man whom congressmen have liked to name to ethics posts: personally honest, but not ready to believe anything bad about his colleagues unless he is forced to."[9]

In the Sixth District in the northeastern corner of South Carolina, John L. Napier, listed as one of the New Right, defeated incumbent John W. Jenrette, Jr., who had been convicted in the Abscam scandals. Again, Napier was represented by Atwater's Baker & Associates, who painted him as conservative as possible. The New Right organizations including NCPAC and Richard Viguerie and Paul Weyrich's Committee for the Survival of a Free Congress helped Napier, whose experience included having served on Strom Thurmond's staff as a legislative assistant for six years. An attorney, he was appointed to serve on the House Agriculture Committee.

In 1980 Newt Gingrich of Carrollton was the lone Republican from Georgia to be elected to the House of Representatives. A persistent, transplanted native of Harrisburg, Pennsylvania, the jovial Gingrich, according to fellow House member Trent Lott, "can be a deceptive politician. Like most of the New Southern Republican leaders, he has the ability, will outwork his opponents, and looks toward a bright future for his party in the South."[10] After the 1970 redistricting shifted the Sixth District from a primarily rural vote to suburban Atlanta, Gingrich tried twice before he won in 1978 with fifty-four percent of the vote. He widened his margin in 1980. A former professor at West Georgia College in Carrollton, Gingrich earned his Ph.D. from

Tulane University. He became ranking Republican on the Joint Committee on the Library and Joint Committee on Printing. He was fourth-ranking member on the House Administration Committee and eighth on the Public Works and Transportation Committee. He worked diligently to help the Reagan administration with the Southern Democratic Boll Weevils who ultimately voted for Reagan's economic recovery program.

The first of two new Republican congressmen elected in Florida in 1980 was Bill McCollum of the Fifth District, which stretches from Orlando west to the Gulf of Mexico. A fast-growing metropolitan and suburban area, it tended during the seventies to be more and more Republican oriented. For six years the Fifth was represented by Richard Kelly, another victim of the Abscam scandals. He was shown on television with the undercover FBI agent disguised as an Arab sheik. After receiving cash, Kelly was videotaped stuffing his pockets with the greenbacks. Bill McCollum was an attorney from a suburb of Orlando, chairman of the local Republican executive committee, and an able thirty-six-year-old campaigner. Serving on the Banking, Finance, and Urban Affairs Committee and Judiciary Committee, McCollum won his race in the general election by close to the fifty-nine percent Ronald Reagan carried the district.

Down in Fort Lauderdale, where conservative Republicanism had had a strong hold in the Twelfth District since the mid-sixties, E. Clay Shaw, Jr., former mayor, city commissioner, city judge, and city prosecutor, beat his opposition 55-to-45 percent while Ronald Reagan won the district with 56 percent to Carter's 36 percent and Independent John Anderson's 8 percent. Shaw was seated in Congress on the Merchant Marine and Fisheries Committee as well as the Public Works and Transportation Committee.

In the Sixth District around St. Petersburg, where transplanted Midwesterners carried Pinellas County for Eisenhower in 1952 and elected a Republican to Congress two years later, C.W. "Bill" Young has held a strong position since 1970. Although blue-collar workers moving into the county by 1980 allowed Reagan to win the district with fifty-three percent of the vote, Young did have opposition. The former member of the Florida Senate was the fifth-ranking Republican on the Select Committee on Intelligence and eighth on the Appropriations Committee.

L. A. "Skip" Befalis of Fort Myers Beach, who was first elected to Congress in 1972, won easily—seventy-nine percent to twenty-one percent—over his Democratic opposition in 1980. In 1978 he did not face opposition. A former banker from Boston, Befalis served in both the Florida House and Senate before losing a bid for the governor's chair in 1970. He was eighth-ranking Republican on the Ways and Means Committee in the U.S. House. In early 1982 he was mentioned as a Republican contender for governor of Florida.

The newest member of Congress elected in Alabama was Albert Lee Smith of Birmingham, who defeated an incumbent Republican, John H. Buchanan, Jr., in the primary and edged out his Democratic opponent with fifty-one percent of the vote. A former member of the John Birch Society, Smith was counted as a member of the New Right. According to Viguerie's *New Right Report* in the fall of 1981, in an effort to show solid support for the president's economic program, Smith "secured 154 Republican signatures, including the entire Republican leadership, on a letter to President Reagan urging him to stick by his guns, even to the point of exercising vetoes if necessary to assure passage of his overall program."[11]

One of two Alabama Republican congressmen elected in the Goldwater sweep of the South in 1964 who remained incumbents into the eighties, William L. "Bill" Dickinson maintained a strong hold on the Second District, including the capital of Montgomery, south to Dothan, and east to the Georgia state line. As ranking member of the Committee on Armed Services, Dickinson kept Fort Rucker near Enterprise as the army's primary helicopter training center and Air University on Maxwell Air Force Base near Montgomery as one of the leading military-warfare educational institutions. Second-ranking Republican on the House Administration Committee, Dickinson continued to be an outspoken proponent of less and less federal government regulation. A strong supporter of Reagan, he won with sixty-one percent of the vote in the general election, while Reagan carried fifty-two percent in the district where Carter had won with fifty-three percent in 1976.

Jack Edwards of Mobile was the other remaining Republican who won in 1964. An attorney, Edwards was another of the strong, silent types who swung more than his weight in the House. Ranking minority member of the Defense Appropriations Subcommittee, he was also third-ranking Republican on the Appropriations Committee. "Congressman Edwards is looked up to by the membership, whether Republican or Democrat," assessed fellow member Trent Lott. "As vice chairman of the House Republican Conference, his power is unquestioned." [12]

In the First District of Louisiana Robert L. Livingston was elected in a special election in August of 1977 to the Congressional seat that

F. Edward Hebert had held for eighteen consecutive terms. The Tulane University Law School graduate won the seat that had been held by Richard Tonry, who was convicted of election fraud. In the district that included St. Bernard and Plaquemines parishes, Bob Livingston won in the regular election in 1978 with eighty-six percent and in 1980 with eighty-eight percent of the vote. With a seat on the Appropriations Committee, he was well established as a Republican officeholder in southeast Louisiana.

Louisiana's only other Republican congressman was elected in 1975. W. Henson Moore, an attorney from Baton Rouge, won two subsequent elections with an overwhelming ninety-one percent of the vote in the Sixth District. An active member of the House Ways and Means Committee, Moore has been outspoken in favor of fiscally conservative programs such as those pushed by the Reagan administration. He was one of the first from his area to speak out for the candidacy of Ronald Reagan in the middle and late 1960s. If he remained satisfied to run for Congress every two years, he was confident of wins into the distant future.

Texas, with five out of its twenty-four seats in Congress belonging to Republicans, elected James M. Collins in 1968. A businessman from the north side of Dallas, Jim Collins was the third-ranking Republican on the Energy and Commerce Committee with a solid base of support in his district. Bill Archer, an attorney and banker, became George Bush's successor in Congress from Houston's Seventh District. When political experts in the South said Bush wasn't a Southerner but a refugee from the Northeast, Texans stated emphatically that he came from the richest, finest, most plantationlike big-city area in the South. Although George Bush's father was a senator from Connecticut and Bush himself went to Yale, he stated that he was from the best of two different worlds. He maintained that his home was in Houston, although he kept a summer place in New England. Bill Archer didn't argue the point. A born-and-bred Texan, he was a Democrat in the State Legislature before he turned Republican and ran for Congress. Winning his last two challenges with more than eighty percent of the vote, Archer, as third-ranking Republican on the Ways and Means Committee, was a proud Republican who saw nothing but good things ahead for the party in Texas.

Jack Fields was a lawyer and member of the Texas governor's Small Business Advisory Assistance Council when he was elected to the U.S. House from the Eighth District in 1980. Representing downtown Houstoners and blue-collar oil-refinery workers, Fields beat incumbent Democrat Bob Eckhardt fifty-two to forty-eight percent at the same time that Jimmy Carter defeated Ronald Reagan in the area. But over in the sparsely populated hill country of central Texas north of San Antonio, in the German-settled towns of New Braunfels and Fredericksburg near the LBJ Ranch, a young man named Thomas G. "Tom" Loeffler beat out a Democratic opponent in 1978 and won with relative ease in 1980 in the Twenty-first District, where Reagan carried sixty-four percent of the vote. Loeffler was one of the top Reagan administration supporters in 1981 and acted as go-between to seal the votes of Boll Weevil Phil Gramm, the conservative Democrat from College Station. And in the Twenty-second District, including the boomtown area south of Houston, a physician named Ron Paul won in 1976 and barely squeaked past Democratic opposition in 1978 and 1980. From Lake Jackson, Ron Paul never ceased to speak out for his conservative views in putting the U.S. back on the gold standard. Not as safe in his seat as other Texas Republicans, Dr. Paul continued to talk about his pet beliefs.

Over in Arkansas John Paul Hammerschmidt had held the reins of the Third District in the northwest corner, the heart of the Ozark Mountains, in 1966. Hammerschmidt, who had been state chairman of the Republican party, kept up the tradition of the only section in the state that had for most of the twentieth century maintained a two-party system. He was Arkansas' only Republican congressman until 1978, when Ed Bethune won the Second District seat in and around Little Rock. He was the first Republican to be elected from the area on the Arkansas River in 110 years, since the big fights following the Civil War. A former FBI agent, this mountain Republican who came to the city to practice law was reelected to his seat in 1980 with seventy-nine percent of the vote.

With Jimmy Quillen from the far northeastern corner of the state, Tennessee laid claim to the ranking Republican on the House Rules committee. First elected in 1962, James H. Quillen won in 1980 with eighty-six percent of the vote. A quiet steadfast conservative, Quillen was the founder and publisher of the Kingsport *Mirror* before he went into real estate business and later became director of a Kingsport bank. He also served in the Tennessee House of Representatives from 1955 to 1962. Elected in 1962 from the old-time Republican Second District, with Knoxville in its center, was John L. Duncan. An attorney and former mayor of East Tennessee's largest city, Duncan became the second-ranking Republican on the House Ways and Means Committee on Taxation. In the Sixth District, which runs through central Tennessee from the outskirts of Nashville to the outskirts of Memphis, Robin L. Beard, Jr., was elected in 1972. Living in suburban Franklin, the former state personnel commissioner won without opposition in 1980 after taking seventy-five percent of the vote in 1978. Fourth-ranking Republican on the Armed Services Committee, he was second-ranking member of the Select Committee on Narcotics Abuse and Control.

A Youthful Tomorrow

When Ronald Reagan's Southern strategist predicted in the summer of 1981, "When the revolution occurs, it will be among the young people," he grinned widely and added, "It has happened!"[1]

Lee Atwater did not look back at the beginning of that revolution of the 1980s. The great-grandfathers and great-grandmothers of the children of the eighties were mostly poor people across the South. They had grown up thinking that the Democratic party was the *only* party that would give the white people and their region a political break. They had been taught that they were from the only part of the United States that had fought a war and been defeated, and the Democratic party understood them, but the Republican party could care less. And in the throes of the Great Depression the poor white people of the South joined hands with the poor black people, and together they voted a solid Democratic South. They had their savior, Roosevelt, and he would lead them to better times.

After World War II, when the men came home from the fighting and the women came home from working in defense plants, when black boys came home to the farms after being in the army and when white boys began making money for the first time in their lives, many of them migrated to the urban areas of the South. There was trouble among the blacks and the whites because the whites thought the blacks should continue to live the way they had always lived—in servitude to white people—and because the blacks were beginning to make some money, live in better housing, see a new and better world, and didn't want to return to yesterday's conditions.

Many of these new townspeople voted for Dwight Eisenhower in 1952. They voted for him because he was different. He was not the same old Democrat their mamas and daddies had voted for. He was a war hero. And, too, he represented someone fatherly. After all, any good Southerner knew you couldn't get away from daddy without finding a substitute daddy somewhere else; that was a part of life, growing up, wandering out into the world.

Most of the South continued to vote Democratic with Kennedy in 1960, but many urban areas where these children of the Depression now lived went for Nixon. And four years later they revolted strongly, using those old racist feelings of distrust toward the blacks, who now believed strongly in Lyndon Johnson's Great Society; the whites went with Goldwater across the South. They continued their racist feelings for the most part in 1968, giving George Wallace the bulk of their votes, but with many of the cities going for Nixon again.

And, finally, the children of these people who were beginning to make a change in their national voting habits came of age in the late seventies and early eighties. They grasped the conservative Republican revolution that was being broadcast by the professionals. They lent the sounds of the revolution their listening ears. They went another step toward fulfilling the revolution their mothers and fathers had started back in 1952.

Not wholly understood by sociologists, political scientists, and social psychologists, their vote was amazingly strong for Ronald Reagan in 1980. Across the South college and university students spoke out their preferences. And in surveys conducted at major campuses from Austin, Texas, to Charlottesville, Virginia, youthful Southerners reiterated their feelings of belief in the Republican party.

"There is a movement among the youth of the United States that is basically conservative, basically Republican, and looking toward the future with a hope that the old ideals will be put into play," stated Lee Atwater when he looked back on his own college days ten years earlier and sighted the days to come. "These people know that the old concepts have to be put to work in a new way. If Ronald Reagan can't do it, they will go with another conservative, another Republican. That is my prediction for the near future. And if conservative Republicanism works this time, it will be at work for a long time to come. Who can tell in politics? Anyone who predicts the future in politics will be wrong. Anyone!"[2]

Prominent Washington, D.C., attorney Charles Morgan, Jr., a former leader of Young Democrats in Alabama and Georgia, said, "Young persons of today are making a total turn-around in the South. They have seen the liberalism at work, and they have been turned off by it. There is too much false about what they have been told up to this point, and if there is anything they don't like, it's phonyism. They are now searching for positive movements within their lives to build upon. If the Democratic party is to survive in the South it will have to turn around for the people. It cannot afford to continue along a false path. It has too long been self-serving for the politicians themselves."

In his days at the University of Alabama in Tuscaloosa Morgan had been a champion of civil rights who helped Autherine Lucy in her attempts to integrate the school in the early 1950s. In 1981 seated in his comfortable Capitol Hill townhouse, he said:

> You know, politics is sort of like lawyering. If you don't do it for the good of your constituent or client, you ain't going to get constituents or clients. It's as simple as that. Look around this city. Most lawyers are politicians of sorts, and not many of the politicians have been all that good at their game, either. Out of more than 31,000 lawyers in Washington, D.C., only a little more than 1,000 have ever had trial experience. *Can you believe that?* I would be ashamed if I didn't march into a courtroom before I was a year out of law school. And when they get up here, most of the politicians forget the people back home. When they do that, they ought to be voted out of office. Democrat or Republican. I guess, as much as anything else, that is what the young people see; that's what they don't like. All young people whether in the University of Alabama or Notre Dame or working at the local filling station don't like hypocrisy; when they see it in politics, they vote against it.[3]

The lawyer, who was born in Kentucky and raised on the north Alabama mountain outside Birmingham overlooking the steel mills in the distance, who carried the banner for Dr. Martin Luther King, Jr., Muhammad Ali, Julian Bond, and other leaders who were unpopular among Southern whites, worked in the 1980s for the university system of North Carolina in a suit brought against the U.S. Department of Health, Education and Welfare. "The students can easily see that the school system of North Carolina should not have to comply with 'de jure criteria'—regulations written by a bunch of Democratic liberals—

when that school system has a higher level of desegregation than most other institutions of higher education North or South. When they see this kind of prejudice, singling out the South the way that has been happening since Reconstruction, most of them know they have to vote in the opposite way. It is up to the Democrats to change their way of doing things. It is not up to the kids. But they see, and they vote." He pointed out that during 1980 North Carolina's predominantly white campuses had a greater percentage of black students than Harvard. North Carolina had 6 percent, Harvard 5.2; and in North Carolina's professional programs, medicine and law, blacks totaled more than 9 percent.

But the problem appeared to be the multimillions slated to be spent for new academic programs and buildings at five of the state's predominantly black campuses, where at least seventy percent of the state's 20,500 black students were enrolled. The Carter administration insisted that North Carolina should transfer programs—departments and schools—to predominantly black schools to force white students who wished to study these subjects to transfer to the black schools in order to even out the ratio in all of the state's colleges. However, Morgan saw it differently. If the white students were forced to attend the black schools, he said, more than sixty percent of the blacks would be driven out because they would not attend college. "The students can see it," he said, and he pointed to the fact that most college-aged white students in North Carolina voted for Ronald Reagan in the fall of 1980 and that most college-aged black students in the state did not bother to vote. "They feel that the big government is fighting against them," Morgan stated. "I fight big government. I fight for students."

The man who was instrumental in taking the one-person one-vote case to the Supreme Court from Alabama, who spoke out against the white apathetic citizens of Birmingham after four little black girls were killed in the Sixteenth Street Baptist Church bombing, continued to believe that the young people "know what is right for them. I hope they will always continue to fight—whether it is as Democrats or Republicans. I believe they will fight for their rights and for their representation in Florida, Louisiana, North Carolina, or any other place."

And at North Carolina State University at Raleigh, Young Republican leader Matthew Barr said, "Students are tired of the mockery of government. In 1980 we voted for Ronald Reagan because we were tired of false promises. We didn't like the self-righteousness of a leader who stood up in front of us with a Bible in his hands and swearing that he will never tell us a lie and, in the next breath, says something totally ridiculous and foolish about the Middle East. As far as we were concerned, Carter made a fool of himself in that regard."[4]

A bright young business major at the University of Mississippi at Oxford, Jeanne Morrison, made straight A's during her junior year. She had done fairly well during her freshman and sophomore years, but with a peaches-and-cream smile she said, "I spent most of those days having fun, enjoying sorority life, going to football games in the winter and the beach in the spring. I had a big time." A native of Tupelo whose family had moved to Memphis, where her father was vice president of a major bank, Ms. Morrison explained her politics:

> My father has always been a Republican, but he never was very politically inclined. My mother was a housewife who busied herself raising me and my brothers, and she never ever talked to us about politics. I didn't even know anything at all about politics until last year when I started dating a Sigma Nu who was running for president of his class. We talked and talked, and all he could talk about was Barry Goldwater and Ronald Reagan and Trent Lott from down around Biloxi, and during spring vacation we went up to Washington and he introduced me to Congressman Lott, who I think is a super person. People criticize him because he's too conservative. But they've got another think coming, doing that! He's a great type of person who will some day be a major political leader in the United States, not just Mississippi. I don't think he's racist simply because he doesn't want to give the mint away to black people who don't want to work. I don't owe anything to the North. I don't owe anything to the black people. As far as I know, my great-great-grandparents didn't even own slaves. They were good, hard-working people, like my grandparents, like my parents, and like I hope I am going to be. Yes, I like conservative politics. I don't believe the way to accomplish something positive is by burning down a building or a town but by burning down old institutions like giveaway programs.
>
> All of my friends and I voted for Ronald Reagan in 1980, and I think we will continue to vote Republican for the rest of our lives. My boyfriend will be a Republican leader in the Delta. I think he will continue to go to law school here at Ole Miss until he graduates, then he'll go home to Yazoo City and run for the State Legislature. And I hope that someday he will even be a Republican governor from Mississippi. I think that would be fantastic. I think by the time we get into our mid-twenties or early thirties, nearly all of the white people of Mississippi and a good number of the black people who get over their welfare syndrome will be voting Republican. It will be a Solid Republican South.[5]

A random poll of sample students at the University of Mississippi showed Republicans at a higher percentage than any other surveyed school in the South. PR Associates, Inc., sampled more than 500 students, sixty-three percent of whom stated they preferred the Republican party. An even thirty percent marked the Democratic preference, and seven claimed to be independent in their voting choices.

Another of the young Republicans interviewed, Larry L. Snider of Vicksburg, said:

> I don't care what the poll shows, it will not have the Republican preference high enough. I have never yet seen an accurate polling of Southern people, whether they are students or blue-collar workers. Southerners are still stuck in the Democratic mold, thinking they are Democrats while they *think* Republican and *vote* Republican in national elections but might still vote Democratic in local elections. Just look at Mississippi's congressional delegation. Until 1978 the state had not had a Republican senator since Reconstruction. Finally Thad Cochran was elected. A graduate of Ole Miss, born in Pontotoc, lives in Jackson, practiced law there for seven years, served in the House of Representatives, and thinks and votes the way most white Mississippians do, and it is only right and natural that he is in the Senate. Our other senator for more than thirty years has been John C. Stennis, who has always run on the Democratic ticket, but he has basically voted conservative Republican; he has been against heavy welfare spending, for strong defense measures, against the giveaway of the Panama Canal, and against basic business regulations. Our senior House member, Jamie Whitten, from Charleston, has been pretty much a Democrat, but he has also voted the conservative lines: for strong military defense, against strengthening labor, and all that. Then you have Congressman Sonny Montgomery from Meridian, who has been in the House since 1966, and he is about our strongest Republican voter, although he is a Democrat; he has always voted along conservative Republican lines and was one of the strongest Democratic defenders of former President Richard Nixon. He has voted against everything the national Democrats have been for and for everything the Republicans have sponsored. He *should* be a Republican.[6]

Southern Democrats remain strong in many areas. At the University of Alabama, where a survey conducted in the fall of 1981 showed the GOP down ten points, Grayton George explained that students throughout the South

> are Democrats by nature. Perhaps many of my Democratic friends voted for Ronald Reagan last year, I do not think they will remain Republican; I don't think that is a permanent switch. It is more or less like voters who pulled the lever in the South for General Eisenhower in 1952 and 1956, but in that same election they might have switched over to vote for Democratic congressmen in Alabama and Democratic county commissioners and city

councilmen. Once the voter learned how to crossover, he or she became an independent.

With a wide grin, George, a Kappa Alpha fraternity leader, added, "There is nothing a Southerner likes better than thinking he is an independent. It would surprise me if you didn't find more independents than great majorities who believe they are either Democratic or Republican." [7]

But the survey at the Alabama school showed only six percent independent. At the University of South Carolina in Columbia, slightly more than twelve percent of those polled stated they were independents. A female graduate student from Atlanta, Marjorie Tankersley, said:

I used to think I was a Republican. My father and I sat down one evening and talked about the difference between the two parties. "What is the *real* difference?" he asked. I thought about it. He said, "Maybe Governor George Wallace is right." And he was no fan of George Wallace by any means. "Maybe he's right that there's not a dime's worth of difference in them," my father said. I thought about it in terms of what the two parties have done and what they have not done, and I came to the conclusion that he was probably right. It is the man that counts. I voted for Jimmy Carter in 1976 because he was an outsider, and my family thought he was a good governor when he was in Georgia. But I voted for Ronald Reagan in 1980 because Carter had been too wishy-washy. It took him too long to make a decision, and then he would try and straddle a fence. I know it is difficult when you are president, but I want somebody there who *is* the president. I don't want to think that he is human and makes mistakes like me. I want to believe he is above the human frailties. Perhaps that is too high a standard, but it is my standard.[8]

At the University of Texas in Austin, where the Republican margin over the Democrats was a bare percentage point, a twenty-one-year-old junior from Amarillo said, "Every girl in my dorm that I know voted for Ronald Reagan. We also voted for Bill Clements for governor. Most of them voted for John Tower for senator. And last time I voted for a Republican for Congress. I plan to keep on voting Republican. It's the party of Abraham Lincoln and it still holds to those same principles."[9]

A black student at the University of Arkansas in Fayetteville stated:

The last time I voted for Jimmy Carter for President. I liked him. I think he was good for the entire country, not simply the black people. But just because I'm black doesn't mean I will always vote Democratic. I want to look and see what each party and its president is doing and has done and what they plan to do. And I'm not talking about just civil rights. I want to know what they are doing about the economy. I think that's the biggest thing young people in college today are worrying about, whether they are going to Arkansas, Harvard, or Stanford, they want to know they can make a good living when they finish school. What the hell am I spending all this time and all this money for if I can't get a good job, earn a decent living, buy a house, build a future? I mean, that's what going to college is all about. Right now, I don't know. When I get out of college in a year or so, I won't be able to buy a house if things keep going up, up, up like they are right now. But if Ronald Reagan and the Republicans bring inflation under control, get interest rates down to a reasonable level, keep the world peaceful, then, what the hell, I might vote Republican next time. If they don't, I will vote Democratic, if the candidate looks worth anything.[10]

Jason Morgan, a junior in the School of Education who grew up in Memphis and worked in Little Rock in summers, said he was not unlike many other black students who attended U. of Arkansas.

When you get an education, I think you are supposed to learn to think. You try to keep from becoming one-sided in your beliefs. Most of my fellow students, black and white, try to judge which way they will vote. They read and listen. But if the economy keeps getting worse under the Republicans, we know we will vote Democratic next time. Frankly, I think that's the basic reason why Jimmy Carter got beat in 1980: people saw his economic programs weren't working; they felt the crunch, and they voted against him. When during the debates Ronald Reagan looked over at Carter and out at the people and said, "Ask if you are doing better today than you were four years ago," and most people automatically said, "No, I'm doing worse." But I was doing better, having a great time, going to school, enjoying my life, and I voted for Carter.[11]

According to the survey forty-eight percent of the students at Fayetteville were Republican, forty-six Democrat, and six independent.

Twenty-eight-year-old Carroll Lee Evans, native of Houston, former marine, putting himself through the University of Florida by tending bar in Gainesville, said:

I have never voted. I don't intend to vote until the candidates become higher class than we saw last year. I guess I would have voted for John Anderson if I thought he had any kind of chance. At least he didn't talk down to the people like we were all a bunch of morons. I resent the fact that Jimmy Carter or Ronald Reagan talked like nincompoops on the so-called debates. I think George Bush is a bright man, I think he knows where he's coming from, but generally all politicians automatically put themselves in a class of fools, in my estimation. When Jimmy Carter made the statement that he was talking to his little daughter Amy about nuclear proliferation, that made my stomach turn. He suddenly showed himself to be the kind of idiot he obviously was.[12]

However, Jimmie Morton, a senior in philosophy at the University of Tennessee in Knoxville, believed she made the right choice with Carter:

The Democratic party has brought the South out of the dark ages of Reconstruction. Without the Democratic party taking the leadership role in American politics, the Republican party would still be playing footsie with the South. For ever so long the Republicans played games with the black voters of the South, promising them the rose garden and giving them the outhouse. Finally along came two Southern presidents—Lyndon Johnson and Jimmy Carter—and the black voters had the best friends they have ever had in the White House. The Republicans took advantage of this, and they are currently taking advantage of it, and they are again playing racist politics. The 1980 election was a prime example of negative politics. They pointed all the key words and phrases at Carter like they were warhead missiles. I maintain that it was not by accident that Ronald Reagan pointed out publicly that Jimmy Carter was speaking in the birthplace of the Ku Klux Klan when Carter opened his campaign in Tuscumbia, Alabama. Of course Ronald Reagan and his smart advisers knew the KKK was born in Pulaski, Tennessee, and not in Tuscumbia. Of course they knew Carter would point out their little teeny-weeny mistake. Of course they knew that would take up several days of news while the newspeople would wring it out for every headline and six-thirty television moment it was worth. All it did was confuse the issue, paint poor old Carter in a corner, and while Carter gloated over being right, Reagan went on to some real issue up North. It was demagoguery played to the hilt by the Republicans. It was quiet demagoguery, and Ronald Reagan played his role better than any he had ever played in the movies.[13]

Ms. Morton, who was born in Huntington, West Virginia, and studied at Ohio University before transferring to Tennessee, said she did not believe the Republican party would become a permanent fixture in the South.

In this part of Tennessee, where Reconstruction took place while the rest of the South was still fighting the Civil War, Republicanism is a part of history. It is very ingrained into the philosophy of the hill country people, who never owned slaves in the beginning and had no use for slavery. They sort of look down their noses at the rest of the South. I think that here, where Senator Howard Baker is as strong as Jesus, the Republican party will never go away. But let's face it, with all the influx of Northern workers, engineers, college professors, construction people, and executives from the Midwest and the East into the Sun Belt, there will become a two-party system. But I do not think the Republican party will move in and take over. First of all, seeing the obvious coming, the old political bosses will become stronger than before. They will get together just like they did after the Civil War, when Yankee Reconstructionists brought their carpetbag governments with them, and they will become more unyielding than before. And tied in with them now will be the black politicians who have also gained strength with their people through the Democratic party. They will not allow their people to escape and run to the Republicans. That simply will not happen. When push comes to shove, the blacks and the whites of the South will join hands to fight the outsiders. And that's still the way they view Republicans: as outsiders.[14]

A twenty-one-year-old English major at the University of North Carolina at Chapel Hill pointed at passersby on the main street next to the old, brick-building campus:

Not ten percent of the average college-aged people in the United States give one hoot in hell about politics. They could care less about who the president is, as long as he keeps us out of war and lets these people keep on going to school. Most campuses—and I've been to four as a student—are filled with people who are completely apathetic about the state of the world. They care about drinking beer, screwing around, making their grades, and getting a little kinky on Saturday night. And these things that fill their minds do not necessarily come in that line of order. I think maybe the kinky is first, the drinking beer is second, the screwing around is third, etcetera, etcetera.[15]

Jonathan McAdams, who said that he was writing a novel about "the know-nothing, do-nothing students of my generation," is the son of a Washington attorney and a veteran of Georgetown University and the University of Virginia. He continued his criticism:

Not one dorm or fraternity house out of fifteen can you find a political discussion at any nine P.M. You're lucky to find talk about literature or philosophy, much less politics. Who the hell is Ronald Reagan other than an actor who has become president? That's what he is. That's what these folks know and care about. If he gets us some money or something, he's good. If he takes money away from us, he's bad. I don't think people of my generation think anything about race anymore. They look at a black, they see a black; they don't turn green around the ears or anything, it's just natural to be around people of different colors. I don't think the South is Republican or Democratic, it's just south of north; it's geography.[16]

Campus coordinator for Young Republicans Max Graham of Emory University in Atlanta said that he and most of the youthful Republicans that he knew "will have to go along with Kevin Phillips' 'Emerging Republican Majority.' "

We think that Phillips was right in 1969. He was right on target when he said that the Republican party would continue to thrive for the rest of the twentieth century—in the South and the West and most of the Midwest. It was not his fault that Richard Nixon and Watergate interrupted the logical progress and put Jimmy Carter in there for a short period of time, then he sealed it for the Republicans in the South. The only thing that will stop Southern Republicans from becoming the dominant party in the region in the next twenty years is the people and the organization itself. If it turns inward and is not responsive to the people, it will lose. But I believe the GOP today is a grass-roots movement in the South, not a country club thing like it was in the distant past, and the people who sit around in coffee shops, greasy-spoon eateries, bars down on the stateline, and your everyday meeting places are no longer afraid to speak out and say, "Look at me, I'm a Republican," and he's no longer viewed as a freak. He's a real live human being. Then those other people who don't think about it much one way or another until somebody asks them, they look at themselves in the mirror and say, "You know, that doesn't sound too bad." And before long there's this long echo heard all the way across the South: "I'm a Republican," "I'm a Republican," "I'm a Republican."[17]

South Carolina Congressman Carroll Campbell, whose shaggy-short, sandy hair and wide-open, bright eyes and rugged good looks made him appear five or six years younger than his forty years, was still attending night classes one day a week in the autumn of 1981, going after a master's degree in political science. He expressed strong belief in the youth of the South, who "today are not interested in tearing down; they're interested in building up and being a part of something positive. They've had an awful lot of bad leadership for a long time." As the state legislator who introduced a bill to lower the voting age in his state to eighteen, he became a champion of Democratic and Republican young people.

I ran all over the state speaking at colleges and universities and high schools, and I watched the attitude of young people change. For a while the only Republicans you saw were the ones who couldn't go anywhere else. Then you began to see them out there working, growing with enthusiasm. They were still outnumbered, but slowly and surely we began to make a move. That's where you have to get your people, from the youth, from high schools. I go to high schools all the time. The problem we [conservative Republicans] have in most colleges and universities and high schools is with the liberal professors. Most of them are active, practicing Democrats. They start any assumption with the belief that everybody should be a liberal Democrat. When I speak in many hotbeds of the Democratic party, the way I did when Ronald Reagan was running for president, afterward many of the kids came up to me and said, "You know, I didn't know that," or "I never have heard that before, it's interesting," and there is this interest. You can see it coming out.[18]

Like the generations that preceded them, the voting patterns of the new Southern electorate continued to fluctuate. As their fathers and mothers had broken with the historical trends, it appeared that no absolute political label could be attached to the new voters.

Afterword

The author has made no predictions concerning the future of the Republican party in the South. Many of the Republicans interviewed expressed a positive attitude, thinking that House seats will be picked up, governor's chairs will be won, mayoralties and city council positions will be gained.

In my travels around the South I discovered more and more Republican organizations becoming stronger and stronger, while most of the Democratic groups had a frazzled membership, people grasping for a new hold on an old rope.

Needless to say, the Democratic party was still strong in the South—particularly among the local and state factions. There was an element of enthusiasm among the people who talked about rebuilding. But the tightly knit organization that once controlled the Deep South with an iron fist no longer existed.

Republicans were not simply country club politicians or peckerwood plutocrats; the individuals discussed meaningful political advances made against adversity. Many were young people looking toward a bright future of progressive Republicanism. Others had already tied their futures to the New Right leaders and saw conservatism as tomorrow's hope.

One thing was certain, as they always used to say around the courthouse squares: Politics are going to be interesting this year.

Notes

1 The First Republican

The first chapter is written entirely from the author's memory from childhood with the help of his mother, Mrs. Lee Able Greenhaw Brown. A portion also came from the remembrances of the author's two aunts, Mrs. Ida Greenhaw Taylor and Miss Lucy Mae Greenhaw of Town Creek, Alabama.

2 Groundwork for a Winner

1. Interview with Senator Jesse Helms, *Charlotte* (N.C.) *Observer*, July 23, 1978.
2. A. Wigfall Green, *The Man Bilbo*. Baton Rouge: Louisiana State Univ. Press, 1963.
3. Speech by Ronald Reagan, Kiwanis Club, Clemson, S.C., April 1966.
4. *Orlando* (Fla.) *Sentinel-Star*, June 23, 1967.
5. Wayne Greenhaw, *Watch Out for George Wallace*. Englewood Cliffs, N.J.: Prentice-Hall, 1976.
6. M. Stanton Evans, *The Future of Conservatism*. New York: Holt, Rinehart and Winston, 1968.

3 A Mixture of Madness

1. M.B. Schnapper, *Grand Old Party: The First Hundred Years of the Republican Party*. Washington, D.C.: Public Affairs Press, 1955.
2. Ibid.
3. Ibid.
4. John Hope Franklin, *The Militant South*. Cambridge, Mass.: Harvard Univ. Press, 1956.
5. Ibid.
6. Schnapper, op. cit.
7. Ibid.
8. Francis Butler Simkins, *The South Old and New: A History 1820–1947*. New York: Alfred A. Knopf, 1947.
9. J. Langford Baggett, *Southern Political Dissidents*. Privately published doctorial dissertation, Jackson State University, Mississippi, 1954.
10. Hanes Walton, *Black Republicans: The Politics of the Black and Tans*. Metuchen, N.J.: Scarecrow Press, 1975.
11. Benjamin Quarles, *Lincoln and the Negro*. New York: Oxford Univ. Press, 1962.
12. Walton, op. cit.
13. Simkins, op. cit.
14. Ibid.
15. Ibid.
16. Ibid.
17. Frank Luther Mott, *American Journalism: A History 1690–1960*. New York: Macmillan, 1962.
18. Ellis Merton Coulter, *The South During Reconstruction*. Baton Rouge: Louisiana State Univ. Press, 1947.
19. Ibid.
20. Simkins, op. cit.

4 Republican Takeover

1. Hanes Walton, *Black Republicans: The Politics of the Blacks and Tans*. Metuchen, N.J.: Scarecrow Press, 1975.
2. Ibid.
3. Ibid.
4. Ibid.
5. Sarah Woolfolk Wiggins, *The Scalawag in Alabama Politics:* 1865–1881, University, Ala.: Univ. of Alabama Press, 1977.
6. James S. Pike, *The Prostrate State: South Carolina Under Negro Government*. New York: The New Edition, 1935.
7. M.B. Schnapper, *Grand Old Party: The First Hundred Years of the Republican Party*. Washington, D.C.: Public Affairs Press, 1955.
8. Schnapper, op. cit.
9. C. Vann Woodward, *Origins of the New South 1877–1913*. Baton Rouge: Louisiana State Univ. Press, 1951.
10. Walton, op. cit.

5 Compromised Reconstruction

1. M.B. Schnapper, *Grand Old Party: The First Hundred Years of the Republican Party*. Washington, D.C.: Public Affairs Press, 1955.
2. George Brown Tindall, *The Disruption of the Solid South*. Athens: Univ. of Georgia Press, 1972.
3. Ibid.
4. Ibid.
5. Ibid.
6. *New York Times*, December 18, 1887.
7. Tindall, op. cit.
8. Francis Butler Simkins, *The South Old and New: A History 1820–1947*. New York: Alfred A. Knopf, 1947.
9. Allan A. Michie and Frank Rhylick, *Dixie Demagogues*. New York: Vanguard Press, 1939.
10. Tindall, op. cit.
11. Ibid.
12. *New York Times*, May 3, 1901.
13. The official minutes of the Alabama Constitutional Convention, Montgomery, Alabama, 1901.
14. Ibid.
15. Robert P. Steed, Laurence W. Moreland, and Tod A. Baker (eds.), *Party Politics in the South*. New York: Praeger, 1980.
16. Schnapper, op. cit.
17. Ibid.

6 A New Division

1. M.B. Schnapper, *Grand Old Party: The First Hundred Years of the Republican Party*. Washington, D.C.: Public Affairs Press, 1955.
2. Ibid.
3. George Brown Tindall, *The Disruption of the Solid South*. Athens: Univ. of Georgia Press, 1972.
4. Francis Butler Simkins, *The South Old and New: A History 1820–1947*. New York: Alfred A. Knopf, 1947.
5. Ibid.
6. *New York Times*, July 15, 1948.
7. *New York Times*, July 18, 1948.
8. *New York Times*, November 6, 1952.
9. *U.S. News and World Report*, November 19, 1954.
10. *New York Times*, July 13, 1960.
11. *New York Times*, November 10, 1960.
12. *New York Times*, September 17, 1963.
13. *New York Times*, July 17, 1964.
14. *The Nation*, February 1965.
15. *New York Times*, May 10, 1964.
16. Wayne Greenhaw, *Watch Out for George Wallace*. Englewood Cliffs, N.J.: Prentice-Hall, 1976.

17. *New York Times*, August 23, 1964.
18. *New York Times*, September 17, 1964.
19. *New York Times*, September 18, 1964.
20. *New York Times*, November 5, 1964.
21. *The Alabama Journal*, November 1964.
22. *Syracuse Herald-Journal*, November 6, 1964.
23. *New York Times*, November 8, 1964.
24. Ibid.
25. *New York Times*, November 11, 1964.

7 Enter: The Good Guy

1. Nick Thimmesch, *The Condition of Republicanism*. New York: W.W. Norton, 1968.
2. Ibid.
3. Ibid.
4. Ibid.
5. Ronald Reagan and Richard C. Hubler, *Where's the Rest of Me?* New York: Elsevier-Dutton, 1965.
6. *Los Angeles Times*, July 1968.
7. Reagan and Hubler, op. cit.
8. Ibid.
9. Thimmesch, op. cit.
10. Ibid.
11. Reagan and Hubler, op. cit.
12. Ibid.
13. Author interview with William J. Mooney, Atlanta, Georgia, April 14, 1981.
14. *San Francisco Examiner*, June 1966.
15. *The Sacramento Bee*, April 1966.
16. Thimmesch, op. cit.
17. *New York Times*, June 9, 1966.

8 Dixie Republicans Rise Again

1. Author interview by telephone, November 1966; *The Alabama Journal*, Montgomery, Alabama.
2. *St. Petersburg Times*, August 1966.
3. Author interview by telephone.
4. *The Nation*, May 15, 1967.
5. *Harper's*, May 1968
6. *Time*, December 15, 1967.
7. *Saturday Evening Post*, July 29, 1967.
8. Ibid.
9. *Time*, December 15, 1967.
10. *The Nation*, May 15, 1967.
11. *Time*, August 18, 1967.

9 The Southern Strategist

1. *New York Times*, August 8, 1968.
2. Wayne Greenhaw, *Watch Out for George Wallace*. Englewood Cliffs, N.J.: Prentice-Hall, 1976.
3. Private conversation between author and source who wished to remain anonymous.
4. *New York Times Sunday Magazine*, May 17, 1970.
5. Kevin P. Phillips, *The Emerging Republican Majority*. New Rochelle, N.Y.: Arlington House, 1969.
6. Kevin P. Phillips, *Mediacracy: American Parties and Politics in the Communications Age*. Garden City, N.Y.: Doubleday, 1975.
7. *New York Times Sunday Magazine*, May 17, 1970.
8. Speech, Harvard University, November 1972.
9. *New York Times Sunday Magazine*, May 17, 1970.
10. Phillips, *The Emerging Republican Majority*, op. cit.
11. George Brown Tindall, *The Disruption of the Solid South*. Athens: Univ. of Georgia Press, 1972.
12. Phillips, *The Emerging Republican Majority*, op. cit.
13. Author interview with Charles Morgan, Jr., Washington, D.C., June 1981.
14. *Anaheim* (Calif.) *Bulletin*, January 1979.
15. *New York Times Sunday Magazine*, May 17, 1970.
16. Ibid.

10 A Conversion to Republicanism

1. *New York Times*, November 7, 1968.
2. *New York Times*, December 7, 1969.
3. Ibid.
4. *Nashville Tennessean*, February 1970.
5. *New York Post*, February 1970.
6. Interview with author, Birmingham, Alabama, July 3, 1981.
7. Ibid.
8. Ibid.
9. Statement of Principle, House of Representatives, Montgomery, Alabama, January 12, 1966.
10. Ibid.
11. Interview with author, Birmingham, Alabama, July 3, 1981.
12. Ibid.
13. Speech to Alabama Republican party, "The Spirit of 1966: Alabama Conservatism and Political Conversion," February 1966.
14. Interview with author, August 1981.
15. Speech to Alabama Republican party, "The Spirit of 1966: Alabama Conservatism and Political Conversion," February 1966.
16. Interview with author, Montgomery, Alabama, September 1981.
17. Interview with author, Birmingham, Alabama, July 3, 1981.
18. Ibid.

11 Mississippi by a Mile

1. *New York Times*, August 6, 1971.
2. Interview with author, Washington, D.C., June 16, 1981.
3. Ibid.
4. Ibid.
5. Interview with author, Washington, D.C., June 16, 1981.
6. *Washington Post*, April 14, 1981.
7. Ibid.
8. Telephone interview with author, July 14, 1981.
9. Interview with author, Washington, D.C., June 16, 1981.
10. Ibid.
11. Ibid.
12. Ibid.

12 A Kinetic Chaos

1. *New York Times*, November 7, 1974.
2. Correspondence with author, June 1978.
3. Correspondence with President Nixon, June 1978.
4. Ibid.
5. Correspondence with author, June 1978.
6. Author correspondence with President Nixon, June 1978.
7. *New York Times*, March 9, 1975.
8. *New York Times*, August 19, 1976.
9. *Raleigh* (N.C.) *Observer*, August 1976.

13 New Southern Strategist

1. All quotations from Lee Atwater in this chapter are from an interview with author, Washington, D.C., July 28, 1981.
2. Interview with author, Charleston, S.C., August 23, 1981.
3. Interview with author, Washington, D.C., July 28, 1981.
4. *Charleston* (S.C.) *News and Courier*, November 1980.
5. *Columbia* (S.C.) *Evening Sun*, October 1980.

14 Marching toward Victory

1. All quotations from Carroll Campbell in this chapter are from an interview with author, Washington, D.C., September 29, 1981.

2. Telephone interview with author, October 7, 1981.
3. Telephone interview with author, October 8, 1981.
4. Telephone interview with author, October 9, 1981.
5. Telephone interview with author, October 7, 1981.
6. Spartanburg (S.C.) *Herald*, May 1981.
7. *Charleston* (S.C.) *Evening Post*, May 1981.
8. Telephone interview with author, October 8, 1981.
9. Press release, Congressman's Washington office, August 3, 1981.
10. *Washington Post*, September 12, 1981.

15 Jesse the Juggernaut

1. *Raleigh* (N.C.) *Observer*, June 1978.
2. Interview with author, Monroe, North Carolina, June 7, 1981.
3. *Time*, September 14, 1981.
4. Jesse Helms Archives, Univ. of North Carolina, Chapel Hill.
5. Telephone interview with author, July 18, 1981.
6. Jesse Helms, *When Free Men Shall Stand.* Grand Rapids, Mich.: Zondervan, 1976.
7. Ibid.
8. *Time*, September 14, 1981.
9. Telephone interview with author, September 22, 1981.
10. Ibid.
11. Interview with author, Montgomery, Alabama, September 1981.
12. *Time*, September 14, 1981.
13. Ibid.
14. *The Wall Street Journal*, July 1981.
15. Video tape, PTL Club, October 1978; also reported in *Charlotte* (N.C.) *Observer*, October 1978.
16. Interview with author, Raleigh, North Carolina, June 8, 1981.
17. Congressional Record, October 1975.
18. *The Alabama Journal*, June 1978.
19. *Newsweek*, September 28, 1981.
20. Speech, Greensboro, South Carolina, October 1978.
21. *Newsweek*, September 28, 1981.
22. *Congressional Record*, October 1981.
23. Associated Press, October 1981.
24. *The New Yorker*, July 20, 1981.
25. Interview with author, Washington, D.C., June 14, 1981.
26. *Time*, September 14, 1981.
27. Syndicated column, September 1978.
28. Helms, op. cit.
29. Speech, Winston-Salem, North Carolina, October 1978.

16 The Way to the Top

1. *Time*, September 14, 1981.
2. *Greensboro Daily News*, October 1980.
3. *Charlotte* (N.C.) *Observer*, December 1974.

4. *Charlotte* (N.C.) *Observer*, March 1977.
5. *Greensboro Daily News*, October 1980.
6. *Conservative Digest*, December 1980.
7. *Greensboro Daily News*, October 1980.
8. *Tarheel*, January 1981.
9. *Greensboro Daily News*, October 1980.
10. Ibid.
11. Ibid.
12. Telephone interview with author, October 21, 1981; also Richard A. Viguerie, *The New Right: We're Ready to Lead*. Falls Church, Va.: The Viguerie Company, 1981.
13. *Charlotte* (N.C.) *Observer*, September 1978.
14. *Charlotte* (N.C.) *Observer*, October 1978.
15. *Charlotte* (N.C.) *Observer*, November 1978.
16. *Conservative Digest*, December 1980.
17. *Charlotte* (N.C.) *Observer*, October 1978.

17 Southern Sex Czar

1. *Mobile Press-Register*, June 1979.
2. Speech, Selma, Alabama, September 1980; also, Jeremiah A. Denton, Jr., and Edwin H. Brandt, Jr., *When Hell Was in Session*. Clover, S.C.: Riverhills Plantation Commission Press, 1976.
3. Denton and Brandt, op. cit.
4. Ibid.
5. Interview with author, Mobile, Alabama, May 16, 1981.
6. Denton and Brandt, op. cit.
7. Ibid.
8. Ibid.
9. Ibid.
10. Ibid.
11. *Washington Post*, December 7, 1980.
12. Telephone interview with author, September 30, 1981; also, interview with author, Washington, D.C., July 28, 1981.
13. Interview with author, Montgomery, Alabama, November 13, 1981.
14. Associated Press, November 1980.
15. *The Wall Street Journal*, December 4, 1980.
16. Speech, Montgomery, Alabama, November 1981.
17. *The Wall Street Journal*, December 4, 1980.
18. *Conservative Digest*, July 1981.
19. Ibid.
20. Interview with author, Washington, D.C., September 29, 1981.
21. Ibid.

18 The Damning of Dixie

1. Speech, Ku Klux Klan rally, Decatur, Alabama, September 1980.
2. Interview with author, Montgomery, Alabama, August 1981.
3. *Nashville Banner*, August 1980.

4. Speeches, June, July, August 1979.
5. *Nashville Banner*, October 1980.
6. Interview with author, Raleigh, North Carolina, June 8, 1981.
7. Patsy Sims, *The Klan*. New York: Stein & Day, 1978.
8. *New Orleans Times-Picayune*, May 1980.
9. Bulletin, privately published, Metairie, Louisiana, June 1980.
10. Ibid.
11. *The Truth Forum*, privately published, Metairie, Louisiana, May 1980.
12. Speech, Pulaski, Tennessee, October 1980.
13. *Miami* (Fla.) *Herald*, October 1980.
14. Ibid.
15. *Thunderbolt*, published by the Ku Klux Klan, summer 1981.

19 The New Religious Right

1. *New York Times*, August 23, 1980.
2. *New York Times*, October 4, 1980.
3. Ibid.
4. Richard A. Viguerie, *The New Right: We're Ready to Lead*. Falls Church, Va.: The Viguerie Company, 1981.
5. Interview with author, Washington, D.C., September 18, 1975.
6. Viguerie, op. cit.
7. Ibid.
8. *The New Right Report*, vol. 10, number 19, 1981.
9. *Time*, October 1, 1979.
10. Speech, capitol steps, Montgomery, Alabama, May 1980.
11. Interview with author, Montgomery, Alabama, June 1981.
12. Interview with author, Montgomery, Alabama, August 1981.
13. *Time*, October 1, 1979.
14. *Los Angeles Times*, March 4, 1981.
15. Interview with author, July 29, 1981.
16. Speech, capitol steps, Montgomery, Alabama, May 1980.
17. Ibid.
18. Interview with author, Lynchburg, Virginia, September 19, 1981.
19. *Conservative Digest*, July 1981.
20. Ibid.
21. *Playboy*, August 1981.
22. Alan Crawford, *Thunder on the Right*. New York: Pantheon Books, 1980.

20 The New Old Republican Order

1. Interviews with author in Habersham and Kilsyth, Tennessee, October 13, 1981; Abernathy Johnson and Joe Langtree.
2. Neil MacNeil, *Dirksen: Profile of a Public Man*. New York: World Publishing Co., 1970.
3. Myra MacPherson, *The Power Lovers*. New York: G.P. Putnam's Sons, 1975.
4. MacNeil, op. cit.
5. Ibid.
6. *Time*, July 15, 1974.

7. *New York Times Sunday Magazine*, November 4, 1979.
8. Speech, Washington, D.C., March 1980.
9. *New York Times*, August 19, 1976.
10. *New York Times Sunday Magazine*, November 4, 1979.
11. *The New Yorker*, November 26, 1979.
12. *Esquire*, January 1980.

21 The Long-Distance Runner

1. Interview with author, Columbia, South Carolina, July 18, 1981.
2. John D. Hicks, *The Populist Revolt*. Minneapolis: Univ. of Minnesota Press, 1931.
3. *The Saturday Evening Post*, October 8, 1955.
4. Interview with author, Columbia, South Carolina, July 19, 1981.
5. *Time*, October 11, 1948.
6. Ibid.
7. Ibid.
8. *Time*, October 4, 1948.
9. *Baltimore Sun*, September 1948.
10. *Time*, October 4, 1948.
11. *Time*, October 11, 1948.
12. Ibid.
13. Ibid.
14. Ibid.
15. Jack Bass and Walter DeVries, *The Transformation of Southern Politics*. New York: Basic Books, 1976.
16. *Current Biography*, 1948.
17. Ibid.
18. Ibid.
19. Ibid.
20. *The Saturday Evening Post*, October 8, 1955.
21. *Time*, July 24, 1950.
22. *The Saturday Evening Post*, October 8, 1955.
23. Ibid.
24. *U.S. News and World Report*, March 23, 1956.
25. *Columbia* (S.C.) *State*, April 1956.
26. *U.S. News and World Report*, November 19, 1954.
27. *New York Times*, September 17, 1964.
28. Ibid.
29. *The New Yorker*, October 3, 1964.
30. Bass and DeVries, op. cit.
31. *Newsweek*, September 13, 1971.
32. *Life*, July 16, 1971.
33. *Life*, September 19, 1969.
34. Telephone interview with author, November 30, 1981.
35. Ibid.
36. *Newsweek*, August 3, 1970.
37. *Columbia* (S.C.) *State*, September 1978.
38. *New York Times*, October 25, 1981.
39. *Newsweek*, September 13, 1971.

40. *New York*, May 18, 1981.
41. Interview with author, Charlotte, North Carolina, political writer, June 8, 1981.

22 Some Other Southern Republicans

1. *Atlanta Weekly*, *Atlanta Journal and Constitution* Sunday magazine, June 14, 1981.
2. Interview with Winifred Green, September 5, 1981.
3. Telephone interview with author, October 9, 1981.
4. *Texas Monthly*, May 1981.
5. Ibid.
6. Telephone interview with Governor Treen's press secretary, Sally A. Nungesser, May 14, 1981.
7. Speech by Governor David C. Treen, Louisiana State University, Baton Rouge, Louisiana, May 16, 1980.
8. *Arkansas Gazette*, August 1980.
9. Michael Barone and Grant Ujifusa, *Almanac of American Politics*, Washington, D.C.: Barone & Company, 1982.
10. Interview with author, June 16, 1981.
11. *New Right Report*, autumn, 1981.
12. Interview with author, June 16, 1981.

23 A Youthful Tomorrow

1. Interview with author, Washington, D.C., June 28, 1981.
2. Ibid.
3. Interview with author, Washington, D.C., June 14, 1981.
4. Interview with PR Associates, Inc., Southern College Survey, Raleigh, North Carolina, March 1981.
5. Interview with PR Associates, Inc., Southern College Survey, Oxford, Mississippi, March 1981.
6. Ibid.
7. Interview with PR Associates, Inc., Southern College Survey, Tuscaloosa, Alabama, April 1981.
8. Interview with PR Associates, Inc., Southern College Survey, Columbia, South Carolina, July 1981.
9. Interview with PR Associates, Inc., Southern College Survey, Austin, Texas, February 1981.
10. Interview with PR Associates, Inc., Southern College Survey, Fayetteville, Arkansas, April 1981.
11. Ibid.
12. Interview with PR Associates, Inc., Southern College Survey, Gainesville, Florida, May 1981.
13. Interview with PR Associates, Inc., Southern College Survey, Knoxville, Tennessee, June 1981.
14. Ibid.
15. Interview with PR Associates, Inc., Southern College Survey, Chapel Hill, North Carolina, June 1981.

16. Ibid.

17. Interview with PR Associates, Inc., Southern College Survey, Atlanta, Georgia, April 1981.

18. Interview with author, Washington, D.C., September 29, 1981.

Selected Bibliography

Anderson, Jack, and Pearson, Drew. *The Case Against Congress*. New York: Simon and Schuster, 1968.

Ayers, Brandt, and Naylor, Thomas H., eds. *You Can't Eat Magnolias*. New York: McGraw-Hill, 1972.

Baker, Tod A.; Moreland, Laurence W.; and Steed, Robert P. *Party Politics in the South*. New York: Praeger Publishers, 1980.

Barnard, William D. *Dixiecrats and Democrats*. University, Ala.: University of Alabama Press, 1974.

Barone, Michael. *The Almanac of American Politics*. New York: E.P. Dutton, 1977.

Barone, Michael, and Ujifusa, Grant. *The Almanac of American Politics 1982*. Washington, D.C.: Barone and Company, 1981.

Baroody, William J. *America's Continuing Revolution*. Washington, D.C.: American Enterprise Institute for Public Policy Research, 1975.

Bass, Jack. *Porgy Comes Home*. Columbia, S.C.: The R.L. Bryan Company, 1972.

Bass, Jack, and DeVries, Walter. *The Transformation of Southern Politics*. New York: Basic Books, 1976.

Billington, Monroe Lee. *The American South*. New York: Charles Scribner's Sons, 1971.

———. *The Political South in the Twentieth Century*. New York: Charles Scribner's Sons, 1975.

Bonadio, Felice A. *Political Parties in American History*. New York: G.P. Putnam's Sons, 1974.

Broder, David S. *The Party's Over*. New York: Harper Colophon, 1972.

Broder, David S., and Hess, Stephen. *The Republican Establishment: The Present and Future of the GOP*. New York: Harper & Row, 1967.

Brown, Gene, ed. *Political Parties: The Great Contemporary Issues*. New York: Arno Press, 1977.

Cash, W.J. *The Mind of the South*. New York: Alfred A. Knopf, 1969.

Chandler, David Leon. *The Natural Superiority of Southern Politicians: A Revisionist History*. New York: Doubleday & Company, 1977.

Chapman, Bruce K., and Gilder, George F. *The Party that Lost Its Head: The Republican Collapse and Imperatives for Revival*. New York: Alfred A. Knopf, 1966.

Coulter, Merton E. *The South During Reconstruction: 1865–1877*. Baton Rouge: Louisiana State University Press, 1947.

Crawford, Alan. *Thunder on the Right*. New York: Pantheon Books, 1980.

Denton, Jeremiah A. *When Hell Was in Session*. Edited by Ed Brandt. Clover,S.C.: Riverhills Plantation Press, 1976.

DeSantis, Vincent P. *Republicans Face the Southern Question: The New Departure Years 1877–1897*. Baltimore, Md.: Johns Hopkins University Press, 1959.

Drew, Elizabeth. *Portrait of an Election*. New York: Simon and Schuster, 1981.

Eaton, Clement. *A History of the Old South*. New York: Macmillan, 1949.

Egerton, John. *The Americanization of Dixie*. New York: Harper's Magazine Press, 1974.

Elliot, Florence. *The Dictionary of Politics*. Baltimore,Md.: Penguin Books Inc., 1974.

Evans, M. Stanton. *The Future of Conservatism*. New York: Holt, Rinehart and Winston, 1968.

———. *The Politics of Surrender*. New York: Devin-Adair Company, 1966.

Fairlie, Henry. *The Parties: Republicans and Democrats in this Century*. New York: St. Martin's Press, 1978.

Fowler, Hubert R. *The Unsolid South*. University, Ala.: Bureau of Public Administration, 1968.

Frady, Marshall. *Southerners*. New York: New American Library, 1980.———. *Wallace* New York: World Publishing Company, 1968.

Franklin, John Hope. *The Militant South*. Cambridge, Mass.: The Belknap Press, Harvard University Press, 1956.

Frazer, Janet, and May, Earnest R., eds. *Campaign '72: The Managers Speak*. Cambridge, Mass.: Harvard University Press, 1973.

Freidel, Frank. *America in the Twentieth Century*. New York: Alfred A. Knopf, 1976.

Gates, Gary Paul, and Rather, Dan. *The Palace Guard*. New York: Warner Communications Company, 1975.

Germond, Jack W., and Witcover, Jules. *Blue Smoke & Mirrors: How Reagan Won and Why Carter Lost the Election of 1980*. New York: Viking Press, 1981.

Gold, Victor. *I Don't Need You When I'm Right*. New York: William Morrow & Company, 1975.

Gray, Daniel S., and Starr, Barton. *Alabama: A Place, A People, A Point of View*. Dubuque, Iowa: Kendall/Hunt, 1977.

Green, Wigfall A. *The Man Bilbo*. Baton Rouge: Louisiana State University Press, 1963.

Greenhaw, Wayne. *Watch Out for George Wallace*. Englewood Cliffs, N.J.: Prentice-Hall, 1976.

Griffith, Lucille. *Alabama: A Documentary History to 1900*. University, Ala.: University of Alabama Press, 1972.

Gulliver, Hal, and Murphy, Reg. *The Southern Strategy*. New York: Charles Scribner's Sons, 1971.

Hadden, Jeffrey K., and Swann, Charles. *Prime Time Preachers*. Massachusetts: Addison-Wesley, 1981.

Haley, Evetts J. *A Texan Looks at Lyndon: A Study in Illegitimate Power*. Canyon, Texas: Palo Duro Press, 1964.

Hamilton, Virginia Van der Veer. *Alabama: A History*. New York: W.W. Norton & Company, 1977.

Heard, Alexander. *A Two-Party South?* Chapel Hill, N.C.: University of North Carolina Press, 1952.

Hicks, John. *Populist Revolt: A History of the Farmers' Alliance and the People's Party*. Minneapolis: University of Minnesota Press, 1931.

Hofstadter, Richard. *The American Political Tradition*. New York: Vintage Books, 1974.

Holmes, Joseph R. *The Quotable Ronald Reagan*. San Diego, Calif.: JRH & Associates, 1975.

Hubler, Richard C., and Reagan, Ronald. *Where's the Rest of Me?* New York: Dell Publishing Company, 1965.

Josephy, Alvin M., Jr. *On the Hill: A History of the American Congress*. New York: Simon and Schuster, 1979.

Jones, Bill. *The Wallace Story*. Northport, Ala.: American Southern Publishing Company, 1966.

Key, V.O., Jr. *Southern Politics*. New York: Alfred A. Knopf, 1949.

Lachicotte, Alberta. *Rebel Senator: Strom Thurmond of South Carolina*. New York: Devin-Adair Company, 1963.

Lewinson, Paul. *Race, Class & Party: A History of Negro Suffrage and White Politics in the South*. New York: Russell & Russell Inc., 1963.

Lewis, Anthony. *Portrait of a Decade: The Second American Revolution*. New York: Random House, 1964.

Lipset, Seymour Martin, and Raab, Earl. *The Politics of Unreason*. New York: Harper & Row, 1970.

Ludberg, Ferdinand. *Scoundrels All: The Mad World of Political Nonsense*. New York: Lyle Stuart Publishers, 1968.

MacNeil, Neil. *Portrait of a Public Man*. New York: World Publishing Company, 1970.

MacPherson, Myra. *The Power Lovers*. New York: G.P. Putnam's Sons, 1976.

Manchester, William. *The Glory and the Dream: A Narrative History of America 1932–1972*. Boston: Little,Brown and Company, 1973.

Marcus, Robert D. *Grand Old Party: Political Structure in the Gilded Age: 1880–1896*. New York: Oxford University Press, 1971.

Mazmanian, Daniel A. *Third Parties in Presidential Elections*. Washington, D.C.: Brookings Institution, 1974.

Morgan, Charles, Jr. *One Man, One Voice*. New York: Holt, Rinehart and Winston, 1979.

Morison, Samuel Eliot. *The Oxford History of the American People*. New York: Oxford Press, 1965.

Novak, Robert D. *The Agony of the G.O.P. 1964*. New York: Macmillan, 1965.

Peirce, Neal R. *The Deep South States of America*. New York: W.W. Norton & Company, 1974.

Phillips, Kevin. *The Emerging Republican Majority*. New Rochelle, N.Y.: Arlington House, 1969.

Potter, David M. *The South and the Sectional Conflict*. Baton Rouge: Louisiana State University Press, 1968.

Robertson, Wilmot. *The Dispossessed Majority*. Florida: Howard Allen Enterprises, 1973.

Roland, Charles P. *The Improbable Era: The South Since World War II*. Kentucky: The University of Kentucky Press, 1975.

Roland, Charles Pierce, and Simkins, Francis Butler. *A History of the South*. New York: Alfred A. Knopf, 1963.

Rosenbloom, David Lee. *The Election Men: Professional Campaign Managers and American Democracy*. New York: Quadrangle Books, 1973.

Rusher, William A. *The Making of a New Majority Party*. Aurora, Ill.: Green Hill Publishers, 1975.

Sarauf, Frank J. *Party Politics in America*. Boston: Little, Brown and Company, 1968.

Schnapper, M.B. *Grand Old Party: The First Hundred Years of the Republican Party*. Washington, D.C.: Public Affairs Press, 1955.

Schoenebaum, Eleanora W. *Profiles of an Era: The Nixon/Ford Years*. New York: A Harvest/Harcourt, Brace Jovanovich Book, 1979.

Stern, C. A. *Republican Heyday*. Ann Arbor, Mich.: Edwards Brothers Inc., 1962.

Stewart, John Craig. *The Governors of Alabama*. Gretna, La.: Pelican Publishing Company, 1975.

Thimmesch, Nick. *The Condition of Republicanism*. New York: W.W. Norton & Company, 1968.

Thurmond, Strom, Senator. *The Faith We Have Not Kept*. San Diego, Calif.: Loeffler & Company, 1968.

Tindal, George Brown. *The Disruption of the Solid South*. Athens, Ga.: University of Georgia Press, 1972.

Underwood, Oscar W. *Drifting Sands of Party Politics*. New York: The Century Company, 1928.

Viguerie, Richard A. *The New Right: We're Ready to Lead*. Falls Church, Va.: Viguerie Company, 1981.

Walton, Hanes. *Black Republicans: The Politics of the Black and Tans*. Metuchen, N.J.: Scarecrow Press, Inc., 1975.

Wattenberg, Ben J. *The Real America*. New York: Doubleday & Company, 1974.

Watters, Pat. *The South and the Nation*. New York: Pantheon Books, 1969.

Whalan, Richard J. *Catch the Falling Flag*. Boston: Houghton Mifflin Company, 1972.

White, Theodore H. *The Making of a President 1960–1972*. New York: Atheneum Publishers, 1960–1972.

Wiggins, Sarah Woolfolk. *The Scalawag in Alabama Politics: 1865-1881*. University, Ala.: University of Alabama Press, 1977.

Williams, J. Earl. *Plantation Politics: The Southern Economic Heritage*. Dr. J. Earl Williams, privately published, 1972.

Woodward, C. Vann. *Origins of the New South: 1877–1913*. Baton Rouge: Louisiana State University Press, 1951.

———. *The Burden of Southern History*. Baton Rouge: Louisiana State University Press, 1960.

Index

Abortion bill, 156–57, 163
Abscam scandals, 127, 242, 243
Advance (magazine), 55
Agnew, Spiro, 78, 87, 99, 110, 211
Aiken, William, 16
Alcorn, James, 28
Alexander, Lamar, 240
Allen, James (senator), 155–56
Allen, Jimmy (churchman), 196
Allen, Richard V., 134
Allen, Steve, 179–80
Almanac of American Politics, The (Barone and Ujifusa), 242
American Independent party, 78, 193
Amnesty Act (1872), 29
Anderson, John, 243
Andrews, T. Coleman, 53
Apple, R. W., Jr., 111
Archer, Bill, 245
Armageddon and the Coming War with Russia (Falwell), 198
Arthur, Chester Alan, 37–38
Askew, Reubin, 114
Atlanta Constitution, 40–41
Atlanta *Journal-Constitution*, 236
Atwater, Harvey Lee, 117–31, 182, 232, 233, 242
  background of, 117–21
  Negative Factor Theory of, 122–24, 128
  in Reagan camp, 117, 121, 129–30, 135, 139, 140, 233, 248
Azbell, Joe, 176–77

Bacon, Mary, 185–86
Baggett, J. Langford, 20
Bailes, George Lewis, 177
Bailey, Douglas, 212
Bailey, James H. "Pou," 161
Baker, Cynthia, 206–207
Baker, Danice Joy Dirksen, 206–207
Baker, Howard H., Jr., 114, 167, 202–13
  background of, 204–207
  Dirksen's relationship with, 208–209
  presidential ambitions of, 211–13
  in Senate campaign, 207
  as senator, 208–13
  on Watergate Committee, 210–11
Baker, Howard Henry, Sr., 204–205

Baker, Irene Bailey, 205
Bakker, Jim, 154
Bankhead, William, 43–44
Banks, Nathaniel, 16
Barkley, Alben W., 51
Barkley, Evans, 147–48
Barnet, Richard J., 84–85
Barnett, Ross, 54
Barr, Matthew, 251–52
Bass, Jack, 230, 242
Beard, Robin L., Jr., 247
Befalis, L. A. "Skip," 243–44
Before the Mayflower (Bennett), 30
Bell, John, 19
Bemus, George, 127
Bennett, Lerone, Jr., 30
Bernstein, Carl, 110
Berryhill, William I., 154–55, 162, 163
Bethune, Ed, 246
Bilbo, Theodore G., 11
Bingham, Chester Arthur, 32
Black, Charles, 201
Black and Tan Republican party, 36, 46, 47
Black Codes, 24, 58
Black Republicans, 20
Blacks, 88–89, 148, 208, 222–24, 230, 251
  Democratic party supported by, 48, 54, 60–61
  disfranchisement of, 38–47
  at 1868 Republican convention, 26
  Hayes' position on, 35
  plans for colonization of, 20–21
  in Republican Reconstruction coalitions, 27, 28, 33
  in Senate, 30–31
  suffrage for, 21, 22, 23, 24, 26–27, 31, 222
  after World War II, 248–49
Blaine, James G., 36, 38, 40
Blair, Francis P., 20
Blanton, Ray, 210, 240
Boggs, Hale, 239
Boll Weevils, 142, 143, 192, 243
Bovay, Alvin E., 15–16
Boyd, James, 81
Breckinridge, John C., 19
Brock, Bill, 116
Broder, David S., 70
Brooks, Preston S., 16
Brown, Edgar A., 225, 226
Brown, Edmund G., 69–70, 73
Brown, H. Rap, 74–75
Brown, Joseph E., 27
Brown, William Garrott, 45
Brownlow, William G. "Parson," 21–22, 25, 204
Brown vs. *Board of Education*, 53, 227
Broyhill, James T., 241
Bruce, Blanche K., 31
Bryan, William Jennings, 42
Buchanan, James, 17
Buchanan, John H., Jr., 244
Bumpers, Dale, 114
Burns, Haydon, 71
Bush, George, 216, 245
Butcher, Jake, 240
Butler, Andrew, 16
Buzhardt, J. Fred, 231
Byrd, Harry F., 50, 53
Byrnes, James F., 51–52, 224–25

Campbell, Carroll Ashmore, Jr., 126, 132–45, 233, 258–59
  background of, 132–33, 137–39
  as congressman, 141–45
  in Reagan campaign, 133–37, 139–41, 233
  in state politics, 137–38, 139
Carmichael, Gil, 108
Carpetbaggers, 27–28
Carswell, G. Harrold, 209–10
Carter, Jimmy, 194–95, 246, 251, 256
  Baker's relationship with, 211–12
  in 1976 presidential election, 114, 116, 164, 244
  in 1980 presidential election, 86, 141, 213, 243
  Reagan's accusations against, 182, 183
Case, Byron A., 94–95
Charlotte *Observer*, 166–67
Chase, Salmon P., 26
Chicago Tribune, 24
Chiles, Lawton, 237
Chowder and Marching Club, 141
Christopher, George, 64, 69

Civil War, U.S., 21–22
Clements, Bill, 238–39
Cleveland, Grover, 38, 40, 41
Clinton, Bill, 240
Coalition for Decency, 175
Cochran, Thad, 236–37
Colfax, Schuyler, 26
Collins, Don, 89–97, 98, 176
 background of, 90–91
 Republican conversion of, 90, 92–97
Collins, James M., 245
Colmer, William, 99, 101, 102
Committee for the Survival of a Free Congress (CSFC), 198, 199–200, 237, 242
Comprehensive Employment and Training Act (CETA), 166
Connally, John, 84, 114, 140, 193, 212, 233, 239
Conservative Digest, The, 178–79
Constitution, U.S.
 Fourteenth Amendment of, 22, 23, 25
 Fifteenth Amendment of, 26–27, 31
Coolidge, Calvin, 46–47
Corrington, J. Edgar, 3, 5
Covington, Howard, 163, 165
Cox, Archibald, 156–57
Crane, Phil, 191, 192, 193
Crawford, Alan, 200
Crouch, Jean, 219–20, 228

Dalton, John, 200
Danton, Maurice, 236
Dart, Justin, 69
Davis, Jefferson, 19, 21
Davis, John W., 47
Dayton, William L., 16–17
Deardourff, John, 212–13
Dees, Morris, 193
Defense Department, U.S., 102
Democratic party
 black support for, 48, 54, 60–61
 civil rights issues in, 50–51, 53–54, 59
 Dixiecrat break from, 50–51
 in Reconstruction, 29, 30, 31–32, 37
 Southern move away from, 47, 87–88, 89
 Southern support for, 48–49, 50, 53–54, 248, 261
 student support for, 253–54, 255
Dent, Harry, 78–79, 88, 231
Denton, Jeremiah, 95, 170–80, 181, 198–99
 background of, 170–72
 in congressional campaign, 176–77
 as congressman, 177–79
 KKK support for, 181–82
 on Security and Terrorism subcommittee, 178–79
 in Vietnam, 172–74
 Weyrich's support for, 198–99
Depression, Great, 48, 248
DeVries, Walter, 230
Dewey, Thomas E., 2, 50, 51
Dickinson, William L., 244
Dirksen, Everett, 74, 206, 208–209
Dixiecrats, 50–51, 53, 221–22, 229
Dolan, Terry, 198, 199, 200
Dole, Robert J., 116
Dorn, William Jennings Bryan, 125
Dornan, Bob, 191, 192
Douglas, Helen Gahagan, 63, 67
Douglas, Myron, 66–67
Douglas, Stephen A., 17, 19
Douglass, Frederick, 27
Drew, Elizabeth, 158
Duke, David, 183–86
Duncan, John L., 246
Dunston, William B., 184

Eagleton, Thomas F., 99
East, John, 139, 167–68, 183
Eastland, James, 113
Eckhardt, Bob, 246
Edens, J. Drake, Jr., 228–29
Edens, William, 120
Education Act (1972), 210
Edwards, Edwin, 114, 239
Edwards, Jack, 244
Edwards, Jim, 138
Edwards, Mickey, 134, 191, 192
Eisenhower, Dwight D., 5, 7, 52, 54, 57, 67, 74, 206, 225, 249
Ellis, Thomas, 154, 155, 161–63, 164, 165, 167–68
Emancipation Proclamation (1863), 20–21

Emerging Republican Majority, The (Phillips), 80, 81–83
Energy Department, U.S., 241
Ervin, Sam, 210
Eskew, Tucker, 123, 131
Ethridge, James G., 215
Evans, Carroll Lee, 255–56
Evans, Thomas R., Jr., 134, 135
Everett, Edward, 19
Evers, Charles, 236

Fair Employment Practices Committee (FEPC), 220, 224
Falwell, Jerry, 177, 190, 191, 194–95, 196–98, 199
Family Protection Act, 199
Farmer, James, 61
Farmers' Alliance, 41–42
Faubus, Orval E., 57
Federal Elections Act (1871), 36
Fields, Jack, 245–46
Finch, Cliff, 108
Fino, Paul, 79, 80, 81
Fitzmorris, James E., 239
Flaherty, David, 166
Fletcher, A. J., 149, 152, 155
Folsom, James E., 8, 181
Folsom, Jim, Jr., 176, 177
Force Bill, 40
Ford, Gerald R., 78, 110, 114, 115, 116, 134, 164, 211, 233
Frankel, Max, 87
Freemen's Bureau, 23
Fremont, John Charles, 16, 17

Galifianakis, Nick, 154, 155
Gallion, McDonald, 94
Gallup polls, 75, 110–11
Gardner, James C., 77
Garfield, James A., 35, 36–37, 38
Garrison, William Lloyd, 35
General Electric Corporation, 67, 68, 69
George, Grayton, 253–54
George, Walter, 50
Gibson, Virginia, 237
Gingrich, Newt, 242–43
Godfrey, James, 164
Goldwater, Barry, 11, 64, 99–100, 209
in 1964 presidential election, 72, 230
Reagan's support for, 13, 60, 62, 69
Southern support for, 13, 54–55, 56–57, 60, 249
Thurmond's support for, 229–30
Graham, Frank Porter, 149–50
Graham, Max, 257–58
Gramm, Phil, 191, 192, 246
Grange (Patrons of Husbandry), 41
Grant, Larry, 183
Grant, Ulysses S., 25, 26, 27, 29, 34, 36
Greeley, Horace, 15, 29
Green, Winifred, 237
Grenier, John, 57
Griggs, Jere, 183
Gudger, Lamar, 241
Gunther, John, 223

Hamer, Fannie Lou, 57–58
Hamlin, Hannibal, 19
Hammerschmidt, John Paul, 246
Hampton, Wade, 35, 36
Hancock, Winfield S., 37
Hanna, Mark, 42
Harding, Warren G., 46
Harper's Weekly, 29
Harrigan, Stephen, 238
Harrison, Benjamin, 40–41
Harris poll, 89
Hartnett, Thomas F., 126, 242
Hatfield, Mark, 208
Hawkins, Paula, 199, 237
Hayes, Rutherford Birchard, 34–35, 36, 37
Haynsworth, Clement F., 88, 209–10
Helms, Dorothy Coble, 148
Helms, Jesse, 115–16, 139, 146–60, 161, 183
background of, 146–50
as congressional aide, 150
in John East's campaign, 167–68
local support for, 162, 163, 164, 168–69
in radio appeals, 151–53
on Reagan, 10–11
in reelection campaign, 163–66
Republican conversion of, 153–55
as senator, 155–60, 164

in Wallace campaign, 153
Hendon, William M., 241
Hendricks, Thomas, 34
Herbert, F. Edward, 245
High, Robert King, 71
Hill, Gladwin, 55, 56
Hill, John, 238
Hill, Lister, 55
Hoar, George F., 29–30
Hobby, Wilbur, 166
Holden, William H., 23
Hollings, Ernest, 230
Holshouser, Jim, 164
Holton, Linwood, 88
Hooks, Benjamin, 210
Hoover, Herbert, 47, 48
Howard, Oliver O., 24
Howard, Perry, 46, 47
Howell, Henry, 200
Hubbard, John H., 32
Humphrey, Hubert Horatio, 13, 50, 58, 77, 78, 222, 229
Hunt, James B., Jr., 164, 166–67

Independents, voters as, 254
Ingram, John, 165, 183
Inside U.S.A. (Gunther), 223
Izvestia, 178

James, Fob, 195
Jaworski, Leon, 127–28
Jenrette, John W., 127, 242
Jenrette, Rita, 127
Johnson, Al D., 111
Johnson, Andrew, 21, 22, 23, 25–26
Johnson, I. S. Leevy, 233
Johnson, James Everett, 27
Johnson, Lyndon Baines, 53, 54, 55, 94, 153, 229, 237, 249
  in 1964 presidential election, 58, 60
  Southern perceptions of, 12–13
Johnson, Paul B., 57
Johnston, Gene, 127
Johnston, Olin D., 51, 221, 224, 229
Jordan, Everett, 154
Jordan, Hamilton, 114
Jorgensen, Earl, 69
Justice Department, U.S., 141

Kansas-Nebraska Act, 15, 16
Kefauver, Estes, 5, 207
Kelley, Oliver H., 41
Kelly, Kent, 166
Kelly, Richard, 243
Kemp, Jack, 134
Kendrick, Benjamin B., 36
Kennedy, Edward M., 114, 156, 209
Kennedy, John F., 54, 55, 60, 127, 171, 249
Kennedy, Robert F., 67, 77
Kennon, Robert F., 51–52
Key, David M., 35
Khachigian, Kenneth L., 111–12, 113
Kilpatrick, James J., 159–60
King's Row, 66
Kirk, Claude Roy, Jr., 71–76, 88
Kirk, Erika Mattfield, 72
Klan, The (Sims), 183
Knox, John B., 44–45
Kornegay, Horace, 127
Ku Klux Klan (KKK), 33, 149–50, 181–88, 216
  Denton supported by, 181–82
  Duke's work in, 183–86
  Reagan supported by, 182–83, 187–88
  younger leaders in, 183–85

LaFollette, Robert M., 47
Lake, I. Beverly, Jr., 166–67
Lambert, Louis, 239
Landers, Josh, 119
Landon, Alfred Mossman, 48
Lane, Joseph, 19
Langhorn, John Jeffers, 219
Larson, Arthur, 53
Lattimer, Jake, 89
Laxalt, Paul, 115, 134, 199, 213
Lee, Jack, 165
Lee, Robert E., 45, 216
LeMay, Curtis, 78
Lemmon Slave Case, 37–38
Lenzner, Terry, 210
Lewis, Anthony, 54
Lily-White Republican party, 36, 46, 47
Lincoln, Abraham, 17–19, 20–21, 22, 23

Lindsay, Robert Burns, 32
Litton Industries, 102
Livingston, Robert L., 191, 192, 244–45
Lodge, Henry Cabot, 40
Lodge, Henry Cabot, Jr., 54, 55
Loeffler, Thomas G. "Tom," 246
Logue, Sue S., 218
Long, Huey P., 49, 239
Lott, Trent, 99–109, 111, 242, 244
  background of, 99–101
  as congressman, 101–109
  philosophy of, 104–109
Lucy, Autherine, 250

McAdams, Jonathan, 257
McAteer, Edward, 189
McCarthy, Joseph R., 150, 153
McClure, Jim, 191–92
McCollum, Bill, 243
McCorvey, Gessner T., 52
McCullough, R. Alex, 231
McDonald, Larry, 126, 191, 192
McGinnis, Joe, 81, 82
McGovern, George, 13, 98–99
McKinley, William, 42
MacPherson, Myra, 175, 207
McVeay, Jimmy, 104
Mangrum, Dennis, 182–83
Mann, Horace A., 47
Martin, James D., 55
Martin, James G., 241
Martin, James L., 194
Mattingly, Mack, 200, 235–36
Maybank, Burnet, 53, 225
Mediacracy: American Parties and Politics in the Communications Age (Phillips), 81
Mencken, H. L., 221–22
Miami Herald, 73
Miller, Andrew P., 238
Miller, William E., 56
Mitchell, John, 79, 80, 84
Mondale, Walter, 116
Montgomery *Daily Advertiser*, 28
Mooney, William J., 67–68
Moore, Dan K., 59
Moore, W. Henson, 245
Moral Majority, 177, 191, 196–97, 199
Moren, Edward H., 32
Morgan, Charles, Jr., 83–84, 250–51
Morgan, Jason, 255
Morgan, Robert, 167–68, 183
Morganville, Jackson Lee, 26
Morris, Earle, 125
Morrison, Jeanne, 252
Morrison, Lawrence, 146
Morton, Jimmie, 256–57
Moss, Frank E., 159
Muldihill, M. J., 46
Muskie, Edmund S., 78

Napier, John L., 126–27, 242
Nast, Thomas, 29, 33, 34, 35
National Affairs Briefing, 191
National Association for the Advancement of White People (NAAWP), 184, 185
National Conservative Political Action Committee (NCPAC), 198, 200, 242
National Constitutional Union, 19
National Pro-Life Political Action Committee, 201
National Republican Candidates Committee, 201
National States' Rights Committee, 51
New Deal, 48, 49–50
New Reconstruction, 12, 220
New Religious Right, 189–201, 237
  organizations in, 190
  political funds provided by, 191–92, 200–201
  Reagan supported by, 189–91, 194–95, 197
  Viguerie's work for, 191–94
New Republican Victory Fund, 200-01
New Right, 11, 163, 164, 191, 192, 194, 237, 244
New Right Report, The, 194, 244
Newsweek, 84
Newton, Norman, 89
New York Times, 18, 38–40, 55–56, 57, 58–59, 224
New York *World-Telegram*, 224
Niemoeller, Martin, 179
Nixon, Richard M., 5, 52, 67, 68, 69, 154, 176

on Goldwater's candidacy, 61–62
in 1960 presidential election, 54
in 1968 presidential election, 77–78, 80, 81, 87
in 1972 presidential election, 99
as president, 98
Reagan's support for, 77–78
resignation of, 110, 111, 174
Southern strength of, 13, 111–14, 249
Supreme Court nominations by, 88, 209–10
Thurmond's support for, 230, 231
in Watergate affair, 210
Nofziger, Lyn, 129, 140
North Carolina Congressional Club, 162–63, 164–65, 166–67, 168–69

O'Connor, Sandra Day, 158, 187, 199, 216
O'Neill, Tip, 143
Operation Dixie, 55, 57

Page, Walter Hines, 45
Palmer, B. J., 65
Panama Canal treaty, 178, 212
Parker, Marshall, 230
Paul, Ron, 246
Percy, Charles, 208
Perez, Leander, 52
Perry, James M., 177
Phillips, Kevin P., 79–86
background of, 79–81
Reagan supported by, 84
Southern Republican strategy devised by, 80–83, 85–86, 87
Phillips, William, 80
Pierpont, Francis H., 22
Pike, Albert, 31
Pike, James Shepherd, 28
Pinchback, Pinckney Benton Stewart, 28
Polk, Leonidas L., 41
Populist party, 40, 42
Pornography, 174, 175–76
Potter, I. Lee, 55
Powell, Adam Clayton, 181
Powell, Jody, 114
Pravda, 178
Preyer, Richardson, 127–28
Progressive party, 45, 47
Prostrate State, The (Pike), 28

Quackenbush, James H., 129
Quillen, Jimmy, 246

Raines, Howell, 190–91
Rainey, Joseph Hayne, 33
Raleigh Progressive Farmer, 41
Raleigh Times, 149
Range, Peter Ross, 199
Ravenel, Charles "Pug," 125–26, 242
Rawle, David L., 126
Rayburn, Sam, 53–54
Reagan, Nancy Davis, 67
Reagan, Ronald, 9–14, 63–70, 95
Atwater's work for, 117, 121, 129–30, 135, 139, 140, 233, 248
background of, 64–67
Baker's relationship with, 212, 213
Campbell's work for, 133–37, 139–41, 233
congressional support for policies of, 236, 237, 243, 244
Eisenhower supported by, 67
in Goldwater campaign, 13, 60, 62, 69
as governor, 9
in gubernatorial campaign, 63–64, 69–70
KKK support for, 182–83, 187–88
as movie star, 9, 59–60, 65–67, 68–69
New Religious Right support for, 189–91, 194–95, 197
in 1976 presidential campaign, 114–16
in 1980 presidential election, 86, 141, 213, 243, 244
Nixon supported by, 77–78
O'Connor appointed by, 158, 187, 199, 216
Phillips' support for, 84
Southern support for, 11, 12-13, 86, 249
tax reduction proposed by, 142–44
Thurmond's support for, 233
TNG strategy for, 133–35

Reconstruction, 21, 22–24, 25–33, 34–38
Reconstruction Acts, 32, 60
Redmond, S. D., 46
Reed, Roy, 88
Reeves, Ann, 182–83
Reeves, Richard, 212–13
Religious Roundtable, 189, 190, 191
Republican party
  black support for, 26
  early campaigns of, 16–17
  1880 convention of, 36–37
  founding of, 15–16
  in Nixon's second term, 110–11
  racial split in, 36, 46, 47
  Reagan's advancement of, 13, 14
  in Reconstruction, 22, 23, 25–33, 34–35, 36
  Southern gains of, 51–53, 54, 55–56, 58–59, 87–88, 89, 249, 261
  young voters' support for, 249–53, 255
Revels, Hiram Rhoades, 30–31
Richards, Richard, 116
Rivers, Mendel, 216
Robertson, Pat, 191
Robinson, J. Kenneth, 200
Rockefeller, Nelson, 61, 64, 75–76, 114, 115
Rockefeller, Winthrop, 88
Rogers, Will, 148
Roosevelt, Franklin D., 1, 2, 3, 5, 122
  Southern support for, 48–50, 56–57, 220, 248
Roosevelt, Theodore, 42–43, 45
Russell, Donald S., 229
Russell, Richard, 221

Scalawags, 27–28
School desegregation, 53
School prayer bill, 157–58
Scott, Hugh, 82, 210
Sears, John, 136
Selden, Armstead, 176
Selling of the President 1968, The (McGinnis), 81, 82
Seward, William H., 18
Shaw, E. Clay, Jr., 243
Sherman, William Tecumseh, 216
Shivers, Allan, 52, 53
Shriver, Sargent, 99
Shuster, Bud, 103
Simkins, Francis Butler, 49
Sims, Patsy, 183–84
Sitton, Claude, 58–59
Smith, Albert Lee, 244
Smith, Alfred E., 47
Smith, "Cotton Ed," 49, 50
Smith, William French, 68, 69
Smith, William H., 32
Smith, Willis, 149–50, 155, 162
Snider, Larry L., 253
Social Security, 142
South
  in Civil War, 21–22
  political heroes in, 11–12
  in Reconstruction, 23–24, 25–33
  secession of, 19–20
  after World War II, 248–49
Southern Loyalists, 22
Southern Manifesto, 53
Southern Poverty Law Center, 182
Sparkman, John, 6, 7, 52
Spence, Floyd, 124–25, 242
States' Rights party, 51, 52, 221
Stennis, John, 102, 113
Stephens, Alexander H., 19
Stevens, Ivy Baker Priest, 77
Stevens, Thaddeus, 21, 23, 24, 25
Stevenson, Adlai, 5–6, 7, 52, 53, 54, 225
Stevenson, Adlai E., 41
Stewart, Donald, 176
Stockman, David, 142
Stoner, J. B., 186–87
Strauss, Robert, 111
Strom, Eleanor Gertrude, 217
Strom, James, 217
Stuckey, Bill, 235
Sumner, Charles, 16, 19, 21, 24, 25
Supplementary Reconstruction Act (1866), 25
Syracuse Herald-Journal, 61

Taft, Robert, 5, 52, 115, 206
Taft, William Howard, 45
Talmadge, Herman, 236
Tankersley, Marjorie, 254

Tax-reduction bill, 142–44
Taylor, Elizabeth, 238
Tennessee Valley Authority (T.V.A.), 209
Thimmesch, Nick, 64, 68
Thunderbolt, 187
Thunder on the Right (Crawford), 200
Thurmond, George Washington, 216
Thurmond, John, 216, 217
Thurmond, Nancy Moore, 231
Thurmond, Strom, 11, 58, 59, 199, 214–34
  Atwater's work for, 118–19, 131
  background of, 216–17, 219
  on *Brown* vs. *Board of Education*, 227–28
  Dixiecrat walkout led by, 51, 221
  Goldwater supported by, 229–30
  in local politics, 217–18, 219–20, 223–24
  Nixon supported by, 78
  racism denied by, 222–23
  Reagan supported by, 233
  Republican conversion of, 89, 228–31, 233–34
  in senate campaigns, 214–16, 225–27, 232–33
  as senator, 216, 227, 233–34
  Southern Manifesto sponsored by, 53
  in States' Rights party, 51, 221–23
  as write-in candidate, 225–26
Thursday Night Group (TNG), 133–36
Tilden, Samuel, 34
Tillman, Benjamin R. "Pitchfork Ben," 41–42, 216–17, 221
Time, 78, 195, 196, 221, 222
Timmerman, George Bell, 226–27
Tindall, George Brown, 82–83
Tonry, Richard, 192, 245
Tower, John G., 56, 237
Transformation of Southern Politics, The (Bass and DeVries), 230, 242
Treen, Dave, 239–40
Trible, Paul S., Jr., 240–41
Truman, Harry S, 1, 2, 3, 50, 52, 66, 220–21, 223, 224, 225
TRUTH: The Whole Truth and Nothing But the Truth, 37
Turnipseed, Tom, 242
Tuttle, Holmes, 69
Tweedy, John, 29

Viguerie, Richard A., 164–65, 166, 191, 192–94, 242
Voting Rights Act (1964), 60
Voting Rights Act (1965), 106, 107, 141–42, 210

Wackenhut, George A., 72–73
Walker, Deloss, 195
Wallace, George C., 8, 13, 64, 72, 75, 97, 222, 249
  attempted assassination of, 98
  Helms' work for, 153
  in 1974 primaries, 114
  popular appeal of, 11–12
  as third-party presidential candidate, 57, 78, 87
  Viguerie's fund raising for, 191
Wallace, Lurleen Burns, 72
Wall Street Journal, 114
Wampler, William C., 241
Warner, John W., 237–38
Warren, Earl, 152
Washington, Booker T., 42
Washington Post, 104, 110
Watergate, 84, 95, 110, 210–11
Watson, Thomas E., 42
Weyrich, Paul, 101, 170, 175, 176, 177, 198–200, 237, 242
Wheeler, William A., 34
When Hell Was in Session (Denton), 171–73
Where's the Rest of Me? (Reagan), 64
White, Frank, 240
White, Horace, 18
White, William S., 52–53
Wide Awakes, 17
Wilkins, Landry, 147
Wilkinson, Bill, 182
Will, George, 101
Williams, Randall, 182
Willkie, Wendell, 50
Wilson, William A., 69
Wilson, Woodrow, 45
Winter, William F., 108
Wirthlin, Dick, 140
Wofford, Thomas A., 227

Wood, Leonard, 46
Woodward, Bob, 110
Wooten, James T., 98
Workfare program, 144, 159
Workman, W. D., 229
World War II, 50
Wrenn, Carter, 164
Wright, Fielding L., 51, 221
Wright, Loyd, 68
Wyman, Jane, 12, 66, 67

Yancey, William Lowndes, 19
Yarborough, Ralph, 228
Young, C. W. "Bill," 243
Young, Whitney, Jr., 61
Young Americans for Freedom, 193
Young voters, 249–59